# TREES
## for your garden

**Discovering the very best of British Ornamental and Fruit Trees**

**by Nick Dunn**

THE TREE
COUNCIL

First published in 2010 by The Tree Council
71 Newcomen Street London SE1 1YT

Designed by Maitland Associates, York.
Printed and bound by Butler Tanner and Dennis Ltd, Frome and London

ISBN: 978–0–904853–08–7

Cover photographs: Nick Dunn

TREES
*for* LIFE

www.frankpmatthews.com

*for Nikki*

# Forewords

**Hanging over the entrance to the editorial offices of *The Sun* newspaper is a quotation from the late Douglas Bader. It reads, "If you are going to do a job old boy, do it well or not at all".**

This book fulfills that maxim to the letter: the pictures, the selection of trees, cultural advice and asides are all of the highest order. Gardening books need to be grown before they are written and Nick, third generation nurseryman, writes from a love and lifetime of growing trees.

Turning the pages, seeing the eye catching photographs and reading the absorbing text, I can hear the slice of his spade into that rich valley soil, planting and lifting young trees. You can smell the soil under his finger nails, sense the crispness of apples picked and eaten fresh from his stock mother trees and see the innate skills producing those serried ranks of vigorously growing young trees, straighter and more uniform than any parade of guardsmen.

It makes me wonder whether Nick, his father and grandfather before him have had sap rather than blood coursing through their veins. What an amazing job the hundred or so skilled nursery workers in this family business do and could there be a more worthwhile occupation producing living things that clean the very air we breathe.

This book should be on every garden centre advisory desk, in school and college libraries, within easy reach of every landscaper, council parks officer and home gardener. But beware, opening these pages will be a theft of time. I lent the proof copy to my Picture Editor at *The Sun*, and after an hour he brought it back saying, "Here, you must have this back or I will not get any work done today!"

While there is so much to be gained from the earlier pages on ornamental trees, it is as if the best has been kept till last. We have such a wealth of fine, fruiting trees as you will soon see here, it makes choosing a few for our gardens difficult.

Even if you have no garden space to grow trees, the information on say, apples, will fascinate all foodies. I love the fact and folklore paragraphs, for example, "Eat an apple going to bed – knock the doctor on the head".

Most of all I welcome the sound advice contained on every page: how to plant, how to prune, how to train into different forms, how to protect from pest and disease attack, where to find yet more interesting and useful information.

This book will, without doubt, become a classic for our time and I recommend it to everyone, without hesitation.

**Peter Seabrook**

**It will come as no surprise to anyone to learn that I am a firm adherent of the principle that everyone should be able to see a tree from their window.**

It really doesn't matter whether you are in a town, village, city, office or home; the principle holds fast. The question often asked is, "but what should I plant in my (insert description) space?" Now, the answer will be simply, "here – consult this book" – though I predict that the next problem articulated will be a plea for guidance through choice paralysis. Honestly, you can't help some folk!

It's true, though, that these pages offer us all plenty of opportunities for enjoyable vacillation. Planning, thinking about what will look good and where, changing the mind at least five times before arriving at a decision, are all part of the enjoyment of planting a tree.

Trees enrich our lives so much, and nowhere so effectively as where they can be enjoyed every day. For many, that is in the garden or the street outside our homes and workplace. From where I write, at The Tree Council, there was nothing outside our office windows but unrelieved brick and tarmac, so we did what any right-thinking

organisation would do – scraped around for funds to get a tree planted in a suitable position, where we could all have the benefit of it. Our choice for this high, rather narrow pavement space was a *Ginkgo* and it has been an unalloyed source of pleasure. This is nothing to do with its role in taking up air pollution or modifying the local climate. When we look out of the window we don't see a carbon sequestration and storage tool, nor do we see a regulator of the urban microclimate that ameliorates adverse effects of weather or any of the (many) researched and documented guises. We see beauty, growth and renewal. In the spring, this *Ginkgo* gives us a measure of how advanced the season is; in the summer, shade; the autumn colour change is an absolute delight and in the winter, we watch for it to give us the first signs of spring.

So, you may want to plant a tree because you wish to reduce $CO_2$ levels, cut down air pollution, manage storm water, improve soil quality, reduce stress... but never forget that no-one, ever, needs a better reason to plant a tree than just *that they want to*. In the pages that follow, there will be one for *your* space and it's only waiting for you to make the connection. All I ask is that when you hear its call, listen and act.

**Pauline Buchanan Black**
**Director General**
**The Tree Council**

The author, *Nick Dunn*, grew up surrounded by trees, the third generation in a family nursery business established in 1901. He is one of the UK's leading authorities on the propagation and care of both ornamental and fruit trees and is a member of several committees dedicated to the research and development of best horticultural practice.

www.frankpmatthews.com

# Introduction

**This book will hopefully provide an exciting and unusual view on trees. You will find a wide choice described and photographed with many an old favourite but also some very recent introductions.**

I have also included some choice and wonderful rare trees from the distant past which, through inadequate exposure, have never been appreciated to the extent they deserve. This is certainly true of many of the ornamentals described. Fruit trees, however, also epitomise the extremes of old and new where our heritage goes hand in hand with the continual selection and breeding of new varieties for the satisfaction of modern times.

The focus has also been to match those illustrated with the knowledge that they are relatively easy to obtain from specialist tree growers and retailers in the UK. It is easy to enthuse and tempt the reader over a rare beauty but frustrating if it is then hard to find.

This book, in the most part, is written for those who have little knowledge of fruit and ornamental trees but who wish to have easy access to information using the most important selection criteria. I also hope that it is stimulating enough for the knowledgeable enthusiast, providing a few agreeable surprises.

I also have an opportunity to revere some of our treasured natives and best loved parkland specimens to widen our perspective beyond our own garden into the breathtaking world of trees beyond.

As you turn the pages I hope you will have a sense of wonder, as I have done through my life, at the sheer diverse beauty of trees and the sumptuous delights of our fruit heritage. Trees are also amazingly tolerant of their surroundings and become such reliable friends through the years. Like children they take a long time to grow up but the pleasure of nurturing, watching and admiring is similarly priceless and immeasurably satisfying. The ultimate contentment is in the knowledge that those who follow will admire the trees we establish today as we have admired those inherited from our ancestors.

The activity of planting and caring for trees can cause no harm to a living soul and those who carry out this worthy task have no need for conscience or regret. There are few indulgences that could be measured as so completely natural or so beneficial and important to our future. As the world continues to debate our influence on the climate it is those who plant trees who put these well meaning words into action. They also leave a visible mark upon the earth which will give pleasure to many for years to come.

**Nick Dunn**

*In memory of my dad, Andrew Hunter Dunn vmh, who inspired a love of trees and propagation in so many people.*

# Contents

# Contents

# How are trees grown?

It is often the case that the longer things live the longer they take to propagate and nurture to maturity. This is something that trees have in common with us. Trees are reproduced in several ways but two principles prevail: *'varieties'* (cultivars or clones) are propagated from cuttings, budding or grafting and *'species'* from seed. In the 'Naming of Plants' on page 15 we explain the differences between genera, species, varieties and common names. However a tree is propagated, it will have taken up to three years in the nursery before it is ready for planting in the garden.

## Trees from seed

Trees raised from seed will be different from their parent(s) as our children are different from us. This could be in size and shape for fruit or in leaf type, shape or intensity of autumn colour for an ornamental tree and these differences will occur within one species. This is evident in many situations such as native woodland but in principle anywhere where nature controls what lives and dies.

## Trees from cuttings, budding or grafting

As soon as we began to influence our surroundings and look for improvements by plant selection and breeding we had to propagate vegetatively to obtain 'trueness to type' and as these techniques replicate varieties exactly they have remained with us for centuries up and until the present day. Some trees are grown from cuttings in winter or summer, but most are budded or grafted onto rootstocks (either seedlings or cuttings themselves) as the pictures here illustrate. Later in life the 'union' of the tree between rootstock and variety is still visible as shown in 'Humps and Bumps' on page 135.

### Budding

Our team of budders work in pairs (budder and tyer). Each pair can bud between 2,000 and 3,000 trees per day.

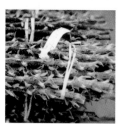

Budwood is prepared, cold stored and delivered to the field for budding.

Each bud is precisely positioned onto a rootstock ensuring good cambial contact. This is then tied in with polythene for 5 weeks.

As the bud begins to grow, various methods are used to ensure the development of a straight tree.

### Grafting

A uniform healthy rootstock is prepared either bare root or individually pot grown (depending on the subject).

Precise matching of graft and rootstock is important.

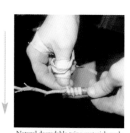

Natural degradable tying materials such as rubber and moisture retentive dipping wax maximise success rates.

The 'union' between scion and rootstock is evident after a successful graft take.

# Choosing your tree...

### First, think about your garden and your neighbours.

Before you choose you will need to make a number of not very difficult decisions. Do you want a fruit or an ornamental tree? Are you after spring blossom, interesting bark, or autumn foliage – or all three? You need to think about your garden, its soil type, the shelter it provides: the things which will determine what will thrive. Think about your neighbours too. Don't choose a tree which, if left un-checked, will block the sun from their garden or their favourite sitting out area.

### Next, find a good garden centre or nursery

Good garden centres and nurseries are like good second hand book shops: they are staffed by knowledgeable people who love the products and they are excellent places in which to browse.

There are some obvious pointers to look out for:

- Make sure that at least some of the staff have secateurs strapped to their belts or in their apron pockets. It's a sure sign that people are caring for the plants and trees as they go about their business.
- Look for printed labels on the tree showing delivery dates so you can quickly tell how fresh the stock is.

- Avoid buying trees that are over 12 months old from delivery date.
- A good garden centre will offer home deliveries within a reasonable distance of their location. After all, a tree isn't the easiest thing to fit into a family car, especially if you have the family on board.
- Look for some sort of replacement guarantee. One year is reasonable and two is excellent. Check this out before you buy.

### Less obvious things to note:

- Trees that have fresh growing tips and healthy foliage are best.
- Avoid trees with signs of stress such as small and tired leaves. These are often associated with both stress and disease infection.
- Avoid trees that show too much bare wood and have leaves primarily at the tips of each branch.

### If you choose to buy your trees mail order:

- Like other mail order shopping, buying trees this way has its advantages and pitfalls. The main advantage is, unquestionably, that you can take your time to make all those important decisions about which varieties to buy – and you need not have the difficulty of transporting that extra large tree home in your car.
- Buy from a company that you know well either from previous experience, or by recommendation.
- Since you cannot see the trees you are buying, companies that specify age and size of tree can be a useful guide to good value.
- Good mail order companies should have knowledgeable and helpful staff on the end of the phone.
- Bare root trees by mail order are generally delivered from November to March, so patience is required if you order in advance. Be suspicious of bare root offers at any other time.
- Seasons vary and in mild autumns bare root trees can often lose their leaves late, delaying autumn lifting and despatch from the nursery: again patience is needed.
- If trees arrive during wet or frosty weather, do not attempt to plant in their final position straight away.

# ...and how to plant it

The best time to plant a container grown tree is from mid August to the end of May. Summer planting (June and July) is possible but weekly watering would be necessary (a bucket a week!). The best time to plant a bare root tree is from November to March.

## Steps to success:

Mark out the diameter of the hole at least twice as big as the container grown pot or bare root tree.

If planting in grass remove the turf entirely, this is best placed upside down on the compost heap.

Dig to a depth that allows the roots to be 1" – 2" below the final soil level. Remember that with fruit trees the union between rootstock and variety should be several inches clear of the soil.

Make sure that the bottom of the hole is well broken up to a fine and kind tilth and also raised in the middle. If very heavy soil then the edge of the hole should be scoured with a fork.

Knock in post for support.

Water container grown trees before planting. If the tree feels light then water extra well.

Root pruning is acceptable for bare root trees in the dormant season, preferable to tucking them round the edge of the hole.

If the roots are dry then soaking in a bucket of water or pond for up to two hours is recommended before planting. Root pruning before soaking increases the uptake of water into the tree more efficiently.

Tease out roots of container grown trees. When in leaf this needs to be done gently retaining most of the root ball intact. In the winter a more robust approach can be taken by breaking out part of the compost and mixing it with the soil backfill.

Add a handful of bone meal on the dug out soil before back filling.

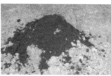

Also add compost if the soil is particularly heavy.

Firm soil gently at the halfway stage for container grown.

Firm the soil well when planting bare root trees.

Make sure all the soil is used to produce a raised area. Leave as a loose tilth to sink on its own.

Apply a suitable tree tie. Fix to the post to hold in position or place above a lower branch.

Spiral guards are an option but take them off once a year to inspect the tree trunk for damage as they also harbour over wintering pests.

Wire guards are a good robust option, one can see the tree trunk at all times and they are more effective. Nail to post as shown.

Bend round tree and fix at two points leaving ragged edges around the top to deter rabbits and hares.

Job complete.

# Understanding the naming of plants

Plant genus (types) can be sub-divided into various categories. We have used various type styles to easily identify these sub-divisions. These are defined, in order of superiority, as follows:

1. **GENUS** (in bold, capital letters, as **PRUNUS** below): "a group of closely related species possessing certain morphological characters in common, by which they are classified and distinguished from all others"

2. *Species* (italicised as *-litigiosa* below): "a sub-division of a genus consisting of plants which have the same constant and distinctive characters, and which have the capacity to interbreed amongst themselves"

3. **Common Name** (in bold as **(Tassel Cherry)** below): the name by which the species is commonly known, not botanical

4. **'Cultivar'** (bold and in single quote marks as in -**'Matsumae-fuki'** below): "an internationally agreed term for a cultivated variety" specifically selected by man because it exhibits different characteristics from the typical species and is worth maintaining in cultivation

5. TRADE/REGISTERED OR SELLING NAME (the plant breeders own plant name as in CHOCOLATE ICE below): appears after the **'Cultivar'** in capitals letters but not bold e.g. -**'Matsumae-fuki'** CHOCOLATE ICE

6. *Hybrid* (in italics, denoted with an x as in *-x subhirtella* **'Fukubana'** below): "a plant raised by the crossing of two genetically distinct plants"

7. Synonym (prefixed with Syn as in Syn: P. 'Weeping Yoshino' below): an alternative name for the same cultivar)

**1. Genus**

**2. Species**

**3. Common name**

**4. Cultivar**

**5. Trade/Registered or Selling Name**

**6. Hybrid**

**7. Synonym**

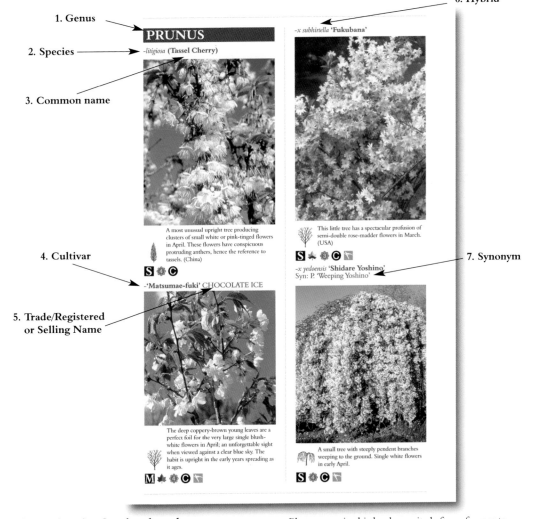

**PRUNUS**

*-litigiosa* **(Tassel Cherry)**

A most unusual upright tree producing clusters of small white or pink-tinged flowers in April. These flowers have conspicuous protruding anthers, hence the reference to tassels. (China)

-**'Matsumae-fuki'** CHOCOLATE ICE

The deep coppery-brown young leaves are a perfect foil for the very large single blush-white flowers in April; an unforgettable sight when viewed against a clear blue sky. The habit is upright in the early years spreading as it ages.

*-x subhirtella* **'Fukubana'**

This little tree has a spectacular profusion of semi-double rose-madder flowers in March. (USA)

*-x yedoensis* **'Shidare Yoshino'**
Syn: P. 'Weeping Yoshino'

A small tree with steeply pendent branches weeping to the ground. Single white flowers in early April.

## Plant registration ® and trademarks ™

As plant registration and trademarks change periodically these symbols are not included in this publication.

Plant names in this book are cited after reference to RHS Plant Finder 2009 Edition and Hilliers Manual of Plants and Trees 2003 Edition.

# Ornamental trees

## Some notes on the symbols used in the ornamental trees section of this Guide

**Most of the symbols in the Ornamentals section are self-explanatory, but we thought it might help if we pointed up the following:**

 A fast growing tree need pose no threat even in a small garden. The trick is to use pruning and coppicing to make the tree work with the space available.

 Slow growing trees are usually well worth the wait. It also means that quite large trees can be enjoyed in small gardens for many years before the need to take remedial action arises.

### Tree heights – after 10 years

An explanation to the tree height estimates in this book.

- Against each tree described there is a rating of VS, S, M and L as an approximate guide to tree size. This rating is after 10 years in a garden situation in reasonably good soil and growing conditions.

**VS** Very Small tree: up to 1.25m/4' in height

**S** Small tree: up to 4m/13' in height

**M** Medium tree: up to 6m/20' in height

**L** Large tree: over 6m/20' in height

### Tree widths

This is more difficult to determine due to proximity of other trees, buildings, shade and exposure. However, by observing the tree shape against each tree it will not be too difficult to estimate width in proportion to tree height.

**The reasons for our guide assessment to be after 10 years:**

- This accounts for the juvenile growth period of a tree when it grows at its fastest.

- After 10 years the growth rate slows and other factors can be more influential to its ultimate size, such as soil type, depth and site. It is these other influences that make tree size unpredictable.

- Pruning, coppicing and pollarding will negate any estimates made and are certainly encouraged with some species to lengthen their life.

 Attractive bark.

 Interesting foliage.

 If two leaf symbols are used the first will indicate spring and summer colours, and the second autumn tints.

 Variegated foliage.

 Scented foliage.

 This is a reasonably accurate guide to flowering month but seasons can vary up to 3 weeks earlier or later. Geographical location and the lie of your land are very influential. For example, central Scotland will be at least a month later than southern England. Flowering will be earlier on sheltered sites and especially if trees are grown in pots. Trees on lighter soils will also flower earlier than those on heavy loam or clay.

 Scented flower.

 Evergreen.

 Apart from attracting wildlife the fruit from most of these trees can be made into jellies, jams, compotes, cheeses and drinks, and much more.

 Prefers acid soil.

 Chalk tolerant.

 Tolerant of clay.

 Needs well draining site.

 Drought tolerant.

 Wet tolerant.

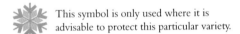 This symbol is only used where it is advisable to protect this particular variety.

Most gardens are positioned amongst buildings, fences, hedges or established large trees, all of which provide shelter. This symbol is used to indicate that this variety can be planted anywhere in this type of environment or where such an environment can be created.

 Suitable for exposed sites.

 Good in coastal site.

 Tolerant of shade.

 Prefers full sun.

Growing trees in patio pots can have an extreme dwarfing effect and for this reason any tree can be grown in a pot – look at Bonsai! We only indicate those which are naturally suitable and are relatively easy to look after. Please remember that all trees in pots need regular watering.

 Trains well against walls.

 Good for hedging.

 Good for topiary.

 These trees can be hard pruned severely at any time without causing any harm to the tree.

 Can be pruned hard after flowering to promote fresh young growth on which flowering is abundant the following year.

 An occasional thinning-out of some of the branches can be undertaken to encourage fresh replacement growth.

 These varieties prefer to be left alone and would not benefit from any regular or structured pruning.

**You will find more information about the Pruning of Ornamental Trees on page 198.**

 Used in the Malus crab apple section to denote disease resistance.

 The Royal Horticultural Society's Award of Garden Merit (AGM) indicates that the plant is recommended by the RHS.

 Trees marked with this symbol are especially suitable for planting in **public spaces**. They will be long lived, robust and have real 'presence' when mature. Those having an upright habit are also suitable for roadside planting.

# ABIES

## (Silver Fir)

Most Silver Firs, though slow-growing at first, eventually become large trees. The following selections, however, are ideal for small gardens. Easy in most conditions and in any reasonably well-drained soil, other than shallow chalk.

### -koreana

 A small, slow growing tree of neat compact habit, leaves dark green, silvery white beneath, producing violet purple, cylindrical cones even on young trees. (Korea)

### -koreana 'Silberlocke'

 Even slower growing, with twisted leaves creating a silvery appearance. Cones develop reliably at a very young age. (Germany)

### -lasiocarpa 'Compacta'

 A slow growing dwarf tree of shrub proportions with attractive blue/grey leaves.

# ACACIA

## (Wattle)

These elegant ornamental trees tolerate poor shallow soils needing good drainage and a sheltered position to perform well.

### -dealbata (Silver Wattle)

 An upright evergreen tree of open habit. The double pinnate bluish-green leaves have a silvery sheen. Clusters of small, rounded, scented, yellow flowers appear in April. Enjoys a well drained soil and a warm, sheltered and sunny site. (Australia)

# ACER

## (Maple)

This is a diverse and mostly hardy group, easy to grow in a wide range of soils. They thrive in sun or partial shade and include such delights as Japanese and snakebark maples. Spectacular leaves, incredibly varied in size, shape and colour, are their predominant feature, with many developing brilliant autumn colour. Newly introduced red maple (A. rubrum) cultivars from North America with more predictable autumn colours to suit the UK climate are also described in this section. For Japanese Maples please see Japanese Maple section.

Although not known as flowering trees, many have attractive, small, delicate flowers in spring before the leaves unfold. These may be followed by colourful fruits in late summer and autumn.

### -campestre (Field Maple)

This round-headed, medium to large size tree with corky light brown stems, is good for hedges but undervalued as a specimen. Five lobed leaves sometimes pinkish-red at first turn yellow, gold, russet, or even dark purple in autumn. Grows on chalk and quite acid soil, also on waterlogged sites. Very hardy.

### -campestre 'Carnival'

The bold, white leaf margins and pink growing tips make this a cheerful and distinctive shrub or small tree all through the summer. Prune hard in winter to increase leaf size for a more dramatic effect. (Holland)

### -capillipes (Snake Bark Maple)

This small tree has striated bark, red turning brown with white streaks. Three lobed leaves are bright green with slightly glaucous undersides. Young growth is coral red. Autumn tints of orange and red. Yellow catkin-like flowers ripen to tiny winged pink and yellow fruit in summer. (Japan)

### -cappadocicum 'Aureum'

The young emerging leaves are a stunning red, turning quickly to golden yellow for many weeks. Wonderful autumn tints. A good spring and autumn tree.

## -cappadocicum 'Rubrum'

 The fiery blood-red young leaves turn green in summer and later assume golden yellow autumn tints. An excellent specimen and garden tree.

## -x conspicuum 'Phoenix'

 An improved form of A. pensylvanicum 'Erythrocladum' with brighter, darker, coral-red winter shoots and striated bark. Slow to grow in the early years and is best planted on good well drained soil. A seedling of A. x conspicuum 'Silver Vein'.

## -x conspicuum 'Silver Vein'

A. davidii 'George Forrest' x A. pensylvanicum 'Erythrocladum' raised in 1961. A very select snake bark maple of impressive white and green bark with particularly large, rich green leaves with red stalks. Butter yellow autumn colours. (Hampshire)

## -davidii 'George Forrest'
## (Snake Bark Maple)

One of the best snake barks grown from seed with green and white striated bark. Leaves shiny dark green, with red stalks. Prefers moisture retentive soil. (China)

## -x freemanii 'Autumn Blaze' JEFFERSRED

A. rubrum x A. saccharinum. A vigorous hybrid with deeply cut leaves and a dense oval head. Spectacular bright orange and red leaves in the autumn. (USA)

## -griseum (Paper Bark Maple)

This small, broadly columnar tree has brown flaking old bark which shows cinnamon coloured new bark beneath. The three lobed yellowish-green leaves turn red and scarlet in autumn. Pale greenish-yellow flowers in late spring. Grows best in sun or light shade and will tolerate chalk soil. A classic border or lawn specimen. (China)

## -grosseri var. hersii (Snake Bark Maple)

A good snake bark with wonderful marbled bark, excellent autumn colours and conspicuous fruits borne on long racemes. (China)

## -japonicum 'Aconitifolium'

The deeply cut green leaves and brilliant crimson autumn colours in some opinions would place this small tree in the Japanese maple section. Small red flowers in spring. Grows best in moist well drained soil and a sheltered site. (Japan)

## -micranthum

A rare, delicate small tree or shrub with five lobed leaves. The finely cut leaves turn bright red in autumn. In the same group as A. rufinerve and A. capillipes. (Japan)

Many species of Acer (maple) are used in medicine to treat general pain, coughs and incorporated into skin care products.

*-negundo* **'Elegans'**

 A fast growing tree when young. The pale green leaves are brightly margined with broad yellow variegations. Good for coppicing like all A. negundo.

*-negundo* **'Flamingo'**

Leaves white variegated with salmon pink edges. This tree can be pruned hard in early spring creating a superb exotic foliage effect in late summer. Attractive grey-white stems in winter. (Holland)

*-negundo* **'Kelly's Gold'**

This beautiful garden tree has fresh golden leaves throughout summer and long, golden tassled flowers in June. Can be pruned hard each spring to enhance ornamental effect or to control size. (New Zealand)

*-pentaphyllum*

A rare and handsome small tree with deeply cut five lobed leaves on long scarlet petioles. Ideal as a patio specimen.

## *-platanoides* **(Norway Maple)**

Large, round-headed, fast growing tree. The five lobed leaves are pale then bright green. Mellow yellow colours in autumn. Clusters of lime green flowers in spring. Good on all soils including chalk soil. Tolerant of pollution and very hardy.

## *-platanoides* **'Crimson King'**

A handsome, round-headed, fast growing tree. Lime green flowers tinged red in April followed by large intense purple leaves turning bright crimson in autumn. Other comparable purple-leaved forms are A. 'Goldsworth Purple' and A. 'Royal Red'.

### Why do leaves turn in autumn?

The bright reds and purples become visible in the autumn when photosynthesis stops and chlorophyll ceases to be made. The chlorophyll masks these colours during the summer. Glucose is also trapped in the leaves and when the conditions are favourable with sunshine by day and colder nights the leaves turn this glucose into red colours. The brown tints are also created from wastes left in the leaves.

## *-platanoides* **'Drummondii'**

A popular garden tree, globe-headed with green leaves and a striking white marginal band. A good foil for purple and gold leaved shrubs. The occasional branch can revert to plain green leaves and should be pruned out.

## *-platanoides* **'Princeton Gold'** PRIGO

A beautiful golden leaved Norway Maple retaining its colour throughout the season. Resistant to scorch in the hottest of summers. A fast growing and worthy tree for any situation.

23

## -*pseudoplatanus* '**Brilliantissimum**'

 A distinctive small mop-headed tree. Spring foliage opens salmon pink, turning green or straw coloured. Slow growing. Suitable for small gardens as a lawn specimen or to add height in borders. Tolerant of exposure and light shade.

## -*pseudoplatanus* '**Gadsby**'

 A compact tree with multi-coloured leaves combining all the features of A. pseudoplatanus 'Brilliantissimum', A. pseudoplatanus var. 'Leopoldii' and A. pseudoplatanus 'Simon-Louis Frères'.

## -*pseudoplatanus* '**Prinz Handjery**'

 A similar form to A. pseudoplatanus 'Brilliantissimum' but more vigorous and open in habit. The salmon pink leaves also last longer and have purple undersides.

## -*pseudoplatanus* '**Worley**'
## (Golden Leaved Sycamore)

 A robust form of sycamore. The golden leaves retain their rich yellow colour throughout summer. A stunning large parkland tree.

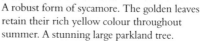

## -pseudoplatanus variegatum 'Eskimo Sunset'

A compact, small tree with bronze-green emerging leaves opening to show pink and green splashes with stripes and startling pink undersides.

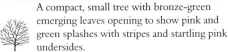

## -pseudoplatanus variegatum 'Simon-Louis Frères'

A slow growing, broadly spreading tree. Leaves brilliant deep pink in spring, becoming green, cream, pink and purple. Can be hard pruned to control size and to enhance the spectacular leaves.

## -rubrum (Red Canadian Maple)

Fast growing, ultimately large, round-headed tree with dark green leaves turning rich red-scarlet in autumn. Dense clusters of small red flowers in spring. Autumn colours are seasonally variable in the UK but will be more predictable on neutral to acid soils.

## -rubrum 'Brandywine'

Probably one of the best A. rubrum varieties for reliably intense autumn colour in the UK climate. Upright and oval in shape, ideal for restricted spaces. The superb red and purple colours last a long time and start early.

### -*rubrum* 'October Glory'

 A dense, round-headed form with glossy green leaves turning brilliant red in the autumn holding on to its leaves quite late. A reliable and often spectacular autumn tree.

### -*rubrum* 'Somerset'

 An impressive and reliable A. rubrum with intense deep red autumn colour even as a young tree. This is a male clone with an ovate crown and is of moderate size.

### -*rubrum* 'Summer Red'

This variety is unique as the summer foliage is very attractive with crimson young leaves and growing tips and deep red stems. Enhanced autumn colours of two tone yellow and crimson.

### -*rubrum* 'Sun Valley'

This is a cousin of A. rubrum 'Somerset' with long lasting autumn colours. It is a vigorous grower when young with a symmetrical ovate crown in later life. Even though late to colour this is still a week before A. rubrum 'October Glory'.

## -rufinerve (Snake Bark Maple)

Broadly columnar, medium to large sized tree with green and white striated bark. Dark green foliage produces bright red and yellow autumn colours. Small upright clusters of yellow-green flowers in spring. Best autumn colour is achieved on neutral to acid soil.

## -saccharinum (Silver Maple)

A fast growing, graceful tree. Delicate cut leaves are silver and downy beneath, producing good gold-yellow autumn colour. Greenish-yellow flowers can appear as early as February. Exposed windswept sites should be avoided as the thin upright branches are liable to break.

Acer saccharinum (the silver maple) described above is often confused with Acer saccharum (the sugar maple). Although the latter does grow reasonably well in the UK the conditions are not ideal for maple syrup production.

## -tataricum subsp. ginnala 'Flame' (The Tatarian Maple)

A shrub or small tree of bushy habit, with bright green leaves turning orange and crimson in autumn. Yellowish-white fragrant flowers in spring. Will tolerate semi-shade. (Afghanistan)

## -triflorum (Three flowered Maple)

This slow growing, broadly spreading tree has pale grey-brown peeling bark. Pale green leaves turn brilliant orange and crimson in autumn. Tiny yellow flowers are in clusters of three in spring. Tolerates semi-shade but colours best in full sun. An attractive and elegant specimen tree.

# JAPANESE MAPLES

There are hundreds of beautiful varieties of Japanese maples. Listed here is a selection encompassing the most distinctive features of this sublime group. Most forms attain large shrub and occasional small tree proportions, will tolerate *some* lime but prefer good loam soils and shelter. Ideal for growing in large pots.

## -*palmatum* '**Atropurpureum**'

 Often used as a generic name for any finely lobed, purple leaved forms similar in habit to its green counterpart.

## -*palmatum* '**Butterfly**'

 Bushy-headed shrub or small tree with grey-green deeply cut leaves, margined cream, pink-tinged when young, turning red-orange in autumn.

## -*palmatum var. dissectum*

 Also often used as a suitable generic name for any rounded, shapely, slow growing shrub with finely lobed green leaves turning a gorgeous orange in autumn.

## -*palmatum var. dissectum* '**Crimson Queen**'

 Leaves very deep reddish-purple, deeply divided into slender, finely cut lobes. Fiery red autumn colour.

*-palmatum var. dissectum* **'Garnet'**

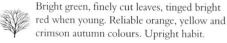 A stronger growing and excellent form with finely dissected, purple leaves.

*-palmatum var. dissectum* **'Seiryu'**

Bright green, finely cut leaves, tinged bright red when young. Reliable orange, yellow and crimson autumn colours. Upright habit.

*-palmatum var. dissectum* **'Tamukeyama'**

Crimson-red dissected leaves which unfold to dark purple throughout summer, turning scarlet in autumn. One of the best and most robust purple dissected forms.

*-palmatum* **'Katsura'**

Attractive five lobed leaves unfolding bright orange-yellow in the spring with enhanced colours in the autumn. The name 'Katsura' means wig.

## -*palmatum* '**Kinshi**'

A most delicate form with finely narrowed, filigree leaves and a gentle weeping habit. Enhanced bronze autumn colours. 'Kinshi' means 'Harp String'

## -*palmatum* '**Orange Dream**'

A lovely cultivar similar to A. palmatum 'Katsura' with seven lobed leaves emerging orange later becoming lemon yellow with orange tinged margins. Autumn colours are bright yellow-gold. (Italy)

## -*palmatum* '**Sango-kaku**' (**Coral Bark Maple**)
Syn: A. *palmatum* 'Senkaki'

One of the most vibrant of small winter trees. Bright coral-red stems in winter. Small palmate, pale green leaves turn gold in autumn.

## -*palmatum* '**Suminagashi**'

Large leaved, upright, well branched tree-like shrub. Leaves rich dark purple in spring, turning bronze-green in summer, crimson-red in autumn.

*palmatum* **'Trompenburg'**

 A graceful form with deep purple-red narrow lobed leaves turning green in the summer and red in autumn. (Holland)

*palmatum* **'Villa Taranto'**

 An A. palmatum 'Linearilobum' type, leaves with five slender leaflets. The reddish, young leaves give contrast to the older, green foliage. Yellow tints in autumn. (Italy)

# AESCULUS

## (Horse Chestnut)

Although most are stately medium to large trees requiring room, some forms described here are compact small trees with variable, attractive flower panicles of differing colours. They are easily cultivated and will thrive in almost any soils, in sun or light shade.

*-californica* **'Blue Haze'**

 This form of the 'California Buckeye' has a pronounced blue cast in its leaves and forms a wide spreading large shrub or small tree. In July the blue-green glossy foliage provides the perfect foil for the large pink tinted, white, fragrant flower spikes.

*-x carnea* **'Briotii' (Red Horse Chestnut)**

 This compact, dome-headed, large tree has a densely leaved habit with deep pink flower bracts. Glossy brown 'conkers' are enclosed in smooth or slightly spiny husks. Slow growing. Resistant to 'Chestnut Leaf Miner'.

## *-hippocastanum*
**(Common Horse Chestnut)**

 Vigorous large tree. Sticky buds progress to large bright green palmate leaves, turning yellow and orange-brown in autumn. Large white 'candle' flowers. Rounded, spiny green husks enclose one or two shiny brown 'conkers' in the autumn. Suitable as a specimen in large gardens and parks. Susceptible to the 'Chestnut Leaf Miner'. Native.

## *-indica* **'Sydney Pearce'**
**(Indian Horse Chestnut)**

A superb more free flowering selection from Kew Gardens that makes a perfect globe-shaped tree with attractive leaves emerging purple then turning dark olive-green in summer. Large panicles of white and yellow flowers suffused pink appear in June and July. (UK)

## *-x mutabilis* **'Induta'**
Syn: A. *pavia* 'Rosea Nana'

 A large shrub or small tree producing a stunning show of apricot and yellow flowers in May and June.

## *-x neglecta* **'Autumn Fire'**
**(Yellow Horse Chestnut)**

This is a lovely small tree, with emerging coppery coloured foliage in spring, turning dark green in the summer and then turning glowing orange and yellow in autumn. It has creamy-yellow flowers in May. (USA)

## -x neglecta 'Erythroblastos'

## -parviflora (Bottle Brush Buckeye)

 A medium to large shrub. Leaves bronze in spring, and yellow in autumn. Slender panicles of white flowers with attractive red anthers. (USA)

## -pavia var. discolor 'Koehnei' (Dwarf Red Buckeye)

 Slender, broadly columnar, slow growing tree. Pointed, finely toothed leaves emerge bright pink, later yellow then dark green, turning orange and red in autumn. Small creamy-white flowers are flushed pink. Best grown in deep, fertile soil.

### Chestnut leaf miner and other problems

Chestnut leaf miner (Cameraria ohridella) has infected trees in the UK since 2002 and has spread (by the adult moth) rapidly northwards. There is no evidence that this pest kills the chestnut tree and all infected trees leaf up perfectly normally the following spring. Many species and their cultivars are resistant including: A. carnea x briotii, A. californica, A. chinensis, A. indica, A. x neglecta, A. pavia.

Chestnut bleeding canker (Phytophthora) is more serious as trees often suffer limb death and occasionally trees will die. Symptoms are weeping tar-like substance on the main trunk. A. hippocastanum is more susceptible, with the ornamental forms seemingly more resistant.

 An unusual dwarf chestnut with emerging bronzy-red leaves and stunning pink and yellow flowers.

## ALBIZIA

### (Silk Tree)

These deciduous or semi-evergreen mimosa-like, small umbrella shaped trees have feathery foliage, stunning fluffy-headed flowers and grow best in warm, sheltered sites on well drained and even impoverished soils. Very suitable for milder parts of the UK.

### -julibrissin 'Ombrella' BOUBRI

An exotic but hardy, small, shrubby tree with delicate feathered leaves. Stunning, dense-headed, deep pink flowers appear from July to September. A quite spectacular and beautiful small tree. Occasionally described as the "Powder Puff Tree".

### -julibrissin rosea

A small, broadly spreading tree, often flat topped. Dark pink flowers appear on top of the dark green feathery leaves in late summer. Growing on a wall can improve flowering. (Korea)

## ALNUS

### (Alder)

Will tolerate almost any soil condition except shallow chalk. Fast and easy to grow, thriving even in waterlogged soil. Excellent for shelter belts. Respond well to coppicing and heavy pruning at any stage.

### -cordata (Italian Alder)

A fast growing tree of neat conical shape. Glossy, deep green, heart-shaped leaves. Showy, long greenish-yellow catkins. Suitable for all soil types. (Italy)

### -glutinosa (Common Alder)

A native tree throughout the Britsh Isles. Once used extensively for the manufacture of clogs in northern England. Has succumbed to widespead Phytophthora infection in recent years not helped by the lack of harvest and coppicing that this tree requires for re-juvenation purposes.

*-glutinosa* **'Imperialis'**

 The most ornamental and graceful form with deeply, fine cut leaves.

*-incana* **(Grey Alder)**

 A conical tree which will broaden with age. The oval leaves are grey underneath. Yellow-red catkins in spring. Small, woody, cone-like fruits in autumn. This very hardy tree is good in cold wet conditions. (USA)

*-incana* **'Aurea'**

 A good yellow leaved form with golden winter shoots and red tinted catkins.

# AMELANCHIER

### (Juneberry, Snowberry or Snowy Mespilus)

Excellent, very hardy, small trees or shrubs for spring flower and in many cases good autumn tints. They will thrive in moist, well-drained, lime-free soil.

*-alnifolia* **'Obelisk'**

 An interesting fastigiate form with a dense branch structure and an intense display of single white flowers in April.

Alnus glutinosa (the common alder) has many uses for making clogs, boats, building materials, gunpowder charcoal, poles for fencing (also used for the underpinning of Venice), tanning and pigments of hides and for the treatment of malaria and rheumatism.

Alders should be encouraged as shelter trees on poor land as they are effective nitrogen fixers for other symbiotic plant life.

## -x grandiflora 'Ballerina'

 A small tree with an upright habit and colourful bronze new leaves. A great profusion of pure white flowers in April. (Holland)

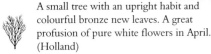

### -x grandiflora 'Robin Hill'

A good, upright form for the smaller garden with emerging pink flowers slowly turning to pure white. More resistant to mildew than other forms.

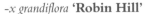

## The Tree Advice Trust

The Tree Advice Trust is an independent charity whose aims are to research and disseminate practical information and guidance on the cultivation, maintenance and care of trees grown for amenity.

The Trust is responsible for the work of the Arboricultural Advisory and Information Service (AAIS). Located at the Forest Research Station near Farnham, Surrey, the Arboricultural Advisory and Information Service has been giving independent and impartial advice to the public and the arboricultural profession for over 20 years.

www.treehelp.info

## -'La Paloma'

This wonderful cultivar (previously distributed as A. laevis) deserves to be widely planted. The pure white, pendulous racemes look sensational against the coppery-red young leaves in April. Forms a round-headed shrub or small tree. Excellent autumn colour.

## -laevis 'R. J. Hilton'

Distinctively pink when in bud opening to large, white flowers, having a stunning contrast to the deep copper-coloured emerging leaves, similar to A. 'La Paloma'. Excellent red and yellow autumn leaf colours. (Canada)

*-laevis* **'Snowflakes'**

A stunning, small tree or large bush of ascending habit. Large, single, white flowers in April appear as a lovely contrast to the emerging copper foliage. Bronze-red autumn leaf colours.

*-lamarckii*

A small tree or shrub with beautiful orange-red autumn colours. A profusion of small, white flowers in spring. Often confused with A. canadensis, A. laevis and A. confusa.

# ARAUCARIA

A genus of evergreen trees from Oceania and S. America with distinctive symmetrical habit.

*-araucana* (**Monkey Puzzle**)

Extensively planted in Victorian times. Long, spidery, spine tipped branches and dark green leaves. Very hardy. Prefers well drained loamy soil. (Chile)

The origin of the popular English name Monkey-puzzle derives from its early cultivation in Britain in about 1850, when the species was still very rare in gardens and not widely known. The proud owner of a young specimen at Pencarrow garden near Bodmin in Cornwall was showing it to a group of friends, and one made the remark, "It would puzzle a monkey to climb that." As the species had no existing popular name, first 'monkey-puzzler', then 'monkey-puzzle' stuck.

Alan Mitchell (1996).

Alan Mitchell's Trees of Britain. Collins. ISBN 0-0021997-2-6.

# ARBUTUS

**(Strawberry Tree)**

Ornamental, evergreen, small trees for many situations.

### -*unedo* (Killarney Strawberry Tree)

Small, evergreen, spreading tree with dark brown shedding bark. Large dark green leaves. Small, 'urn-shaped' white flowers and red 'strawberry' fruit appearing together in autumn. Good for coastal sites and tolerant of lime.

**S B E C I**

### -*unedo rubra*

A pretty form with pink flowers.

**S B E C I**

# ARONIA

**(Chokeberry)**

Both autumn tints and interesting fruit. Not recommended for chalk soil.

### -*x prunifolia* **'Brilliant'**

An attractive shrub with white flowers in spring followed by clusters of red or black fruits. Good autumn colour. (USA)

**S A**

# BETULA (Birch)

Some of the most graceful of all trees with a much wider range of bark features than realised, from dynamic white to chocolate brown, smooth and shaggy. They will succeed on most soils with certain species happy even in wet sites. Although tolerant of chalk soils they will not reach maximum size in these conditions. Best in full sun.

## -albosinensis 'Fascination'
### (Chinese Red Barked Birch)

 This worthy selection has deep orange, satin, peeling bark revealing layers of variable colour. The exceptionally long catkins provide much added interest.

## -albosinensis 'Hergest'

 (Possibly B. albosinensis x B. ermanii). A rare and beautiful selection with light copper-brown shiny bark. (Hergest Croft Gardens, Kington, Herefordshire)

## -albosinensis 'Kansu'
### (Chinese Red Barked Birch)

 A good strong growing form with multi-coloured copper and pink bark, one of the best forms of the albosinensis species.

## -albosinensis var. septentrionalis
### (Chinese Red Barked Birch)

Of upright habit with finely flaking, pink-red marbled bark. The pale green leaves are lance-shaped. (W China)

## -'Edinburgh'

B. utilis x B. albosinensis var. septentrionalis. Found in the nursery of The Edinburgh Botanic Gardens – noted for its vigour and upright habit. Eventually developing a good white bark this selection is also ideal for a multi-stemmed tree.

## -*ermanii*

A graceful, vigorous grower with bright green heart-shaped heavily veined leaves. Attractive creamy white bark. (NE Asia)

## Said the tree to the man

I ask but little of you, light and space that I may grow to serve you. In return, I give you winter shelter from the wind and rain, and grateful summer shade.

I provide the door to your home and the beams and rafters that support its roof. You tread my boards as you cross the floor to eat at my table.

Mine are the logs that blaze upon your hearth, mine your comfortable pipe and the matches with which you tend it. And, when the time for sleep is come, my wooden bed awaits you.

At work, mine are the handles of your tools; at leisure, mine your wheel barrow, your stick, your bat, your newspaper.

At life's start I rocked you in my cradle; and, at your journey's end, my coffin will take charge of your relinquished body.

There has always been music for you in my leaves, beauty in my changing colours, nourishment in my fruits. With trees around, no man is comfortless.

## Said the man to the tree

I will spare you the light and the space that you need.

I will secure that, when you are old, another generation shall replace you. I will tend your offspring in their youth, knowing that my descendants will benefit by their maturity. I will value you as you deserve and, emulating your aspiring boughs, look up, in gratitude, towards the stars.

*Elizabeth Barling*

## -ermanii 'Pendula'

A neat and tidy weeping form with a clean, cream coloured peeling bark and strong yellow autumn tints.

## -ermanii 'Polar Bear'

A strong growing tree quickly developing a pure white trunk. After some years and with a little imagination this tree starts to resemble the polar bear of its name with its typical heavy branch structure. Attractive, long catkins.

## -'Fetisowii'

A lovely hybrid, slow growing and graceful birch. Noted for its smooth, creamy, chalk-white bark. Suitable for the smaller garden. (C Asia)

## -nigra

The river birch is a lovely sight when it develops its shaggy bark. There are several cultivars worth considering with B. nigra 'Wakehurst Place' that is similar to the picture above but with more pink tones in the bark and a recent introduction B. nigra 'Summer Cascade' a more compact weeping form shown below. All nigra forms are especially suitable for damp conditions.

### -pendula (Common Silver Birch)

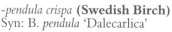
The 'Lady of the Woods'. A graceful slender tree with variable, white peeling bark developing with age and slightly pendulous branches. Diamond-shaped green leaves turn yellow in autumn. Makes an excellent windbreak and specimen tree. Native. (Europe)

### -pendula crispa (Swedish Birch)
Syn: B. pendula 'Dalecarlica'

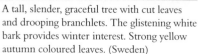
A tall, slender, graceful tree with cut leaves and drooping branchlets. The glistening white bark provides winter interest. Strong yellow autumn coloured leaves. (Sweden)

### -pendula 'Golden Beauty'
Syn: B. pendula 'Schreverdinger Goldbirke'

A true golden leaved form of birch that is bright and cheerful whose leaves do not scorch. Good autumn colour and white bark in winter. Particularly suitable for Scotland and the North. (Germany)

### -pendula 'Long Trunk'
Syn: B. utilis jacquemontii 'Pendula'

A unique form with a wide spreading, graceful, weeping habit eventually becoming dome-shaped. The bark becomes a good white for winter interest.

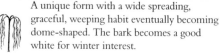

## *-pendula* 'Royal Frost'

This recent hybrid B. 'Crimson Frost' x B. populifolia 'Whitespire' introduction has persistent rich burgundy leaves and in time a good white stem with cinnamon hues. The yellow-orange-red autumn colours are an added feature. (Wisconsin, USA)

## *-pendula* 'Tristis'

A tall, graceful tree with pendulous twisting shoots at the end of the branches. The white bark, as with many birch, develops characteristic black fissures with age. A special tree for its unusual weeping appearance.

## *-pendula* 'Youngii' (Young's Weeping Birch)

A mushroom-headed, medium weeping tree with branches reaching the ground. Rough white bark has black fissures with age. Triangular, serrated, glossy green leaves turn golden yellow in autumn.

## *-platyphylla* 'Dakota Pinnacle' FARGO (Asian White Birch)

Ideal for urban areas due to its unusually narrow pyramidal habit. Dark green leaves are retained late into the autumn. The bark ultimately changes to creamy-white from orange in the early years. Particularly suitable for difficult conditions where soils are heavy or drought prone.

### The Perfect Shade Tree

A 'Shade Tree' is a generic North American term for most trees in gardens and the landscape. Its literal meaning is not considered often especially in the UK as we have too few bright sunny days when trees could be considered absolutely necessary as protection from the sun. However, 'dappled' rather than heavy shade is very desirable in our gardens and the Birch tree is the perfect tree in this respect. Even in the height of summer the naturally small leaves and lightly structured branches of most varieties are perfect for this purpose.

*-utilis var. jacquemontii*
**(The Himalayan White Birch)**

A popular distinctive form of the 'white' birch. Ascending branches form a spreading head, and the coppery-brown bark on young wood eventually peels to leave a distinctive white bark. The dark green serrated leaves are gold-yellow in autumn.
(N. India and N. and W. Nepal)

*-utilis var. jacquemontii* **'Doorenbos'**
See B. *utilis* 'Snow Queen'

*-utilis var. jacquemontii* **'Grayswood Ghost'**

A striking form with bright white bark, upright branches and glossy green leaves. Propagated from a tree in Grayswood Hill, Surrey. One of the best white barked selections.

*-utilis var. jacquemontii* **'Jermyns'**
One of the more vigorous and healthy white barked forms, broadly conical and with large catkins. The whiteness in the trunk takes a little more time to develop than some of the more select forms. A Hillier Nursery selection. (Hampshire)

## Multistems... a challenge!

Birch are the classic trees to use as multistems. Other attractive bark forms include the snake bark maples (see Acer section) and Prunus serrula. Most trees are capable of producing multistems and the best ones are seen in the wild that come naturally from young damaged trees grazed by animals. They are actually very hard to produce when contrived.

Two methods can be used: where a single tree is encouraged to produce multi-stems, as in the picture on the left; and where 3 individual trees are planted close together, as in the picture on the right.

## *-utilis var. jacquemontii* **'Silver Shadow'**

## *-utilis var. jacquemontii* **'Trinity College'**

A good new selection with a gleaming white trunk from an early age. This form is upright, graceful and light in form. Good for small spaces.

Ⓜ Ⓑ ● ◑ 🐪 🐸 ☒

## *-utilis* **'Moonbeam'**

Striking white bark and large drooping dark green leaves. One of the loveliest birches with dazzling white stems. The origins of this selection are from some of the earliest grafted trees of B. jacquemontii by Hillier Nursery, Hampshire.

Ⓜ Ⓑ ● ◑ 🐪 🐸 ☒ 🏆

This birch has a fine white trunk and is considerably smaller than other forms making it ideal for the small garden. Propagated from a fine specimen at Wakehurst Place, Sussex.

Ⓢ 🐌 Ⓑ ● ◑ 🐪 🐸 ☒

Betula *utilis* 'Snow Queen'

*-utilis* **'Snow Queen'**
Syn: B. *jacquemontii* 'Doorenbos'

This exceptional tree produces a lovely white stem within three years. Ideal for planting as a specimen, multi-stemmed or in clumps. Strong yellow autumn tints.

*-utilis* **'Wakehurst Place Chocolate'**

One of the darkest barked birch with true plain chocolate bark in the early years changing to all shades of brown as it ages. (Wakehurst Place, Sussex)

## Pleaching

Pleaching is a form of art that could be used much more as 'friendly and natural' barriers between neighbours. Used as 'hedges in the air' they are versatile and attractive garden features. The best trees are those with soft pliable shoots that are forgiving and respond well after hard pruning, such as limes (Tilia). Hornbeam (Carpinus) and beech (Fagus) have the added advantage of holding their leaves in winter.

# CARPINUS

## (Hornbeam)

These attractive and easily grown trees are suitable for heavy, wet or chalky soils, hedging, topiary and pleaching.

*-betulus* **(Common Hornbeam)**

A medium-large tree with grey fluted trunk and ovate, serrate, ribbed leaves turning yellow in autumn and then brown. Green catkins in late spring to autumn, followed by winged nuts. Will tolerate heavy soil and can be used as hedging. Native.
(Europe and Asia Minor)

*-betulus* **'Frans Fontaine'**

A medium sized tree of pyramidal habit, narrow when young and broadening as it matures. Good autumn colours of mellow yellow. A classic narrow neat tree for landscape and garden. Other forms include C. betulus 'Fastigiata' but this is the better compact form. (Holland)

## -betulus 'Pendula'

 A very graceful, mushroom-headed tree with steeply pendant branches.

## -fangiana

A rare and wonderful hornbeam named after Fang Wen-pei and only introduced in the last twenty years. It has large handsome leaves that are boldly ribbed and orange tinted when emerging in the spring. The very long pendulous fruiting catkins, persisting for several months, are a wonderful additional feature. We are indebted to Roy Lancaster for introducing this tree to our nursery. (SW Sichuan, China 1992)

## -japonica

 A very beautiful, spreading, small tree or large shrub with corrugated leaves and conspicuous fruiting catkins. A very elegant and worthy small garden tree. (Japan)

## -turczaninowii

 An attractive, small, shrubby tree with slender stems and dainty leaves emerging bright red in spring. (N China. Korea. Japan)

### Trees fall into 2 categories:

#### Angiosperms
- where the seed is hidden inside the fruit i.e Apple, Pear and Thorn (Crataegus).

#### Gymnosperms
– where the trees have naked seeds i.e Ash (Fraxinus), Maple (Acer) and Birch (Betula).

We see the use of the prefixes 'angio' and 'gymno' elsewhere: for example, an angiogram helps us track blood flow which is hidden from the human eye whilst the word gymnasium comes from a type of school in ancient Greece where young men trained as athletes – naked!

# CASTANEA

## (Chestnut)

These long-lived trees of stately appearance are good on light soils and are moderately lime tolerant.

### -*sativa* (Spanish or Sweet Chestnut)

 A fast growing large tree. Distinctive twisting bark on mature trees. Oblong, toothed leaves and yellow catkins in July. Rich brown edible nuts, encased in a prickly shell. Will tolerate drought. Very important as a timber tree especially for traditional coppicing for railings. Naturalised in the British Isles. (S Europe)

Chestnut fencing as 'post and rail' or 'paling' as shown here are traditional uses for a timber that is high in naturally preserving tannins and the ease in which it splits evenly down the grain. Its fruit can also be ground into gluten free flour.

### -*sativa* 'Albomarginata'

 A striking broadly columnar form. The leaves have creamy-white margins and turn yellow in autumn. Tiny creamy-yellow flowers in summer. Edible brown nuts in prickly shells in autumn.

### -*sativa* 'Variegata'
Syn: C. *sativa* 'Aureomarginata'

 Leaves are bordered with a broad yellow band. Can scorch in very hot summers. Ideally suited to partial shade and can be pruned hard for large succulent leaves.

# CATALPA

These deciduous trees and shrubs require well drained soil and full sun. They are very tolerant of urban pollution. Worth pollarding occasionally to contain size and enhance leaf size.

*-bignonioides* **(Indian Bean Tree)**

Large heart-shaped leaves and white 'foxglove' type flowers with attractive purple and yellow speckles borne in large panicles in July and August. These result in long bean-like pendulous pods up to 30cm long. (E.USA)

*-bignonioides* **'Aurea'**
**(Golden Indian Bean Tree)**

Low spreading habit with domed crown. Large heart-shaped golden velvety leaves fade to green. Prune in winter to increase the leaf size which is magnificent. Panicles of white flowers similar to C. bignonioides although less profuse. There is also a more dwarf form C. bignonioides 'Aurea Nana'.

*-bignonioides* **'Nana'**

A compact dense headed tree often seen in garden and landscape planting in Europe. A formal, architectural tree, ideal for small gardens and worthy of wider use.

*-x erubescens* **'Purpurea'**

 The young leaves and shoots are dark purple, almost black, gradually becoming dark green. Contrasts well with C. bignonioides 'Aurea'. Prune hard in winter.

## CEANOTHUS

**(California Lilac)**

Evergreen, lime tolerant shrubs or small trees. Some are relatively hardy, good for walls and seaside locations.

*-arboreus* **'Trewithen Blue'**

Large panicles of deep blue slightly scented flowers in spring. A vigorous rangey form, not the most hardy but certainly one of the most beautiful.

## CEDRUS

**(Cedar)**

These large conifers thrive in well drained soils and are tolerant of drought.

*-atlantica* **'Glauca' Group (Blue Cedar)**

 This spectacular blue conifer is popular for specimen planting. Pyramid-shaped when young becoming flat-topped later. Dark grey fissured bark and silvery-blue leaves. Best suited to the larger garden. (SW Asia and Syria)

### -atlantica 'Glauca Pendula'

 A superb, small to medium tree with narrow weeping branches and glaucous leaves. A special tree that gives good contrasting perspective in landscape and garden plantings.

### -deodara 'Aurea' (Golden Deodar)

 Golden-yellow leaves in spring fading to green in the late summer. A graceful drooping leader distinguishes itself from other species.

### -libani (Cedar of Lebanon)

 A slow growing, evergreen, large, wide-spreading, majestic tree. Green or grey-green foliage. Barrel-shaped cones are purple-green then brown. Will tolerate both dry acid and alkaline soil and cool summers.

## CERCIDIPHYLLUM

These trees are grown for their foliage and prefer moist, fertile soil and dappled shade.

### -japonicum (Katsura Tree)

 A fast growing, spreading tree. Small, heart-shaped, pale yellow to smokey-pink foliage in autumn, scenting the air with a burnt sugar aroma. Best colour is achieved on lime free soil. (Japan and China)

*-japonicum pendulum*

 A rare and unusual form with long pendant branches and healthy attractive heart-shaped leaves. A stunning weeping tree.

*-japonicum* **'Rotfuchs'** RED FOX

 An attractive purple-red leaved form, less vigorous and of more upright habit than the common Katsura. Raised from seed in Germany.

# CERCIS

## (Redbud)

These trees or large shrubs require well drained soil and full sun. The various species are from N. America, China and the Mediterranean.

*-canadensis* **'Forest Pansy'**

 A splendid selection with deep reddish-purple foliage, velvet to the touch. An attractive specimen for the small garden. Leaves take on gold and purple hues in autumn. Small, pea-like pink-mauve flowers appear in May.

*-canadensis* **'Hearts of Gold'**

 The distinctively bright golden leaved form with lavender flowers even on young plants. The first emerging leaves are red to add to its charm. Retain in full sun to maintain good golden leaf colour. (USA)

## -canadensis 'Lavender Twist'

A very special weeping redbud with somewhat contorted and arching branches. Foliage and flower is typical of the species, with the flowers being a more pinkish-purple. (USA)

## -chinensis 'Avondale'

A beautiful small tree with shiny rich green leaves that produces rosy-lilac pea-like flowers profusely from an early age. Hard pruning after flowering is recommended to maintain a small dynamic shrub.

## -reniformis 'Oklahoma' (Oklahoma Redbud)

Brilliant rose-magenta flowers and thick lustrous green leaves make this one of the best and robust flowering forms of the 'Redbud'.

## -reniformis 'Texas White'

A stunning white flowering selection with particularly large flowers.

## -siliquastrum (Judas Tree)

Small, rounded, bushy tree with glaucous green leaves. Clustered, rosy-lilac, pea-like flowers, followed by purple tinted seed pods. Heavy clay soil should be avoided.

## *-siliquastrum* 'Bodnant'

 A superior form of C. siliquastrum with very deep purple flowers.

Cercis can be pruned hard in the spring after flowering to produce vigorous growth and large succulent leaves from mid summer onwards.

# CHAMAECYPARIS

## (False Cypress)

The false cypresses native of the USA, Japan and Taiwan. Described below are unusual forms of good merit.

### *-nootkatensis* 'Green Arrow'

 A very narrow upright form with occasional informal weeping branches coming from the main stem. Very architectural in appearance.

### *-nootkatensis* 'Jubilee'

 Similar to 'Green Arrow' but more regular in its weeping habit. Narrower than C. nootkatensis 'Pendula'.

# CLADRASTIS

### -*kentuckea* (Yellowwood)

 A handsome tree producing long panicles of fragrant wisteria-like white flowers in June. The large attractive pinnate leaves turn clear yellow in the autumn. (SE USA)

# CLERODENDRUM

### -*trichotomum*

 A strong growing shrub or small tree with fragrant white flowers enclosed in maroon calyces in August and September, followed by bright blue fruit. (China and Japan)

# CORNUS

## (The flowering Dogwoods)

These beautiful trees are very hardy and tolerant of most conditions preferring well drained fertile soils to perform at their best. Both winter and spring flowering they give exceptional good value for their long flowering period over several weeks.

### -*controversa*

 A majestic tree-like species with the horizontal branches clothed in cream coloured flowers followed by black autumn fruits. 'Pagoda' is a fine vigorous form with large fruits and purple plum autumn colour. (Japan, China, Taiwan)

### -*controversa* 'Variegata' (Wedding Cake Tree)

 Small, slow growing tree has striking silver margined leaves displayed on horizontal branches. Clusters of cream-coloured flowers in May. A spectacular tree.

58

## -'Eddies White Wonder'

C. florida x C. nuttallii. A superb, upright shrub or small tree, with slightly glossy dark green leaves turning red and purple in autumn. Large white flowers in spring. Tolerates some shade. Not suitable for shallow chalk, best grown in deep fertile soil. Regarded as the very best white flowering Cornus. (USA)

## -florida
## (North American Flowering Dogwood)

A large shrub or small bushy tree. Dark green foliage richly coloured red and purple in autumn. White petal-like flowers (bracts) in May. Not suitable for shallow chalk soil.

## -florida 'Cloud Nine'

Large snow white bracts very free flowering even at a young age.

## -florida 'Daybreak'
## CHEROKEE DAYBREAK

An upright branching form with variegated leaves, creamy-white margins and good autumn colour. Flower bracts are pure white with green flower centres.

## -florida 'Rainbow'

Handsome yellow marginal leaves. Pure white bracts. Rich autumn colours.

## -florida rubra

 A generic name for various red and pink bract forms. Round-headed shrub or small tree. Flowers are pink to red with similar autumn colours to C. florida.

## -florida 'Sunset' CHEROKEE SUNSET

 New growth has pinkish-red tips that matures to a broad green leaf with wavy yellow margins. Good red bracts and pink to reddish purple autumn colour.

## -kousa var. chinensis

 An elegant tree, very often a show stopper when in its prime. Spectacular white bracts fading pink over a considerable period from June into early July, followed by strawberry-like fruits. One of the best forms is to be seen at RHS Wisley now named C. kousa var. chinensis 'Wisley Queen' (pictured below). (China)

*C. kousa var. chinensis 'Wisley Queen'*

## -kousa 'Weisse Fontaine'
Syn: C. *kousa* 'White Fountain'

 A spectacular show of pure white flower bracts which weigh the branches down to justify its descriptive name.

## -mas (Cornelian Cherry)

Spreading, open habit. Oval dark green leaves turn to reddish-purple in autumn. Tiny yellow flowers appear in February. There are several 'fruiting' forms selected for their abundant astringent pearl drop fruits that make excellent compotes and jams. See our fruit section under 'Cornelian cherry'. (C. and S. Europe)

## -'Norman Hadden'

 A semi-evergreen variety with large white long lasting flower bracts in June, turning deep pink with age and red fruits in autumn. (Porlock, Somerset)

## -nuttallii

The 'Mountain' dogwood from North America. The stunning white flower bracts occasionally become flushed pink and the leaves turn yellow and red in autumn. There are several exceptional cultivars available. For this tree to do well the soil needs to be moist and fertile. Avoid shallow chalk.

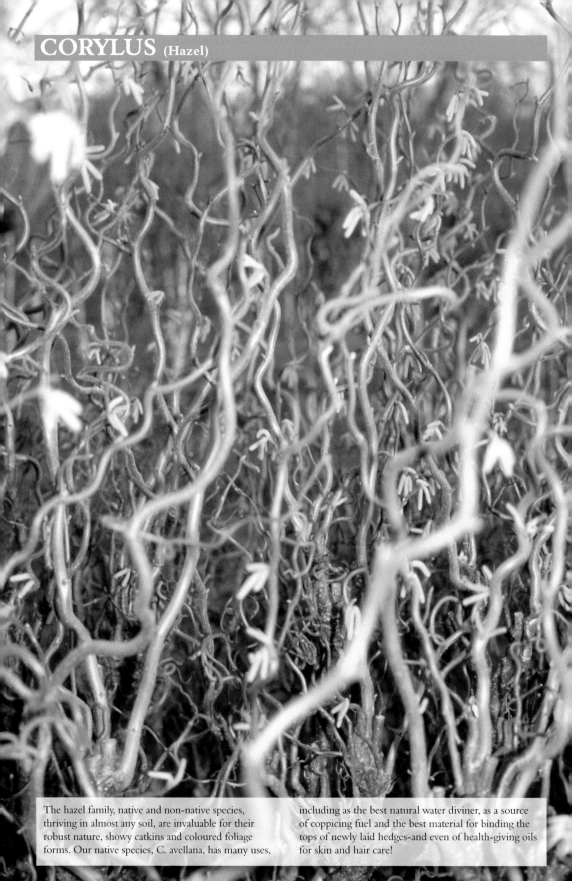

# CORYLUS (Hazel)

The hazel family, native and non-native species, thriving in almost any soil, are invaluable for their robust nature, showy catkins and coloured foliage forms. Our native species, C. avellana, has many uses, including as the best natural water diviner, as a source of coppicing fuel and the best material for binding the tops of newly laid hedges-and even of health-giving oils for skin and hair care!

## -avellana 'Aurea'

A soft yellow leaved form excellent as a contrast to the red forms such as C. avellana 'Red Majestic' and C. maxima 'Purpurea'. Yellow catkins in February.

## -avellana 'Contorta'
## (Harry Lauder's Walking Stick)

Also known as the 'corkscrew' hazel with curled and twisted shoots and a fine show of yellow catkins in late winter-early spring. A covering of winter frost makes a cheery sight. Prune hard at will!

## -avellana 'Heterophylla'
## Syn: C. avellana 'Laciniata'

A form with deeply lobed and textured leaves.

## -avellana 'Pendula'

A graceful weeping form creating a small but dense dome-shaped tree.

## -avellana 'Red Majestic'

 A striking red leaved form of the popular C. avellana 'Contorta'. Similar corkscrew curled and twisted shoots, dark purple leaves. Purple catkins eventually turning purple-green in mid-late summer. Prune hard at will!

## -colurna (Turkish Hazel)

A remarkable tree of symmetrical, pyramidal form. The corky corrugated bark is an interesting feature. Eventually grows into an imposing strong tree.
(SE Europe and W. Asia)

## -maxima 'Purpurea' (Purple-leaf Filbert)

 Large vigorous shrub to small tree. Striking long claret red catkins and purple foliage. Edible purple fruits. Contrasts well with C. avellana 'Aurea'.

## -'Te-Terra Red'

 A vigorous upright tree with deep red purple young leaves ageing dark green. This two toned colour effect is enhanced further when rustled by a gentle summer breeze. The wonderful purple-pink catkins drape the branches like curtains. Also shares the attractive bark of C. Colurna.

# COTINUS

## (Smoke Tree)

The smoke trees succeed best in any well-drained, preferably not too rich soil, in full sun. Their size can be maintained to shrub proportions with occasional hard pruning that also encourages large succulent leaves.

### -*coggygria* 'Golden Spirit'

 A distinctive bright golden leaved form well suited to a sunny position. (Holland)

### -*coggygria* 'Royal Purple'

 This form has deep wine-purple leaves, translucent in the sunshine. The colour is more enhanced towards autumn. Fawn coloured flower plumes in June and July.

### -*coggygria* 'Young Lady'

 A pretty, large shrub or small tree with frothy pink blooms covering every inch of this plant from early summer until autumn. The green summer leaves turn yellow by late September.

### -'Grace'

 One of the 'Dummer' hybrids named after the breeders wife, with soft purplish-red leaves, purple-pink flower clusters in summer and scarlet leaves in the autumn.

# COTONEASTER

Indispensable hardy ornamentals, they are tolerant of almost all soils, sites, positions, treatment and are invaluable for foliage, flowers and fruit.

## *-frigidus* **'Cornubia'**

Semi-evergreen strong growing small tree of tall spreading habit, with large, rich green leaves and very large red fruits that weigh down the branches. A versatile tree with all round interest.

## -**'Hybridus Pendulus'**
Syn: C. *salicifolius* 'Pendulus'

A worthy small tree for any garden with all year interest. Virtually evergreen this is a small weeping tree with pendulous branches covered in white flowers that produce dense bunches of deep red autumn berries.

## *-salicifolius* **'Exburiensis'**

Semi-evergreen, arching, spreading habit. Lance-shaped bright green leaves and white flowers in May. Apricot-yellow fruits, becoming pink-tinged in winter. Similar to C. salicifolius Rothschildianus. (Exbury 1930)

## *-x suecicus* **'Coral Beauty'**

Small evergreen shrub. Very dense foliage with arching branches. Abundant, bright orange-red fruits in autumn. The top worked grafted form makes an excellent weeping tree.

# CRATAEGUS

## (Thorn)

The Thorns have diverse flowers and fruit, are extremely hardy and ideal for the smaller garden. They are deciduous, occasionally semi-evergreen and will tolerate a wide range of soils, urban pollution and coastal conditions. Known as the 'father of the heart' for its antioxidant properties in flowers, shoots and leaves to help angina and blood pressure. Some fruits are particularly edible such as C. arnoldiana, pedicellata and 'Big Golden Star'. They also make excellent jellies.

### -arnoldiana

 A beautiful small tree with shallow lobed leaves and large fruits like red cherries. Worthy of wider planting. (NE USA)

### -laevigata 'Crimson Cloud'
Syn: C. laevigata 'Punicea'

Dense semi-weeping tree with glossy, dark green foliage. Profuse, small, single, dark red flowers with creamy centres appear in May. Small bright red fruit into late autumn. A very unusual ornamental thorn flowering from an early age. (USA)

### -laevigata 'Pauls Scarlet'
Syn: C. laevigata 'Coccinea Plena'

Small round-headed tree, with lobed, dark green foliage and densely double pinky-scarlet flowers. Small red haws in autumn. (Hertfordshire)

### -laevigata 'Plena'

Small, compact, spreading tree with glossy, lobed, dark green foliage. Small, densely double pure white flowers in May.

### -laevigata 'Rosea Flore Pleno'

A profusion of small, double pink flowers borne in clusters during May. A highly ornamental and robust thorn making an ideal garden specimen suitable for all situations.

### -x lavalleei 'Carrierei'

An upright dense tree with large impressive white flowers, attractive dark green glossy leaves remaining on the tree well into December. Large orange fruits add to its many features.

### -monogyna 'Biflora'
Syn: C. monogyna 'Praecox'
**(Glastonbury Thorn)**

An interesting form of the common thorn that can flower twice (hence 'Biflora'), once in winter and again in spring. It is also semi-evergreen. Legend has it that this tree is linked to Saint Joseph of Arimathea, who when reaching Glastonbury in the 1st Century AD to be the first to introduce Christianity, struck his holy staff of hawthorn into the ground and it miraculously sprouted.

### -orientalis Syn: C. laciniata

A spreading tree with grey flaking bark and glossy green, deeply cut leaves, grey-green downy beneath. Dense clusters of single white flowers. Large orange-red fruits. Leaves remain fresh well into the autumn. (Orient)

### -pedicellata (Scarlet Haw)

This beautiful tree has dark green lobed leaves turning red and orange in autumn. Clusters of small white flowers with red anthers appear in spring producing bright scarlet haws in autumn. (NE and N. America)

### -pinnatifida var. major 'Big Golden Star'

A small (almost thornless) tree with large lobed leaves. Excellent autumn colour and large fruits over 3cm in diameter.

### -'Prunifolia Splendens'

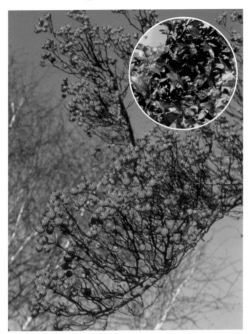

 One of the best thorns with persistent showy orange-red fruits, polished oval leaves and rich autumn colours.

### -schraderiana

 A striking small tree with silver cut foliage, creamy flowers and an abundance of large purple fruits. (Greece and Crimea)

# CRYPTOMERIA
## (Japanese Cedar)

These cedars are worthy of wider planting due to their robust nature, unusual seasonal change in leaf colours and their like for cool damp situations. They also make excellent hedges.

### -*japonica* 'Elegans' Group

 A bushy habit when young with feathery pale green foliage, turning browny-green in summer and an attractive copper-bronze in autumn and winter. (Japan)

### -*japonica* 'Elegans Viridis'

 An attractive finer leaved form of 'Elegans' but with bright golden-yellow foliage.

# CUPRESSUS

## (Cypress)

These conifers grow in any well drained soil in full sun and both have potential for wider planting in gardens.

### -*arizonica var. glabra* 'Blue Ice'

### -*sempervirens* (Italian Cypress)

 A small, slow growing attractive conical tree with striking blue/grey foliage and peeling red bark. It is also much hardier than previously recorded. (New Zealand 1984)

This distinctive tree with its narrow, columnar habit and attractive cones is a familiar site in Mediterranean regions.

## Cupressus leylandii – birth of a suburban legend!

In 1845, the Leighton Hall, Powys Estate was purchased by Liverpool banker Christopher Leyland. In 1847, he gave it to his nephew John Naylor (1813–1889) as a wedding present, who then proceeded to rebuild the house and estate creating a model farm in the process.

Naylor commissioned Edward Kemp, a pupil of Sir Joseph Paxton, to lay out the gardens, which included Redwoods, Monkey Puzzle Trees and two very different species of conifer in close proximity to each other in the estate's Park Wood:

- Monterey Cypress, Cupressus macrocarpa (syn. Callitropsis macrocarpa) from California

- Nootka or Alaskan Cypress, Callitropsis nootkatensis (syn. Cupressus nootkatensis,

Xanthocyparis nootkatensis, Chamaecyparis nootkatensis)

The two species would never have met in the wild as their natural ranges are thousands of miles apart, but in 1888 the hybrid cross occurred when the female flowers or cones of Nootka Cypress were fertilised by pollen from the Monterey Cypress.

The hybrid has since arisen many times, always by open pollination, since the two species are readily compatible and closely related. As a hybrid, Leyland Cypress are sterile so all the trees we now see have resulted from cuttings originating from those few plants.

There are now over forty forms of Leyland Cypress.

# CYTISUS

**(Broom)**

Although the 'Brooms' dominate this family as a very extensive shrub range, described below is a lesser known but highly valuable tree form.

*-battandieri*
**(Moroccan or Pineapple Broom)**

Semi-evergreen, erect habit. Silver downy foliage and pineapple scented cone shaped clusters of yellow flowers appearing in July. Can be wall fan trained or planted as a specimen small tree.

# DAVIDIA

Prefers moist, well drained, fertile soil and tolerates semi shade.

*-involucrata*
**(Pocket Handkerchief Tree)**

This unique and lovely tree produces beautiful large white flower bracts in May giving the appearance of a handkerchief tree. Conical at first becoming tall with upright branching habit. Orange-brown peeling bark. Shiny bright green, heart-shaped leaves with felt undersides. Green rounded berries ripen to purple in the autumn.

# DICKSONIA

**(Tree Fern)**

The origins of Tree Ferns date back to prehistoric times. A native of the temperate forests of South Australia, these spectacular plants can adapt to most conditions and are now found growing in gardens from Cornwall to the Highlands of Scotland.

*-antarctica*

This is the most popular of the Tree Ferns. Hardy to -10°C. Used widely in gardens, patios, sheltered balconies, or as specimens in lawns or by pools and ponds. Best to wrap up for the winter!

## Native and non-native in harmony

Gardens are richly diverse with plants from all over the world and this adds colour, vitality, form, shape and general interest. Trees play their part within this tapestry and as long as they suit the conditions in which they are planted and their arrival here does not threaten their own extinction or that of our native trees, then the likes of tree ferns and monkey puzzles can be welcomed into our landscape.

# DIOSPYROS

An interesting and wide reaching species whose range includes D. ebenum, the ebony, and the date plum and persimmon.

*-kaki* **(Chinese Persimmon)**

A small tree with wonderful orange-red and plum-purple leaf colours in the autumn with the occasional orange-yellow tomato type fruits. Linked to homeopathic remedies and one tree is known to have survived the plutonium bomb dropped on Nagasaki in 1945. Both male and female plants are needed for cross pollination with flowers appearing from July to September. (China)

# ELAEAGNUS

Mostly consisting of shrubs for seaside and exposed sites we include one particular selection as a suitable small garden tree.

*-Quicksilver*

This is an exceptionally good silver foliaged small tree with highly scented dainty white flowers. A good canvass for primary colours. Can sucker. (Poland)

# EMBOTHRIUM

Preferring lime free conditions these beautiful evergreen trees are hardier than generally considered but do thrive better in the milder and wetter districts in the UK.

## -*coccineum* (Chilean Firebush)

Beautiful orange-scarlet flowers appear in May on this semi-evergreen tree. In ideal conditions it may grow to a surprising size and although tolerant of wet conditions would prefer good drainage. (Chile 1846)

### Coppicing

Eucalyptus can dominate their surroundings and sometimes drastic action is necessary. This tree was cut down in April and the new budding shoots are seen here eventually appearing in July. For more information on tree pruning go to page 198.

# ENKIANTHUS

Preferring lime free soil these plants are known primarily for their exquisite autumn colours.

## -*campanulatus*

An erect large shrub with bell-shaped green and pink flowers lasting for three weeks in May followed by autumn colours of every shade. (Japan)

# EUCALYPTUS

## (Gum Tree)

These fast growing evergreen trees will grow in almost any soil except shallow chalk. Coppice for control and effect with the best time for pruning being the spring. The species listed here are all hardy for the UK if grown from the correct seed source.

## -*dalrympleana* (Mountain Gum)

One of the hardiest forms with the attractive patchwork bark becoming white with age. Bronze young leaves unfold to grey-green colours. (Australia)

## -gunnii (Cider Gum)

A conical tree, the peeling bark is greenish-grey and orange, creamy-white beneath. Silver-blue young foliage turns blue-green with age. Clusters of small white flowers in late spring-early summer. Excellent for flower arrangements. One of the hardiest in its group. (Tasmania)

## -pauciflora subsp. debeuzevillei (Jounama Snow Gum)

One of the smaller and hardiest of species. Thick lance-shaped adult leaves. (SE Australia)

## -pauciflora subsp. niphophila (Snow Gum)

Open, broadly spreading habit, with python skin bark. Slow growth with large leathery, grey-green leaves. Clusters of small white flowers in summer. Very hardy and one of the most attractive. (Australia)

## -perriniana (Spinning Gum)

A tree of broadly spreading habit with peeling grey and brown bark. The usually glaucous leaves are in semi-circular pairs united into a single leaf which 'spins'. Adult leaves turn purple then deep blue-green. Clusters of small white flowers in late summer. (S. Australia and Tasmania)

# EUONYMUS

These deciduous and evergreen shrubs or trees will thrive in almost any soil including chalk. The fruits can be harmful if eaten.

## -cornutus var. quinquecornutus

 A remarkable and rare little tree or shrub. Pink tinged fruit with five or six horn-like extensions that appear as 'jester' hats. (W. and SW China)

## -europaeus (Spindle Tree)

 A shrub or small tree of open habit native to hedgerows displaying green stems and good autumn red colour. Scarlet red fruits split to reveal orange seeds. Attractive corky bark.

## -europaeus 'Red Cascade'

 The arching branches often droop under the weight of the rosy red fruits with yellow seed pods. Rich scarlet autumn colour. A good small garden tree.

## -hamiltonianus 'Indian Summer'

 Vigorous growth when young with showy red fruits and superb reliable autumn crimson leaf colours.

## -hamiltonianus 'Koi Boy'

A small tree or large shrub with an arching habit. The white fruits produced in September to November split to reveal striking bright red seeds resembling the similar contrasting colours of the Japanese Koi Carp. The leaves also turn a pure lemon yellow.

## -phellomanus

An unusual and interesting large shrub with fascinating corky-winged stems. The showy four-lobed, pink fruits appear in abundance in autumn. (N. and W. China)

## -planipes

A shrubby small tree with excellent autumn leaf colours and large showy scarlet fruits. A good form of this species now in circulation is E. planipes 'Sancho', with more enhanced leaf colours. (NE Asia)

### Native hedging

Euonymus europaeus (the native spindle) plays an important role in our native hedgerows, providing stem and leaf colour and fruit for wildlife. The following is an approximate guide for a mixed native hedgerow.

Field Maple (Acer campestre)............................15%

Common Dogwood (Cornus sanguinea)............5%

Hazel (Corylus avellana).....................................15%

Crataegus monogyna.........................................40%

Spindle (Euonymus europaeus)...........................5%

Holly (Ilex aquifolium).........................................5%

Sloe/ Blackthorn (Prunus spinosa).......................5%

Wayfaring tree (Viburnum lantana)......................5%

Guelder Rose (Viburnum opulus)........................5%

The spindle is also a very versatile hard wood, easily split and used for spindle machines, skewers, knitting needles and toothpicks and makes high quality charcoal.

# EXOCHORDA

A genus of relatively few species with spectacular white flowers in April. Vigorous shrubs suitable for most soils although thin chalk should be avoided.

### -x macrantha 'The Bride'

 The most choice of selections with abundant racemes of large flowers arching the slender branches under their weight.

# FAGUS

## (Beech)

Eventually growing into large trees although some of the more ornamental forms are slow growers. Many of the varieties offered here have wonderful leaf forms. They will grow in most soils provided they are not waterlogged, and will tolerate most sites except coastal. The milder winters do not suit beech and those in the dryer southern districts are showing signs of discontent but further north there will be increasing opportunities to see them at their best.

### -sylvatica (Common or European Beech)

 A large, noble tree or excellent for hedging, this versatile tree has smooth silver-grey bark. Dark green leaves turn rich golden-copper in autumn. Thrives in well drained acid or alkaline soil and will tolerate semi-shade. (Europe)

### -sylvatica 'Black Swan'

 A good weeping purple beech more compact and with deeper red purple foliage than any other form. Leaves open brown and then go almost black within a few weeks.

### -sylvatica 'Dawyck Gold'

This golden beech is very upright in habit with bright golden leaves that eventually fade to a mellow yellow-green in mid summer. Contrasts well when planted in conjunction with F. sylvatica 'Dawyck Purple.

### -sylvatica 'Dawyck Purple'

A purple leaved upright form that has rich dark purple leaves. Contrasts well with the golden form F. sylvatica 'Dawyck Gold' despite being narrower in shape!

### -sylvatica var. heterophylla 'Aspleniifolia' (Fern Leaf Beech)

Also having the smooth silver grey bark in common with most beech the attractive, narrow, lance-shaped, dark green leaves make this a very graceful form. The leaves turn copper-gold in autumn. Thrives in light shade.

### -sylvatica 'Pendula' (Weeping Beech)

A magnificent large parkland tree taking on many unique informal weeping shapes with the primary limbs draped with hanging branchlets.

### -*sylvatica* 'Purple Fountain'

One of the best selections of the weeping purple beech with a narrow growth habit developing a good dominant central leader. The leaves are rich dark purple. (Holland)

### -*sylvatica* 'Purpurea' Group

Selected seedlings with variable shades of purple leaves. An economical way of planting purple beech hedging and to ultimately raise unique specimen parkland trees.

### -*sylvatica* 'Purpurea Pendula'

A classic weeping tree with dark purple leaves. Often develops as a small dome-shape ideally suited for the smaller garden.

### -*sylvatica* 'Purpurea Tricolor'
### Syn: F. *sylvatica* 'Roseomarginata'

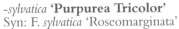

A very attractive form with irregular pink margins to the purple leaves. The tree develops a lighter canopy than most beech.

### -*sylvatica* 'Riversii'

A classic weeping tree with dark purple leaves.
Selected for its very large deep purple leaves. The best dark purple form of all.

# FOTHERGILLA

## (Witch Alder)

These large shrubs are conspicuous due to their bottlebrush flower spikes and autumn colours. They require lime free soil.

*-major*

 The best form with the flowers appearing before the leaves which are glaucous and downy beneath. Wonderful autumn colours. (USA)

The common ash tree (Fraxinus excelsior) is a multi purpose wood used for amongst other things, tool handles, hurling and hockey sticks, long bows, floor boards and curved arches in Gypsy caravans. With shock proof properties it is also used as the main frame of Morgan sports cars. For keeping us warm it is the 'king of logs' told to us in the following poem:

Beechwood fires are bright and clear
If the logs are kept a year,
Chestnut's only good they say,
If for logs 'tis laid away.
Make a fire of Elder tree,
Death within your house will be;
But ash new or ash old,
Is fit for a queen with crown of gold.
Birch and fir logs burn too fast
Blaze up bright and do not last.
It is by the Irish said
Hawthorn bakes the sweetest bread.
Elm wood burns like churchyard mould,
E'en the very flames are cold
But Ash green or Ash brown
Is fit for a queen with golden crown.
Poplar gives a bitter smoke,
Fills your eyes and makes you choke,
Apple wood will scent your room
Pear wood smells like flowers in bloom
Oaken logs, if dry and old
keep away the winter's cold
But Ash wet or Ash dry
a king shall warm his slippers by.
*Anon*

# FRAXINUS

## (Ash)

The Ash are mostly fast growing and tolerant of most soils and sites. They are good on chalk, are naturally shallow rooted, and will withstand shade while young. Ideal for coppice pruning to enhance their variety of striking foliage and are one of the most useful for burning logs.

*-americana* **'Autumn Purple'**

 A reliable form of the 'White Ash' for its splendid autumn colours of dark and light purple tones. (USA)

*-angustifolia* **'Raywood'** Syn: F. 'Flame'

 A fast growing tree of upright and dense habit. Good reliable autumn colours of dark green turning plum-purple.

## -*excelsior* (Common Ash)

*Fraxinus excelsior coppice*

These fast growing, hardy, large trees have lance-shaped dark green leaves turning yellow in autumn. Flowers are small and purple and the winged 'keys' hang in dense clusters. The winter buds are black. A worthy native. (Europe)

## -*excelsior* 'Aurea Pendula'

 A graceful weeping tree with bright yellow leaves and stems forming an umbrella-shaped crown. A good addition to the winter garden.

## -*excelsior* 'Jaspidea'

Both the young shoot growth and autumn leaves are an intense yellow making this a good all seasons tree. Although fast growing, it can be pruned hard (coppiced or pollarded) to control its size and enhance the golden yellow shoots in the winter.

### -excelsior 'Pendula' (Weeping Ash)

 This strong growing tree forms a wide spreading mound of weeping branches with long shoots to the ground. Should not be restricted to churchyard planting.

### -ornus (Manna Ash)

The very ornamental 'Manna Ash', a slow growing tree with profuse large pleasantly scented fluffy cream flowers in May. (Europe and SW Asia 1700)

### -ornus 'Obelisk'

 A very compact, upright and choice form of the 'Manna Ash', which like the species, has large panicles of white candy floss flowers in May.

### -pennsylvanica 'Cimmzam'
Syn: F. pennsylvanica 'Cimmaron'

 A superior form of landscape ash selected for being seedless and for its fine rich green foliage in summer, yellow stems and good burgundy tints in autumn. (USA)

> ## "Ash before Oak,
> ## we're in for a soak
>
> ## Oak before Ash,
> ## we're in for a splash."
>
> Looking into this well known saying further, the ash has been observed rarely if ever to come out before the oak, indicating that our summers should generally be hot and dry!
>
> The ash tree appears to change sex, having all male flowers or all female flowers or a mixture of both in any given year. How this happens is as yet unknown. Perhaps this phenomenon could be used to predict the weather more accurately!

# GINKGO

## (Maidenhair tree)

A survivor from an ancient family stretching back 190 million years. These remarkable deciduous conifers are well known for their unusual leaf shape and tall slender habit. The species could be male or female but selected forms are generally male to eliminate seed production.

### -biloba

 Conical when young, later becoming broadly columnar. The bark is dull grey, ridged and fissured. Fan shaped bright green leaves, yellow in autumn. Needs well drained soil and shelter from cold winds. Female forms will produce seed but only if they are crushed will they produce an unpleasant pungent smell. (Introduced to England 1754)

### -biloba 'Autumn Gold'

 Typical 'Maidenhair' foliage, becoming persistently brilliant golden yellow in autumn. A good male form.

### -biloba 'Pendula' Group

 Unusual weeping forms producing wide arching branches. Needs space to become a remarkable specimen.

### -biloba 'Saratoga'

 The best small, upright and male form with excellent yellow autumn colour.

# GLEDITSIA

These handsome trees, mainly grown for their attractive pinnate foliage, are tolerant of drought, shade and urban pollution. They are suitable for almost all well drained soils.

### -triacanthos (Honey Locust)

 An elegant fast growing tree with a spiny trunk. Feathery bright green foliage turning yellow in autumn with distinctive brown seed pods. (C. and E. USA)

### -triacanthos inermis 'Speczam' SPECTRUM

 An improvement on 'Sunburst' for its leaves which remain yellow for longer into the summer and the young shoots which are also more intensely yellow. (USA)

*-triacanthos* **'Rubylace'**

A small tree with dainty fern-like foliage, bright ruby red leaves turning bronze-green with maturity. Needs to be pruned hard to show off its spectacular foliage. (USA)

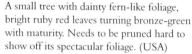

*-triacanthos* **'Sunburst'**

An attractive honey locust with delicate fern-like golden yellow leaves in spring. The older leaves will eventually turn green giving an effective two tone colour to the tree by mid summer returning to yellow-golden in autumn.

# HALESIA

The silver bells or snowdrop trees are similar to Styrax with a preference for lime-free soil.

*-carolina* **(Snowdrop Tree)**

A small spreading shrub-like tree with oval-oblong pointed green leaves becoming mid green later. White nodding bell-shaped flowers and pear-shaped fruits. Will grow well in moist well drained soil with shelter from cold winds.

## Mycorrhiza... friendly fungi... how effective are they?

There is much debate as to the benefits or otherwise of mycorrhiza. These are friendly fungi that attach themselves to roots naturally for the purposes of assisting in the root systems conversion of available nutrients for plants. All plants have these fungi naturally and opinion varies as to whether additionally applied mycorrhiza makes a difference. However, there is general consensus on the following:

• They are likely to assist establishment in the first few years.

• They have more beneficial effects for trees planted on poor soils.

For more about Truffle fungi see page 152.

# HAMAMELIS

## (Witch Hazel)

Large shrubs or small trees thriving in any reasonable soil, but prefering neutral to acid conditions. Very special for their tough but delicate spider-like highly scented winter flowers.

## -x intermedia 'Arnold Promise'

 An upright, strong growing, compact form, with freely borne, bright yellow flowers that open later than other varieties. (USA)

## -x intermedia 'Diane'

 An excellent dark red flowered form with good autumn tints to the leaves. Less fragrant than other varieties. (Belgium)

## -x intermedia 'Jelena'
### Syn: H. x intermedia 'Copper Beauty'

 A more vigorous and spreading habit than most with red autumn foliage. Large clusters of rich, coppery orange flowers in February. (Belgium)

*-x intermedia* **'Pallida'**

 One of the most popular Witch Hazels. The large sulphur-yellow flowers are borne in densely crowded clusters in January and February and have a strong sweet fragrance. Leaves are lustrous and have cheerful yellow tints in autumn.

# HEPTACODIUM

A Chinese shrub related to Abelia. Suitable for a wide range of soils, flowers on one year wood.

*-miconioides*

 A deciduous, Chinese shrub of fairly recent introduction. Small, jasmine fragranced, white flowers are produced in late summer, followed by bright red calyces in good autumns. A vigorous shrub worthy of wider planting. (China)

## The Savill Garden

The Savill Garden is one of our greatest ornamental gardens. Neither a botanical garden, nor a kitchen garden attached to a great house, it is a garden for the garden's sake, enjoyed by horticulturists and enthusiasts alike with 35 acres of contemporary and classically designed gardens and exotic woodland.

The garden was created in the 1930s by Sir Eric Savill, beginning as a woodland garden, with native trees, but evolving to incorporate many new plant discoveries over the years. Uniquely, The Savill Garden has also bred many important garden hybrids; some of these include Rhododendron hybrids.

**www.theroyallandscape.co.uk**

## RHS Garden Wisley

This is undoubtedly one of the great gardens of the world and an inspiration for those who love ornamental and fruit trees. Included in a series of model gardens is one devoted to fruit, whilst Weather Hill and the Conifer Lawn show a huge variety of ornamental trees to spectacular effect. Steeped in the history of plant collecting from every part of the world, a visit to RHS Garden Wisley is an unforgettable experience.

**www.rhs.org.uk**

# ILEX
## (Holly)

These mainly evergreen trees and shrubs thrive in almost any well drained soil, in sun or shade. Most are tolerant of urban pollution and coastal conditions. Male and female flowers are usually borne on separate plants and just to confuse 'Golden King' is female and 'Silver Queen' is male!

- Holly is a 'broad leaved' evergreen and each leaf can remain for up to 3 years on the tree before falling off.

- Holly logs burn like wax.

- Holly is the tree of good luck and protection.

- The largest annual traditional market for Christmas trees, holly and mistletoe is situated near Tenbury Wells, Worcestershire and is held on the last Tuesday in November and the first 2 Tuesdays in December.

- The National Collections of Holly are held at the Crown Estate Commissioners at Windsor Great Park and the RHS Garden Rosemoor in Devon. See www.nccpg.com.

- In legend it is unlucky to step on a holly berry as it is a favourite food of the Robin who acquired its red breast while plucking holly thorns from Christ's brow on his way to be crucified.

- Holly make excellent walking sticks and the straightest coppiced shoots are used as the core for whips.

### -x altaclerensis 'Belgica Aurea'
Syn: I. *x altaclerensis* 'Silver Sentinel'

A small pyramidal shape, ideal for clipping with handsome leaves up to 10cm.
 Conspicuous creamy-yellow margins. Masses of large red fruits and virtually spine free.

### -x altaclerensis 'Golden King'

 Richly variegated golden-yellow leaves are almost spineless with large quantities of reliable bright red berries. Female.

### -aquifolium (Common Holly)

A versatile evergreen hardy multi-purpose tree for screens, hedges and as a specimen. Can reach considerable size in ideal growing conditions. Glossy dark green leaves and red berries on female plants. Native. (W. and S. Europe)

87

## *-aquifolium* 'Alaska'

A small narrow and conical tree with spiny leaves. A female form ideal for shaping that fruits reliably even on young plants.

## *-aquifolium* 'Argentea Marginata'

Bushy and fairly pyramidal in shape with silver margined oval leaves. A heavy fruiting female form making a specimen tree, hedge or topiary.

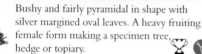

## *-aquifolium* 'Aurea Marginata'

A small bushy tree with shiny leaves margined with yellow. A female form producing ample fruit and interesting purple stems.

## *-aquifolium* 'Handsworth New Silver'

Included in the 'Argentea Marginata' group this cultivar has attractive long, broadly cream edged, deep green mottled grey foliage. A free fruiting female form with bright red berries. An all purpose holly. (1850)

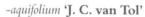

## *-aquifolium* 'J. C. van Tol'

Dark green shining leaves are almost spineless. One of the most reliable self fertile fruiting female forms. Good as a free standing specimen, hedge or for topiary.

## *-aquifolium* 'Limsi'

A naturally pyramidal habit with dark green leaves which vary in shape, mostly with few spines. Heavy crops of orange turning bright red fruit. (Holland)

## -aquifolium 'Myrtifolia Aurea Maculata'

A dense compact form, small attractive dark green leaves with pale green shading and a splash of gold in the centre. Non fruiting. Male.

## -aquifolium 'Silver Queen'
Syn: I. aquifolium 'Argentea Regina'

A good foliage type with a dense shrubby habit. Young shrimp-pink unfolding leaves followed by shiny dark green leaves, margined white. Male.

# JUGLANS

## (Walnut)

The walnut family like deep, well drained soil and full sun or part shade. Speculation on walnuts 'poisoning' the soil for other trees is true with the Black Walnut (J. nigra) which produces 'Juglone', a plant inhibiting substance. It also has other colouring properties used in the cosmetics (hair dye) and food industries. The common walnut (J. regia) produces less juglone and is safe to plant within a respectful distance from other plants, without problems. See below.

Walnut timber: J. nigra grows fast and straight grained producing excellent timber for many uses. J. regia provides the best 'burr' for veneer. This particular highly valuable timber is found at and just below ground level. The aerial timber is less desirable as it is rarely straight, nor does it produce the 'burr' knot qualities. See more walnut facts on page 284.

## -nigra (Black Walnut)

A noble and fast growing tree with deep furrowed bark and large, pinnate, glossy, dark green leaves. Yellow-green male and female catkins in late spring. Edible nuts although a long hot summer is needed to ripen fruits. Grown largely as a timber tree.
(E. and C. USA)

### Juglone

All Juglans species (and hickories & wingnuts) produce a chemical called Juglone which can have an adverse effect on certain plants, although not all. The chemical is released by the roots. The two species that produce the most juglone are the American black walnut (J. nigra) and butternut (J. cinerea). Juglone is not very water soluble and is eventually destroyed by soil bacteria. The common walnut (J. regia) produces much smaller quantities and this should not be a concern.

### -nigra 'Laciniata'

 A black walnut selection with deeply cut leaves making a graceful and less vigorous tree.

### -regia (Common Walnut)

A slow growing tree, valuable for its 'burr' timber and presence. Aromatic leaves are bronze when young, later dark grey. Yellow-green male and female catkins in late spring. Smooth husks enclose edible creamy-white nuts although it takes some years to fruit. (SE Europe and China)

# KOELREUTERIA

Needs well drained soil and a sunny sheltered site.

### -paniculata
### (Pride of India or Golden Rain Tree)

 A very attractive, large-headed tree with reddish leaves in spring turning to dark green, then bright yellow in autumn. Large panicles of small yellow flowers in July followed by bronze-pink or red 'bladder' fruits. (China)

### -paniculata 'Coral Sun'

 A new selection of this very rewarding small deciduous tree. In this form the leaves emerge bright pink-red and turn through a flaming orange-red becoming light green with contrasting red petioles. Bright yellow flowers in August followed by inflated seed pods in good summers. Retains its excellent autumn colour of yellow and orange.

*-paniculata* **'Fastigiata'**

A very rare slow growing form. The growth habit is very fastigiate and dense. Raised at Kew.

 ♞ 🍁 ✿⑦ ⚙ 🪨 ✖

# LABURNUM

Ideal for the small garden, especially arches and pagodas. Suitable for all types of soil. The seeds are poisonous.

*-anagyroides* **'Aureum'**
**(The Golden Leaved Laburnum)**

The leaves are a soft yellow in summer, the older leaves are green giving an attractive two tone effect. Recommended for Scotland and the North as can scorch in full sun in southern districts.

**S** 🍁 ⑥ ✿ ● ⚙ 🪨 🌿 🍂

*-x watereri* **'Vossii'**

An erect spreading tree with pendent chains of scented, golden yellow flowers in early June. A sterile form that sets few seeds. These seeds are poisonous if eaten. Ideal for arches, pagodas and as a specimen.

 **S** ⑥ ✿ Ⓐ Ⓒ ● 🌿 🍂 🏆

# LARIX

## (Larch)

These interesting deciduous conifers are very much trees for all seasons. Containing some surprising ornamental features as well as useful fast growing utility timber trees. Will tolerate most soils except very wet or chalky.

*-decidua* **'Puli'**

A stiffly weeping dwarf form for ornamental gardens.

 **VS** 🍁 ● ⊘

### Poisonous trees

In most cases very large amounts of plant material would need to be digested to cause severe problems but all leaves and seeds should be treated with respect. Of the trees listed in this book the following with known poisonous content are: Euonymus (Spindle), Cotoneaster, Laburnum (seed), Ligustrum (Privet), Taxus (Yew) and Prunus laurocerasus (Laurel).

### Composting poisons

Most leaves decompose well and are indeed a vital part of the successful compost heap. However, it is best to avoid the evergreens Taxus (yew) and Laurel (Prunus laurocerasus). It is ironic that the medicine 'Taxol', a derivative of yew clippings has proved successful in treating cancer.

### *-kaempferi* (**Japanese Larch**)

Broadly conical with scaly red-brown bark. Reddish shoots, bright, fresh green spring foliage and stunning gold autumn colours. Male yellow drooping flowers and female upright creamy-pink flowers on the same plant. Will tolerate poor and/or acid soil. (Japan)

### *-kaempferi* '**Jakobsen's Pyramid**'

A good fastigiate upright form with all the other attributes of the Japanese Larch.

# LAURUS

The 'Bay Tree' is suitable for all types of soil and is often grown in pots on the patio for all those useful culinary purposes.

### *-nobilis* (**Bay Laurel**)

Grown for its aromatic foliage as well as a useful pyramidal or topiary tree. Very forgiving when pruned. Can die back in severe frost but quite hardy otherwise. (Mediterranean)

This is a topiary form in a walled garden.

Apart from its culinary uses this useful evergreen tree provides the laurel crown worn by emperors and poets ('poet laureate').

# LIGUSTRUM

## (Privet)

A large range of useful shrubs both evergreen and deciduous, can grow anywhere and will tolerate shade. We list below specifically the Chinese Privet with an additional explanation of the 3 main 'hedging' privets.

### -lucidum (Chinese Privet)

This species is a useful evergreen tree form with attractive, large, glossy, pointed leaves and lovely panicles of white flowers in autumn. L. lucidum 'Tricolor' and 'Excelsum Superbum' are excellent variegated forms with pale cream-yellow edges to their leaves (S. and E. China)

### The 'Hedging' privets

**Japanese privet (L. japonicum)**
With shiny green leaves similar to the camellia this plant makes an excellent screening hedge with large panicles of white flowers in late summer.

**Oval-leaved privet (L. ovalifolium)**
One of the most popular hedging privets, if left un-pruned, makes a reasonable small evergreen tree only losing its leaves in the coldest areas. The variegated and golden leaved forms come from this species much loved by flower arrangers.

**Common privet (L. vulgare)**
This one particularly likes chalk conditions and is conspicuous for its narrow (lanceolate) leaves and shiny black fruits in the autumn.

# LIQUIDAMBAR

Beautiful picturesque trees with maple-like leaves renowned for their spectacular autumn colours. They need moist but well drained soil and a sunny site.

### -acalycina

A very good summer tree with sumptuous bronze-purple leaves that persist until the autumn. (China)

### -styraciflua (Sweet Gum)

The handsome species grown for its glossy, maple-like leaves that can turn brilliant crimson, purple and orange in the autumn. As this is seed grown there is considerable variation in the intensity of the autumn colours. The older stems have corky bark. (E. USA)

Liquidambar *styraciflua* 'Palo Alto'

*-styraciflua* **'Lane Roberts'**

Shining maple-like green leaves turning rich, blackish crimson-red in autumn.

*-styraciflua* **'Palo Alto'**

The leaves are long, narrowly lobed and the bright, intense autumn colours are superb and very persistent. See image on previous page.

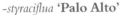

*-styraciflua* **'Slender Silhouette'**

A recently introduced form and one of the first Liquidambars with a very fastigiate habit. The leaves turn yellow to reddish-purple. (USA.)

*-styraciflua* **'Stared'**

A very reliable form for excellent autumn colours with particularly small, delicate, deeply cut seven lobed leaves.

*-styraciflua* **'Worplesdon'**

A beautiful tree with leaves that have long narrow lobes which turn orange and yellow in autumn. One of the best forms with reliable and intense autumn colours.

# LIRIODENDRON

Large, fast growing trees that are happy in most fertile, well drained soils, including chalk. L. tulipifera is native to the USA and is the state tree for Indiana, Kentucky and Tennessee. L. chinensis was discovered by Ernest Wilson in China in 1901.

## -tulipifera (Tulip Tree)

A stately tree, conical at first becoming tall and domed. Unusual angular leaves turning butter-yellow in autumn. Tulip shaped, yellow-green flowers banded with orange appear in June and July but these take many years to appear.

## -tulipifera 'Aureomarginatum'

 The leaves are bordered with bright yellow, turning greenish-yellow in late summer.

## -tulipifera 'Fastigiatum'

© Ronald Houtman

 A useful medium sized compact form of broadly columnar habit.

### Bees and Trees

The Tulip tree is one of many trees to offer pollen for foraging bees even in June when there seems so much choice. Other trees particularly good for bees are crab apple (Malus), cherry (Prunus), holly (Ilex), Indian bean (Catalpa), sycamore (Acer pseudoplatanus), thorn (Crataegus) and willow (Salix). The 'bee symbol' is one of many to guide you to choosing the right tree for the right place. For more on bees see page 288.

### The Bees Knees!

There are several theories for the origins of this saying but none that have total consensus. Options are: 1) As the bee works it gathers pollen in its knee sacks and only the very 'highest quality' is taken back to nest or hive. 2) Ms. Bee Jackson was an American dancer who was credited with introducing the Charleston to Broadway in 1924.

# MAGNOLIA

Some of the most beautiful flowering trees. A large number of species and cultivars exist and listed here are only a few of the finest. Hybrids continue to be introduced at a rapid rate with a full range of colours from pure white to dark almost black reds. These deciduous, semi-evergreen and evergreen trees prefer a well drained site with shelter from cold winds, especially for those that flower early. Tolerant of clay soils and pollution. Some varieties are chalk tolerant depending on parentage and whether on their own roots or grafted on a tolerant rootstock like M. kobus.

## -'Black Tulip'

 This most exceptional of recent introductions has the darkest red of current known varieties. It flowers from a very early age (2-3 year old trees) and occasionally produces a second flowering in mid to late summer. M. 'Vulcan' x M. 'Iolanthe' (New Zealand. 1990s)

## -x brooklynensis 'Yellow Bird'

© Helmut Orth

 A compact, upright tree with very erect medium daffodil-yellow flowers which appear in mid-May for three weeks. (USA.)

## -campbellii 'Charles Raffill'

© Jim Gardiner

 Vigorous, upright, later spreading tree with oblong pointed mid-green leaves. The early large flowers are deep rose-pink in bud, opening rose-purple.

## -'Daybreak'

© Jim Gardiner

 Of neat upright habit this tree is potentially one of the best garden magnolia's. Large fragrant splayed rose pink flowers. From an early age it is very floriferous. One of the finest x brooklynensis hybrids. (USA 1991)

## -denudata 'Yellow River'

 A beautiful variety with large, fragrant, lemon scented, citrus yellow, tulip-like flowers appearing in early May. This is a small compact tree and late flowering. (China)

## -'Elizabeth'

©Jim Gardiner

 A small conical tree with exquisite, fragrant, clear, pale primrose-yellow flowers opening before the leaves in April. (USA)

## -'Galaxy'

 Flowering when quite young this vigorous yet small conical tree has striking, purple-pink to red tulip shaped flowers in mid to late spring. (USA)

## -'Gold Star'

 A M. stellata hybrid with soft yellow multi-tepalled flowers which fade to a creamy white. Young leaves are an attractive bronze. (USA)

## -'Heaven Scent'

 A magnificent small to medium sized tree with sublime pink flowers in April and May with a magenta stripe at the base. Richly scented this is one of the finest of the 'Gresham Hybrids'. (USA)

## -'Joe McDaniel'

One of the best and darkest of the 'Gresham Hybrids' with a good compact habit. Very profuse in its flowering with rich purple-red shapely flowers appearing on very young plants. (USA)

## -'Limelight'

This recently introduced hybrid has long greenish-yellow to chartreuse coloured, tall, narrow flower buds and will produce a vigorous multi-stemmed tree. (USA)

## -x loebneri 'Leonard Messel'

This worthy variety produces a small bushy tree with masses of lilac flowers deeper pink in bud opening with a pale purple line inside. A good fragrant frost resistant variety. (UK)

## -'Peppermint Stick'

© Jim Gardiner

A small upright growing tree with a profusion of white, pink flushed flowers. Erect inner pointed tepals contrast with the outer that are reflexed almost to the horizontal. Another excellent 'Gresham Hybrid'. (USA)

99

### -salicifolia 'Wada's Memory'

This special cultivar has lovely reddish-bronze leaves in bud opening almost black and well after the large floppy petalled, fragrant white flowers. (USA)

### Magnolia

The Magnolia is named after French botanist Pierre Magnol (1638 – 1715) who was Professor of Botany and Director of the Royal Botanic Garden of Montpellier and a member of the Académie Royale des Sciences de Paris.

Magnol is of lasting importance because he was one of the innovators of the current botanical scheme of classification in which groups of plants with associated common features are described e.g. ROSACEAE, GRAMMITIDACEAE, LILIACEAE

### Evergreen Magnolias

The evergreen Bullbay or Loblolly magnolia is ideally suited for sheltered sites or as a wall shrub. Leathery, glossy green leaves set off the most beautiful, huge, creamy white fragrant flowers, appearing from July onwards. (SE USA 1734) The best modern less vigorous upright early flowering forms are M. 'Bracken's Brown Beauty' and M. 'Kay Paris'.

### -sieboldii subsp sinensis

Similar to M. wilsonii this small spreading tree has broader leaves, tomentose beneath and wider, more scented flowers with a bright red staminal core appearing in June. (NW Sichuan, China 1908)

### -x soulangeana 'Rustica Rubra'

 A shrubby tree with lilac flowers which are deeper in bud and have a pale purple line inside. A good frost resistant variety.

### -'Spectrum'

A sister seedling of M. 'Galaxy', this is perhaps superior with larger and deeper pink flowers. A good alternative to M. 'Black Tulip'. (USA)

## -'Star Wars'

 M. liliiflora x M. campbellii. Early to flower as a young tree this is a choice variety. The lovely large rich pink flowers, white inside, appear for six weeks from mid March onwards. (New Zealand)

## -*stellata* **'Royal Star'**

 A superior form of M. stellata with pale silvery-pink buds opening to a clear ice white flower each with up to twenty five tepals. Flowers larger and later than other stellata types. Good for frost prone sites. (USA)

### A Tree Miscellany

There are a host of tree books for suggested reading mentioned on page 318. One of the most interesting and compelling is, *Why are leaves Green?* by Jon Stokes and John White of the Tree Council, with photographs by Archie Miles who has also contributed many fine pictures in this book. It answers all those questions we always wanted to ask!

## -'Susan'

 The flowers are deep purple in bud, opening white stained purple, with a delicate musky scent and flower over a long period through April and May. A compact shrub.

## -*wilsonii*

A large, wide spreading shrub with lance-shaped matt green leaves which are silky underneath. The pendant highly fragrant saucer-shaped white flowers have crimson stamens. Similar to M. sinensis for its wonderful fragrance. (W. China)

# MALUS (Crab Apple)

The most diverse of garden trees. Flower, foliage, fruit and autumn colours. They will grow in almost any fertile soil except waterlogged; although tolerant of some shade, full sun is preferred. Many varieties are offered as mini trees on M27 rootstock. Good disease resistance (specifically against scab) should certainly be a priority in the garden and many of the more uncommon and recently introduced forms have been selected for their healthy constitution and therefore deserve more exposure.

The ✚ symbol indicates the most disease resistant forms.

## -'Adirondack' ADMIRATION

## -baccata 'Dolgo' PINK GLOW

A charming, dwarf, upright growing, shrubby, small tree. Dense clusters of waxy white flowers follow dark carmine buds. Masses of red-bronze fruits lasting well into December. Ideal for restricted spaces and patio growing.

### -baccata

This is the true Siberian crab. Making a rounded crown with oval, finely toothed dark green leaves leaves. A profusion of white fragrant cup-shaped flowers in spring are followed by small egg-shaped red or yellow fruits. (NE Asia)

One of the best early season fruiting crab apples for making jelly and an excellent ornamental. A round-headed tree with strong single white flowers followed by bright pink fruit that look like plums. Although early to fall in mid September it is a very good alternative to John Downie as it is more disease resistant. (USA)

---

## Crab apple facts

**The differences between apples and crab apples**
In this instance size does matter. Apples and crab apples reside in the same genus but what is the difference? It is an unscientific contention that a Malus tree with fruit larger than two inches in diameter is considered an apple, while a Malus tree with fruit smaller than two inches is considered a crab.

**Healthy fruit**
The other obvious difference is that crab apples are very sour compared with their sophisticated relatives and the more bitter they are the better they are for

you... if you could eat them! There is more on the health giving attributes of apples in the fruit section; but Malus crab apples should not be ignored. There is often up to 4 times more antioxidant concentrations in crab apples and high levels of vitamin C and pectin, the latter so useful for setting jellies (see page 109) and aiding other fruits for the same purpose.

**Species Malus**
All 'species' Malus are naturally resistant to disease and generally have small persistent fruit.

## -*brevipes* WEDDING BOUQUET

This is a lovely and charming species with long tapered dark green healthy leaves, single shell-shaped, ivory white flowers and profuse clusters of small transluscent dark red fruits persistent into December.

## -'Butterball'

Heavily laden branches glowing with butter coloured fruit each autumn make this a stunning tree. The apple blossom flowers in spring add to its charm and the fruit are ideal for making crab apple jelly. (N. America)

## -'Cardinal'
Syn: M. *hupehensis* 'Princeton Cardinal'

A beautiful foliage and flowering tree with large, intense pink, sumptuous flowers and dark almost black spring leaves changing to glossy red in summer. Deep red small fruit festoon the branches in the autumn. (USA)

## -'Comtessa de Paris'

The smallish, elliptic, yellow crabs of this special variety usually persist well after Christmas. One of the best persistent yellow crabs of which there are few. (France)

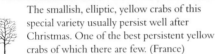

## -coronaria 'Elk River'

An unusual form of crab apple related to M. 'Charlottae' with single, large, soft pink flowers and bright, rich green, mini Granny Smith type crab apples. Excellent autumn tints to the large and handsome leaves.

## -'Coralburst'

A naturally very dwarf variety. The coral pink buds open to pretty double rose pink flowers followed by persistent small bronze fruit in the autumn. Ideal for patios.

## -'Crittenden'

A small semi-pendulous tree. Pale pink flowers are followed by heavy crops of bright scarlet fruit which persist well into winter.

## -'Directeur Moerlands'
Syn: M. *x moerlandsii* 'Profusion Improved'

M. x moerlandsii 'Profusion' is a classic ornamental tree for the garden and landscape. This improved version has more disease-resistant, deeply lobed, shiny leaves and equally fine, dark pink flowers. Persistent small dark fruit.

## -'Donald Wyman'

This variety is quite special as its abundant, small, bright red fruits persist well into February in most years. A strong growing round-headed tree with pink buds, white flowers and dark green foliage.

## -'Evereste' PERPETU

A conical tree with dark green lobed leaves and large soft pink to white flowers. Small red and yellow fruits, rather like mini apples, holding well into winter. An excellent pollinator for apples.

## -*floribunda* (Japanese Crab)

Known as the Japanese crab, a very pretty tree in flower, displaying crimson buds opening to white and pale blush petals which come earlier than most varieties. Small, red-yellow fruit in autumn. (Japan)

## -'Golden Gem'

 Clouds of large bunches of fragrantly scented pure white flowers followed by abundant dainty yellow fruit. Also an excellent pollinator for apples.

## -'Gorgeous'

A small compact tree with scented apple blossom flowers. The fruits resemble the perfect miniature apples persisting well into November. Ideal for tangy pink crab apple jelly.

## -'Harry Baker'

This is a very special variety with exceptionally large, rich, flamboyant pink flowers, dark green-maroon leaves followed by large ruby red fruit with a deep pink flesh lasting into mid October. High in pectin making a superb deep red jelly. (UK)

## -*ioensis* **'Purpurea'** EVELYN
Syn: M. 'Rubra'

A most spectacular purple leaved form of the 'prairie crab' with large lobed dark purple leaves that turn a stunning orange-red in autumn. The flowers are large single pink and fragrant. (North America)

## -'Indian Magic'

Dark red buds open to showy large deep pink flowers. Heavy production of small glossy red fruit changing to orange and persistent until well into the new year. Prominent purple leaves into mid summer. One of the best introductions in recent times. (USA)

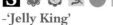

## -'Jelly King'

An exciting new introduction with spectacular large orange-pink fruit that persist much longer than most large fruited crab apples. Strong white blossom covers this vigorous but compact tree in spring. Makes excellent pink jelly. (New Zealand)

## -'John Downie'

A vigorous upright tree when young with bright green young leaves. Attractive white 'apple blossom' flowers in spring and large bright orange and red pear-shaped fruits in the autumn. One of the most popular for crab apple jelly despite its disease susceptibility.

## -'Louisa'

A charming graceful tree, one of the best weeping Malus, forming an umbrella shape. Dark green, glossy leaves, rose coloured buds opening to true pink flowers. Small lemon-gold ripening to golden-orange fruit festoon the branches in the autumn.

# -'Laura'

A naturally dwarf tree with an upright habit, for even the smallest garden. Dark purple-green leaves and stunning pink and white flowers in April. Persistent large, round, maroon fruit perfect for the best crab apple jelly. Bred by Hugh Ermen (Kent).

## Crab apple jelly – a simple recipe

Ingredients: Fruit, sugar and water!

Method:

- For every 454g (1lb) of washed, ripe unsliced fruit add 568ml (1pt) water.

- Simmer until the fruit has cooked to a pulp.

- Strain through a jelly bag. Do not squeeze if you want very clear jelly, but if in a hurry squeeze the bag for quicker extraction (only when Granny is not looking!)

- Add 454g (1lb) of sugar for each 568ml (1pt) juice.

- Bring to the boil and continue for approx. 5 minutes (or estimated setting point). Bottle and store.

- Ideal as an accompaniment with lamb and pork, as a spread on peanut butter or thinly on toast for a quick energy snack at any time.

## -x moerlandsii 'Liset'

A pretty, small tree with purple foliage when young, reddish and glossy later. Deep crimson flowers and small blood-red fruits. (Holland)

## -'Pink Perfection'

 Large double fragrant pink blossom makes this variety quite special.

## -'Prairie Fire'

 A superb small tree upright in habit with vibrant deep pink single flowers, dark purple to green narrow leaves and large attractive small spheroid purple fruit in the autumn. An excellent recently introduced variety.

## -'Red Obelisk'

 A compact upright tree with light pink flowers followed by attractive, conical, red fruits. Foliage is purplish-brown at first, later becoming dark green. Good for crab apple jelly. (Belgium)

## -*x robusta* **'Red Sentinel'**

 A classic crab apple with decorative red fruit. White apple blossom scented flowers and large clusters of deep red fruits that remain on the branches well into January. A lovely winter tree and a true bird feeder from nature. The fruit laden shoots can also be cut for Christmas decoration. For image see next page.

Malus x *robusta* 'Red Sentinel'

### -'Royal Beauty'

A small, steeply weeping tree with leaves copper-red when young, later dark green. Deep pink flowers are followed by small, dark red fruits.

### -'Rudolph'

One of the largest single pink flowers on any Malus variety and stunning when in full bloom. The fresh purple-green leaves during the season also makes this a good summer tree. The fruits are small, dark purple and persistent. (Canada)

### -'Sun Rival'

A charming semi weeping (umbrella-shaped) tree with flower trusses of delicate pink buds opening to white followed by stunning bright red fruits. Apple blossom scented flowers add to its many fine features. (Bristol, UK)

### -*toringo* Syn: M. *sieboldii*

A small, dense, semi-weeping Japanese crab with pink buds opening to masses of small delicate white flowers. Small yellow fruits appear in large bunches. (Japan)

### -*toringo* subsp. *sargentii* '**Tina**'

A charming, small, almost dwarf variety smothered in gold-anthered pure white flowers followed by small cherry-like fruits in autumn. Ideal as a patio tree.

## *-toringo* '**Scarlett**'

A superb 'all seasons tree' combining good leaf, flower and fruiting features. The rich pink blossom contrasts well with the emerging purple, deeply lobed leaves which turn to glossy dark green in the summer and then rich scarlet with purple tints in the autumn, very rare for a Malus. The persistent small purple fruits remain long after leaf fall. (Denmark)

## *-toringoides*

A small but wide spreading tree with deeply lobed leaves providing good autumn tints. Delicately scented creamy-white flowers are followed by red and yellow round-conical fruit. M. toringoides 'Mandarin' is a selected variety of this species with more orange coloured fruit. (W. China)

## *-transitoria*

A wide spreading tree with small, delicate, narrowly lobed leaves. The white star-shaped flowers appear as a white cloud. The fruits are yellow, small and abundant. Good autumn colours of yellow-gold. M. transitoria 'Thornhayes Tansy' is an exceptionally pretty compact dwarf form with finely cut leaves. (NW China)

### -trilobata 'Guardsman'

A rare and very distinctive form of the unusual M. trilobata species. Stiffly erect in habit with deeply lobed maple-like leaves which turn scarlet-crimson in autumn. The white flowers are large and appear late in June. Small moss green fruits. (Mediterranean and NE Greece)

### -'White Star'

Splendid show of white star-like flowers followed by medium golden-russet crab apples which persist into December. A healthy robust tree for all situations. Bred by Hugh Ermen. (Kent, UK)

### -x zumi var. calocarpa 'Golden Hornet'

Small compact tree with an upright habit in its early years. Dark green, broadly oval leaves turn yellow in autumn. Large white flowers flushed pink followed by a large crop of bright yellow fruits maturing early in the autumn.

### Self fertile and pollinators for apples

All fruiting Malus are self fertile. Some are also used for pollinating commercial apple orchards and those with particularly compatible pollen are listed below.

Each variety has a 1-5 flowering period compatible with apples so if you need an ornamental pollinator you can match to suit. See page 287 for more on fruit pollination.

4 M. 'Butterball'

1 M. 'Dolgo' (syn: Pink Glow)

3 M. 'Evereste'

4 M. 'Golden Gem'

2 M. robusta 'Red Sentinel, M. 'Jelly King'

5 M. zumi var calocarpa 'Golden Hornet'.

# METASEQUOIA

These fast growing deciduous conifers, very similar to Taxodium, do well in wet, well drained or chalky soils. They are tolerant of urban pollution.

## *-glyptostroboides* **(Dawn Redwood)**

A large tree of conical habit. Soft flaky cinnamon bark. Bright larch green leaves during summer becoming tawny pink and golden in autumn. Small green cones turn brown when ripe. One of the most rewarding of trees to plant for the future. Only first discovered in China in 1941 despite knowledge of its existence in pre-historic times from fossil records. (C. China)

## *-glyptostroboides* '**Gold Rush**'

A remarkable and lovely form. The delicate filigree leaves remain gold throughout the summer ending in an autumn display of orange and golden tints. It also has the same shaggy soft cinnamon bark as M. glyptostroboides. It is slower growing than the normal 'Dawn Redwood' and produces little shade due to its thin conical shape. Ideal for planting near water as it particularly enjoys moist conditions. (Japan)

### Deciduous conifers?

Conifers (cone-bearing) are generally considered to be evergreen but there are a few that are deciduous. Metasequoia above is one of these and the others are also to be found in this book namely: Larix (larch), Pseudolarix, Taxodium and Ginkgo.

### Worthy of wider distribution.

They all have seasonal interest, with attractive bark, excellent autumn colour and produce little competitive shade for other plant life, being tall and slim with sparse branch systems.

# MORUS

## (Mulberry)

Mulberries will grow in almost any fertile, well drained soil. A warm sunny site is needed for good crops of fruit so gardens are generally a good spot for a mulberry tree. See the Fruit Section for the Black Mulberry (Morus nigra) page 258.

### -alba 'Pendula'

A small weeping tree with steeply falling branches. Large, heart-shaped leaves are glossy dark green, turning yellow in autumn. Small edible white fruits turn reddish-pink.

*Both the white (alba) and black (nigra) mulberries are symbols of the quality of wisdom. Food for silk worms (alba) and fruit from both stimulate the immune system. The white mulberry does fruit but it is inferior in eating quality.*

*The picture here shows an old black mulberry (Morus nigra) all of which is one tree. Mulberries eventually fall over in this way and often rise again from the original root, in some ways a 'phoenix' of nature.*

# NOTHOFAGUS

## (Southern Beech)

An interesting group of deciduous and evergreen trees, from the southern hemisphere, for many uses. Although hardy they are not comfortable on chalk soils and prefer a sheltered site.

### -antarctica (The Antarctic Beech)

An elegant, fast growing large tree with small, round, dark green heart-shaped leaves turning yellow in autumn. (Chile)

### -dombeyi

A valuable evergreen tree with small dainty leaves that are doubly toothed and dark shining green. Can be pruned into a spectacular hedge. May lose its leaves in a hard winter. (Chile and Argentina)

### Nothofagus

Nothofagus is named from two Greek words: nothus meaning false and fagus meaning beech. It is an ancient genus, which we know was present in Gondwana – the land mass which broke up to form – among others - South America, New Zealand, New Guinea, New Caledonia as well as Australia. Fossil records of Nothofagus have also been found in Antarctica.

This tree can still be found in the wild in Argentine Patagonia and central Chile forming dense forests, wherever there is water and soil in abundance. It sometimes forms mixed forests with another import from that region Araucaria araucana (monkey-puzzle trees, see page 38).

# NYSSA

Grown mainly for their autumn colour, these trees should be planted in fertile, moist, neutral to acid soil. Best results are seen in areas with long hot summers.

## -*sylvatica* (Tupelo Tree)

A handsome tree with oval, glossy green leaves which are dark green above and blue green underneath, turning rich scarlet, orange and yellow colours in autumn. It has a columnar habit and will tolerate semi-shade. Several known forms such as N. sylvatica 'Sheffield' are worth planting. (Canada, USA and Mexico)

# OLEA

## (Olive)

Useful in the UK as evergreen shrubs and trees, very tolerant of a wide range of soil conditions provided they have good drainage. Grown extensively in warm climates around the world.

## -*europaea* (Common Olive)

 The Olive is hardy in the UK's mildest areas as a foliage tree. They can be severely pruned even into the old wood and will grow back like an old friend.

### Can we grow olives in the UK?

Fruit production is likely to be precarious and unreliable in the UK but if anything the garden provides the best environment to try. Here are a few tips.

- Grown in pots in a sunny warm spot in the garden or conservatory in a well drained mixture of 50/50 loam and well rotted compost.
- Pot on and increase the container volume every 2 years to balance with the tree size.
- Feed regularly with high nitrogen and phosphate liquid feed – tomato feed is suitable.
- Obtain specific fruiting varieties rather than the 'common' olive mentioned above as these will be more reliable.
- Olives do require some winter chill so leave outside for as long as possible but shelter in a cold greenhouse in winter if the temperature goes below –5°C.
- Olives flower and fruit on the previous years growth.

# OSTRYA

These interesting trees resemble the hornbeam and are suitable for any fertile soil.

## -*carpinifolia* (Hop Hornbeam)

 A bush-shaped tree with ovate, double toothed leaves that turn clear yellow in autumn. Long drooping catkins give rise to nutlets contained in bladder-like husks. (S. Europe and W. Asia)

## Ironwood trees

Both Parrotia persica and Ostyra are known as ironwood trees – something they share with trees from many parts of the world including Carpinus caroliniana, (the American hornbeam) Casuarina equisetifolia, (Common ironwood from Australia) Chionanthus foveolatus, (pock ironwood from South Africa) Mesua ferrea, Rose chestnut or Ceylon ironwood or Nahar and various olive trees. It will come as no surprise that these trees have been thus named for their exceptionally dense and strong wood: hard to work but worth the effort for the strength such timber gave to all manner of structures.

# PARROTIA

These lovely trees are part of the Hamamelis (Witch Hazel) family and are very lime tolerant but grow best in deep, well drained fertile soil. Good autumn colours are their main feature.

## -*persica* (Persian Ironwood)

A large shrub or small tree of wide spreading habit, and grey flaking bark. Large deep green oval leaves turn crimson-gold in autumn. The small delicate crimson flowers in late winter to early spring are often unappreciated. (N. Iran)

*Parrotia persica* **(Persian Ironwood)**

# PAULOWNIA

Requires moist but well drained fertile soil.

## *-tomentosa* (**Foxglove Tree**)

If placed in a sheltered position these broadly columnar trees can become sizeable. The dark green leaves are hairy underneath. Beautiful mauve 'foxglove' flowers are produced in May in the warmer areas of the UK. If flowering is unsuccessful it is recommended to 'stool' this tree by pruning each spring to ground level. This will produce large succulent leaves. (China, Japan)

# PHOTINIA

These very versatile shrubs and trees are mostly evergreen. Grown in tree form they can be regularly trimmed to symmetrical shapes. They will succeed in almost any fertile soil.

## *-davidiana* '**Palette**'

The leaves of this slow growing form are conspicuously blotched and streaked with creamy-white. The young vigorous growth is pink-tinged when young. (Holland)

## *-x fraseri* '**Red Robin**'

## -x fraseri 'Red Robin'

A dense, upright habit if untrimmed. Sharply toothed leaves, brilliant red at the growing tips. Ideal for clipped standards, topiary, hedges and trees. There are other similar forms such as P. x fraseri 'Purple Peter', P. x fraseri 'Canivily'. (New Zealand)

## -villosa

A deciduous species eventually forming a small tree. Hawthorn-like flowers followed by small, egg shaped bright red fruits. Leaves turn a lovely scarlet gold in autumn. Avoid shallow chalky soil. (Japan, Korea, China)

# PICEA
## (Spruce)

A large range of trees including the Norway Spruce, the most common of Christmas Trees. Tolerant of most soils except dry shallow chalk. Only a few gems mentioned here.

## -breweriana (Brewers Weeping Spruce)

One of the most graceful of all the spruces resembling a green fountain at its best with its arching branches and even more slender falling branchlets. Slow to develop. (W. USA)

### Honey Fungus (Armillariella mellea and A. ostoyae)

If this problem has been identified in a garden the following trees and their related cultivars have moderate to good resistance. Acer negundo, Carpinus betulus (hornbeam), Catalpa (Indian Bean), Cercis (various species), Cornus (various species), Fagus sylvatica (beech), Fraxinus excelsior (ash), Juglans nigra (black walnut), Larix kaempferi (Japanese larch), Robinia pseudoacacia (false acacia), Taxus baccata (yew), Prunus laurocerasus (cherry laurel), Sorbus aria (whitebeam).

*-pungens* **'Erich Frahm'**

A very good alternative to P. pungens 'Hoopsii'. Has a denser habit with smaller leaves giving a more conical shape but still an impressive silvery blue foliage. (Germany)

*-pungens* **'Hoopsii'**

A classic garden conifer of densely conical habit, with vividly glaucous blue leaves. P. pungens 'Edith' is a superior alternative well worth seeking.

## The faithful lovers

Down the centuries there have been many stories in different cultures of people being turned into trees. In Greek legend, Daphne turned into a laurel tree when fleeing the advances of Apollo. Lotis, another nymph who fled from unwanted advances, became the lotus tree. But other transformations symbolise eternal love. In another Greek myth, the gods turned Baucis and Philemon, a devoted old couple, into an oak and a lime tree which grew close together and intermingled as a reward for their ready hospitality to the Gods. In Japan, two pine trees growing close together are said to be faithful lovers. Tales from many cultures speak of the dead being reincarnated, or reborn, as trees, and legends and songs often tell of two trees, their branches linked or intertwined, that grow from the graves of lovers.

# PINUS (Pine)

These evergreen trees of all sizes and some with spectacular ornamental cones are very adaptable, requiring only a well drained soil and preferably a sunny position.

**Scots pine (P. sylvestris) in Scotland**

## -flexilis 'Firmament'

 An ornamental form of the five needled 'Limber Pine' with good bluish tints to the foliage, becomes densely furnished and forms a neat pyramidal tree. (W. and N. America)

## -heldreichii (Bosnian Pine)

 A distinctive form with a smooth grey-green bark, ovoid habit and bright blue cones. P. heldreichii 'Compact Gem' is a slow growing dwarf form with dark green leaves.

## -patula

A most beautiful pine with long graceful branches, light tan coloured bark and bright green leaves up to 30cm long. The very large, twisted cones are very conspicuous and the well spaced branches add to its elegance. Hardy in England and Wales and the west of Scotland.

### Strangling roots

*Poor root system*

Most trees grown in pots will 'circle' within the pot especially if they become 'root bound'. In most cases at planting time this can be rectified with deciduous trees especially during the dormant season with some hard root pruning. There is a risk with Conifers that such root interference could actually kill the tree. The pictures here show a poor circled root system from a solid pot and a good fibrous root system from an 'Air' pot. Some tree nurseries have adopted these pots as the ultimate for root development and they particularly come well recommended for coniferous trees.

*Good roots*

### -radiata (Monterey Pine)

An attractive, fast growing tree with deeply fissured, dark brown bark and a dense head of branches. Slender leaves are dark green and the cones are glossy greyish-brown. Ideal for coastal areas. (W. USA)

### -radiata 'Aurea' Group

A lovely slower growing form with bright golden needles. (New Zealand)

---

### Pine trees information

- There are over 100 species of pine trees with only the Scots Pine (P. sylvestris) as native to the UK. They are long lived often to 1000 years and beyond.
- The resin of some species is an important source of turpentine and pitch used for waterproofing.
- The cones mostly deposit their seeds annually but some are only released in forest fires when the parent tree dies.
- One rule on soil selection is that most pines are adaptable to acid and alkaline soils but the five needle pines do less well on chalk soils.
- Most pines dislike shade and polluted atmospheres.
- A collection of pines as in an arboretum situation is called a Pinetum (Pine-e-tum).
- Pine trees have come to represent longevity and steadfastness in many cultures. In China, they are planted on graves to strengthen and stiffen the souls of the departed.

### -sylvestris 'Aurea' Group

A particularly special form of the 'Scots Pine', slow growing with slender blue green leaves that are temperature sensitive, turning bright golden yellow in the winter months returning to blue green in summer.

### -sylvestris 'Chantry Blue'

One of the best blue forms with an upright habit.

125

*-sylvestris* **'Edwin Hillier'**

 A lovely selection with silvery blue-green leaves and reddish stems.

*-wallichiana* **(Bhutan Pine)**

 A very elegant large tree with graceful blue-green foliage forming a broad head with age. The pendant cones are resin smeared. (Himalaya)

# PLATANUS

**(Plane)**

These large trees with maple-like leaves and flaking bark are very fast growing when young.

*-x hispanica* **(London Plane)**
Syn: P. *x acerifolia*

A noble park and city tree with attractive, mottled or patchwork flaking bark and large palmate bright green leaves. Flowers are inconspicuous. Rounded bauble-like fruits hang in clusters of two-four. Best grown in deep fertile soil. Will tolerate urban pollution.

*-orientalis* **(Oriental Plane)**

A large, long-lived tree with a broad head and short broad trunk. The deeply lobed, dark green leaves have downy undersides. Globular seed heads ripening in September. A form with more slender lobes is P. orientalis digitata. (SE Europe)

# POPULUS

## (Poplar)

Large, fast growing trees which will grow anywhere except shallow chalk. Useful as shelter trees but not suitable for very small gardens unless pruned hard. Best planted at a distance from buildings in small gardens as they will compete for valuable moisture in the summer.

### -alba 'Richardii'

 A small growing tree with leaves bright golden yellow above and silver beneath. When russled by the wind the effect is delightful. Treat as a shrub and prune hard in winter.

### -x jackii 'Aurora' Syn: P. candicans 'Aurora'

Large, broad-headed tree. Variegated leaves, creamy-white tinged pink on young growths, balsam-scented in spring. If left unpruned the leaves are significantly less variegated. Annual hard pruning recommended.

### -nigra (Black Poplar)

A large majestic tree naturalised in much of the UK and now considered very much a native. There are two clones from the Welsh Marches area selected from ancient champion trees with interesting historical connections. P. nigra 'Hanging Tree' (male) and P. nigra 'Lady Overton' (female).

### -tremula (Aspen)

An attractive suckering tree that is the most common source of wood for the match industry. Leaves, prominently toothed, appear late, flutter/rustle in the slightest breeze and turn clear butter-yellow in autumn. Has long grey catkins in late winter and spring. P. tremula 'Erecta' has a more columnar habit. (Europe, Asia and N Africa)

127

## The Hardiness of Trees

There is an internationally recognised rating for tree hardiness based on the USDA (United States Department of Agriculture) Plant Hardiness Zone system. This rates trees survival as follows:

**Temperature in Celsius**

| | |
|---|---|
| Zone 1 | Below -45°C |
| Zone 2 | -45°C to -40°C |
| Zone 3 | -40°C to -35°C |
| Zone 4 | -35°C to -29°C |
| Zone 5 | -29°C to -23°C |
| Zone 6 | -23°C to -17°C |
| Zone 7 | -17°C to -12°C |
| Zone 8 | -12°C to - 6°C |
| Zone 9 | -6°C to -1°C |
| Zone 10 | -1°C to 4°C |
| Zone 11 | Above 4°C |

The UK climate is so dominated by the changeable mild Gulf Stream that winter injury is not a subject for continual debate as it would be on a continental land mass and the table above is rarely used as a guide to hardiness. Zones 7-11 are those that effect us in normal winters and possibly Zones 5 and 6 in extreme winters.

Wind (exposure), East (dry) and West (wet) are for us as much and possibly more important a consideration as low temperatures when deciding what will survive. We also do not have predictable hardening off periods as we enter winter and damage to trees and other plant life can often occur on soft un-ripened wood that would survive quiet happily if effected later in the winter.

We mention the hardiness zone in this book in case the reader wishes to use the information when reading other books; but as there are so few trees mentioned here that cannot be planted in the majority of the UK, this will not be used to rate individual trees. However, look out for the ❄ symbol that means frost damage can cause some dieback in shoots at times. Most of these trees can be pruned back into healthy wood and grow away perfectly well the next season.

# PRUNUS

Prunus contains a wonderfully diverse range of deciduous and evergreen trees for the garden. Flowering times ranging from winter to mid summer. There are also some spectacular autumn colours.

They are easy to grow on almost any well drained soil, prefering chalk to acid.

There are over 400 species within this genera and we list a selection of the most diverse and suitable for gardens in the first part of this section. The Japanese flowering cherries, so much the show offs and most exotic of the Prunus are listed in a section of their own from page 142.

### -'Accolade'

A graceful tree of spreading habit bearing masses of pendulous, semi-double, light pink flowers during April. An outstanding cherry for all gardens. The mid green leaves turn orange-red in autumn.

### -*avium* (Wild Cherry)

The 'Gean' or 'Mazzard'. Single white flowers and good autumn colour makes this one of our most attractive native woodland trees. It is the parent of most fruiting sweet cherries and in some years will produce a good crop of fruit itself, not necessarily very sweet but good enough to feed the birds. (Europe and Western Asia)

## -avium **'Plena'** Syn: 'Multiplex'

The double 'Gean'. A profusion of densely-double pure white flowers in May. Leaves are bronze when young, turning dark green then yellow and crimson in autumn. Upright, vigorous growth. This spectacular tree has been grown for over 300 years.

## -x blireana

A beautiful small tree with metallic, coppery-purple leaves and very large fragrant rose pink double flowers appearing in early April.

## -campanulata **'Felix Jury'** (Formosan Cherry)

The best and hardiest form of this lovely early spring flowering tree with rich pink flowers and yellow stamens. (China, Japan, Taiwan)

## *-cerasifera* 'Hessei'

A very unusual and attractive shrubby tree with an abundance of single white flowers in March, followed by mottled white, pink and purple foliage. If pruned hard after flowering the leaves are more vibrant and the flowers more prolific the following spring. (1906)

## *-cerasifera* 'Nigra'

## *-cerasifera* 'Nigra'

A neat round-headed tree with purple leaves and stems throughout the growing season. Myriads of small pale pink flowers appear in late February and early March to herald the arrival of spring. P. 'Vesuvius' is similar. (1916)

## *-cerasifera* 'Spring Glow'

An upright shape with persistent bronze leaves and large single vivid pink flowers in March. One of the first large flowers to appear. The size of the flowers suggests almond and/or peach in its parentage.

## -*cerasus* 'Rhexii'

An unusual non fruiting form of the sour cherry, dating back to the 16th Century. A small shrubby tree with densely double white 'carnation' type flowers. (UK)

## -x *cistena* 'Crimson Dwarf' (Purple Leafed Sand Cherry)

The red leaves and masses of small white flowers make this a very useful shrub for a mixed border or hedging.

## -'Collingwood Ingram'

A seedling of P. 'Kursar' but with even deeper pink flowers appearing 7-10 days later than its parent. It also shares the same excellent autumn leaf colours. (1979)

## -'Hally Jolivette'

A small graceful tree. Its light branch structure is covered with unique semi-double blush white flowers in early spring. (USA)

## -himalaica

A rare tree and a good alternative to P. serrula or P. rufa but with darker mahogany, peeling bark than the former and more serrated leaves than the latter. Collected by Tony Schilling in 1965 who has written a good account of this tree in The RHS Garden Volume 6 part 4 December 2007.

M B 🍁 C ⬤ 🏹

# THE FUJI CHERRIES

All Prunus incisa varieties are the excellent Fuji cherries, so named as they grow wild on the slopes of Mount Fuji ('Shirotae' is perhaps "coincidentally" rather than "inadvertently" named "Mount Fuji"). They are worth a special mention as small garden trees/shrubs for their size, adaptability, ease of growing, versatility and stunning displays of flower and autumn leaf colours. Pictured here is P. incisa Kojo-no-mai (described on this page) grown successfully in a pot. They can be pruned just after flowering to contain their size and improve the intensity of the flowers for the following year. Feeding is important and re-potting every other year is recommended, adding some fresh compost/soil on each occasion.

## -incisa 'Kojo-no-mai'

A small, slow growing shrub with attractive 'zig-zag' shoots and pendulous blush white flowers in April. Attractive red and copper coloured leaves in the autumn. An ideal patio plant.

VS 🐌 🍁 🍃 🍁 C ⬤ 🪴 🏹

## -incisa 'Midori-zakura'
Syn: P. incisa yamadae

A unique and lovely shrubby tree with fresh bright green buds and calyxes opening to pure white bell shaped flowers. (Japan 1916)

S 🍁 🍁 C ⬤ 🪴 🏹

## -*incisa* 'Mikinori'

A small tree or large shrub which displays a beautiful show of delicate pink opening to pure white flowers in March. Finely toothed leaves show rich red autumn tints.

## -*incisa* 'Oshidori' PRINCESSE

One of the best dwarf 'Fuji' cherries displaying profuse double blush white flowers with a delicate pink centre in March. The narrow leaves with serrated edges display rich autumn colours.

## -*incisa* 'Pendula' (Weeping Fuji Cherry)

A very graceful, small weeping tree. The delicate single white flowers densely festoon the branches.

## -*incisa* 'Praecox'

A small tree or large shrub. A fine winter flowering form with white flowers which are pale pink in bud.

## -'Kursar'

*Collingwood Ingram was a leading authority in the west on ornamental cherries during the 20th C.*
*His book 'Ornamental Cherries' published by Hazell, Watson & Viney 1948 is worth seeking out.*

A beautiful small tree with masses of deep pink single flowers in early March, followed by rich autumn leaf colours of red and gold. This variety was raised by Ingram from P. campanulata x nipponica var. kurilensis. Prunus 'Collingwood Ingram' is a similar variety with darker pink flowers. Both are outstanding. (UK)

## -*laurocerasus* (Common or Cherry Laurel)

A vigorous wide spreading large shrub that will take on tree proportions. Produces very attractive terminal racemes of small white flowers. Good for screens, hedges and specimens. Avoid shallow chalk soils.

## -*laurocerasus* 'Caucasica' and 'Rotundifolia'

Prunus 'Caucasica'

There are two forms worth considering of the common laurel. P. laurocerasus 'Caucasica' is highly recommended for its long narrow leaves and far less prone to disease. P. laurocerasus 'Rotundifolia' is less vigorous and more bushy in habit.

## *-litigiosa* (**Tassel Cherry**)

A most unusual upright tree producing clusters of small white or pink-tinged flowers in April. These flowers have conspicuous protruding anthers, hence the reference to tassels. (China)

S 🌼 C ⬤

### Humps and Bumps

Many ornamental trees are budded or grafted (see page 12) on rootstocks just like fruit trees. It is one of the most successful ways to propagate trees true to type. Evidence of this is often seen in older trees. Those near the ground or 'top worked' on stems can still show the rootstock in later life as a familiar swelling between rootstock and variety.

## *-lusitanica* (**Portugal Laurel**)

A dense and spreading tree with oval, rich green leaves with reddish petioles. Small white hawthorn scented flowers are carried in long slender racemes. An ideal patio plant for shaping and trimming. (Portugal)

S 🍁 ⑥ ⚙ E ⚔ C ⬤ ⊘ 🧺 ◉

## *-maackii* '**Amber Beauty**' (**Manchurian Cherry**)

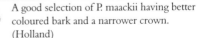

A good selection of P. maackii having better coloured bark and a narrower crown. (Holland)

M 🐎 B 🌼 ④ ⚔ ⬤ 🌿 🌳

135

## -*mume* **'Beni-chidori'**
Syn: P. *mume 'Beni-shidare'*/
P. *mume 'Beni-shidon', P. mume 'Beni-shidori'*
**(Japanese Apricot)**

A delightful February flowering shrub with rich, deep pink flowers, highly and heavenly scented. Prune annually, after flowering. Translated this means 'Flight of the Red Plovers'.

## -*nipponica* **'Brilliant'**
**(Japanese Alpine Cherry)**

A compact, erect, large shrub with bright showy white flowers produced in a stunning display in early April. Good for patio growing.

## -**'Okame'**

A hybrid raised by Capt. Collingwood Ingram. Masses of small, deep shell pink flowers produced in mid March, followed by good autumn colours. (UK)

## -*padus* **'Albertii'**

A very prolific flowering form of the 'Bird Cherry'. Compact and of an upright shape. (Asia and Japan)

## -*padus* **'Watereri'** Syn: P. *padus* 'Grandiflora'
**(Bird Cherry)**

Broadly conical at first becoming rounded. Oval light green leaves turn to yellow in autumn. Almond scented white flowers in May. Small black fruits.

## -'Pandora'

A good, small, all seasons tree for any garden. Compact in habit with ascending branches clothed in pale, shell-pink flowers in late March. Bronze-red leaves in the spring with tints of purple-red in the autumn.

**S** 🍁 🍃 ③ **C** ◐ ⬔ 🏆

## -*pendula* 'Pendula Rubra'

Formally P. subhirtella 'Pendula Rubra' this attractive early pink flowering weeping tree has wide arching branches.

**S** ③ **C** ◐ ⬔ 🏆

## -*pendula* 'Stellata'

A beautiful, spectacular little tree with clear pink star shaped flowers produced in crowded clusters on graceful branches.

**S** ❀ **C** ◐ ⬔

## -*persica* 'Versicolor'

A very unusual flowering peach/almond with separate white, pink, and pink, white mottled flowers on the same tree.

**S** ❀ ❀ ◐ ● ⬚ ⬔

### -'Pink Shell'

 An elegant and worthy small tree. Spreading branches drooping beneath an abundance of cup-shaped shell pink blossoms.

### -*rufa* (**Himalayan Cherry**)

 An ornamental bark tree similar to P. serrula and P. himalaica with peeling reddish-brown and amber bark. Rusty hairy young shoots and small clusters of pale pink flowers. (Himalaya)

### -*sargentii* (**Sargent Cherry**)

 One of the earliest, large flowered cherries and one of the finest for autumn colour. A round-headed, broad spreading habit, bronze-red oval leaves when young, contrasting with the large, single pink flowers in late March. Brilliant red and maroon in the autumn. (Japan, Sakhalin and Korea)

### -*sargentii* '**Charles Sargent**'

 An outstanding form for autumn colour and also for sumptuous dark copper-red new leaves in spring. P. sargentii 'Columnaris' is a good upright form for restricted spaces.

*-serrula* Syn: *P. serrula var. tibetica*

A special tree for all seasons with impressive glistening mahogany peeling bark. Small vigorous and upright in its early years spreading with age. The leaves are narrow, willow-like and small dainty white flowers appear late April. Good small specimen tree for all situations. (W. China)

### -'Shosar'

A strong growing fastigiate tree with clear pink flowers in late March and excellent autumn colours. Another variety bred by Collingwood Ingram. (UK)

### -'Snow Goose'

A narrow, upright small tree of considerable merit. The lovely, large, soft, single, white flowers with long tassle stamens are beautiful in early April. Similar to P. 'Umineko'. Good autumn colours.

### -'Snow Showers'

A lovely, small, profusely flowering dwarf cherry with spectacular dense single white flowers which cover steeply pendent branches in late March. Maintains a small, neat habit. Good autumn leaf colours.

# Prunus 'The Bride'

## -'The Bride'

A lovely compact tree that as the flowers begin to emerge show exquisite little pointed buds, white tipped with carmine. These open to give the most wonderful display of single white flowers with striking red anthers. A choice small tree for any garden.

## -'Spire'

A vase-shaped tree with oval leaves, bronze on emergence, turning orange-red in autumn. Single almond-pink flowers borne in mid spring.

## -x subhirtella 'Autumnalis' and 'Autumnalis Rosea'

 Small spreading bushy trees highly valued for their long season of flowering from late autumn to April, especially during mild winters. 'Autumnalis' becomes white when the flowers are fully open and 'Autumnalis Rosea' retains its pretty pink shades throughout.

## -x subhirtella 'Fukubana'

 This little tree has a spectacular profusion of semi-double rose-madder flowers in March. (USA)

## -'Tilstone Hellfire'

 A remarkable introduction with pretty soft single pink flowers, glossy dark metallic green leaves turning deep red and purple in the autumn. Raised by Donavan Leaman as a hybrid seedling or cross between P. sargentii 'Rancho' or P. Hillieri 'Spire'.

## -'Trailblazer'

 A very interesting ornamental fruiting plum with purple-bronze leaves, white flowers and large purple skinned and fleshed fruit. Probably a hybrid between P. saliciana and P. cerasifera. Leave fruit for as long as possible before attempting to eat. (USA)

## -x yedoensis (The Yoshino Cherry)

 A graceful, wide spreading tree with single almond scented blush white flowers in late March. The national flower of Japan. (Japan)

## -x yedoensis 'Shidare Yoshino'
Syn: P. 'Weeping Yoshino'

 A small tree with steeply pendent branches weeping to the ground. Single white flowers in early April.

# JAPANESE FLOWERING CHERRIES

The Japanese flowering cherries are a distinctive group of varieties separated from those mentioned already due primarily to their country of origin, their age stretching as far back as 1000 years and the high regard in which they are held in their homeland. In Japan they are known as the Sato-zakura meaning 'village-cherries'. Their parentage is mixed and to the layman is probably not too important, but the semi-double flowering forms that dominate this group come from the Oshima cherry (P. serrulata var. speciosa). The Japanese hold these trees in such high esteem that, in Japanese, the word 'flower' means first 'flowering cherries'. Also included are some recently introduced varieties referred to as the 'Matsumae' cherries bred by Matatoshi Asari from the island of Hokkaido. Many excellent books have been written on the subject and these are mentioned in our reference section.

## -'Amanogawa' (The Flagpole Cherry)

 A distinctive columnar tree with erect branches. The oval leaves are greeny-bronze when young, later dark green, then red-gold in autumn. Dense clusters of fragrant semi-double light pink flowers in late April.

## -'Beni-tamanishiki' SPRING SNOW

A small tree with a spreading habit. Clusters of blush white flowers appear like blobs of snow on the bare branches. Coppery young leaves provide a lovely contrast with the flowers. One of the Matsumae cherries.

## -'Beni-yutaka'

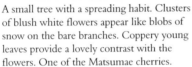

A semi-double, disc-shaped flower in a unique sugar pink colour with a distinctive dark central eye, developing as the flower ages, in early April. Lovely rich red-crimson autumn colours. A spectacular, robust and worthy tree.

## -'Daikoku'

A small tree with strong ascending branches. Large, deep, double, lilac-pink flowers with a central cluster of small green carpels carried in loose drooping clusters. One of a number of special, rarely seen varieties.

## -'Gyoikō'

A strong growing tree with ascending branches and unusual showy creamy-white semi-double flowers with green and pink shades, somewhat similar to P. 'Ukon' but flowers later.

## -'Hokusai'

One of the earliest introductions into the UK around 1860 but certainly not diminished in its splendour due to its age. A vigorous wide spreading tree with large semi-double pale pink flowers contrasting beautifully with the young brownish-bronze leaves.

## -'Horinji'

A small upright tree with soft pink semi-double flowers contrasting with pronounced purplish-brown calyces. Young leaves are greenish-brown. A very beautiful cultivar that is now rare, even in Japan.

## -'Ichiyō'

 Ascending branches and double shell-pink flowers with a frilled appearance borne on long flower stalks. See image on following page.

## -'Kanzan'

One of the showiest and best known varieties, with densely-double, purplish-pink flowers in late April. The spring foliage is coppery-red turning green and then orange in autumn. A strong-growing tree, with an upright, spreading habit.

## -'Kiku-shidare-zakura'
Syn: P. 'Cheals Weeping'

 A very popular small weeping tree with arching branches bearing densely clustered, double rose pink flowers. Lance-shaped leaves are pale green and slightly bronzed at first. Often wrongly referred to as P. 'Cheals Weeping' which has a more steeply weeping habit.

## Prunus 'Ichiyō'

The Japanese word 'Ichiyō'
means: ichi "one" and yo "leaf".

## -'Little Pink Perfection'

 This is a naturally dwarf version of P. 'Pink Perfection' growing to about half normal size, ideal for small spaces and patio tubs.

## -'Matsumae-beni-murasaki' CANDY FLOSS

The very large, double, deep-pink flowers in May have attractively fringed petals which age to the texture of crushed velvet. Coppery-bronze young leaves make a lovely contrast to the flowers.

## -'Matsumae-fuki' CHOCOLATE ICE

The deep coppery-brown young leaves are a perfect foil for the very large single blush-white flowers in April; an unforgettable sight when viewed against a clear blue sky. The habit is upright in the early years spreading as it ages.

## -'Matsumae-hanagasa' PINK PARASOL

One of the most beautiful of the Matsumae varieties. The graceful spreading branches are wreathed with heavy clusters of long-stemmed blooms in late April. These large pale pink flowers have densely packed petals surrounding a centre of bright-green, leafy carpels.

## -'Pink Perfection'

 The double rose-pink flowers are one of the most exotic and long lasting of any of the Japanese flowering cherries persisting for several weeks from early May. A small vase-shaped tree with oval leaves, bronze when young, turning orange-red colours in autumn.

## -'Royal Burgundy'

A vase shaped garden tree, impressive for its contrasting rich burgundy leaves and deep rose-pink double flowers. The leaves also turn a spectacular scarlet-red in autumn. Introduced from the USA as a sport of P. 'Kanzan' but considered worthy of a place within the Japanese cherry section.

## -'Shirofugen'

A majestic wide spreading tree unsurpassed for its beautiful display of large double white fragrant flowers and contrasting copper coloured leaves. The flowers fade to a subtle shade of pink. The latest of all the cherries to flower, this variety is at least 500 years old and is still one of the best.

### Japanese meanings & general terms

**Beni** "red" or "pink" • **Zakura** "cherry"
**Shiro** "white" • **Botan** "double"
**Murasak** "purple"

### Literal translations

**Amanogawa: (Ama-no-gawa)**
"Heavens River" "Ama" is an old word for the abode of the Gods.

**Beni-murasaki**
"pink purple"

**Gyoiko (Ko-Gyo-I)**
"Coloured court robes"

**Ichiyo (ichi yo)**
"one leaf"

**Kiku Shidare-Zakura**
"Chrysanthemum weeping cherry"

**Shogetsu**
"moonlight on the pine trees"

**Tai-Haku**
"big white"

**Ukon**
"Turmeric"

### In memory or recognition

**Daikaku**
One of the Japanese Gods of fortune

**Hokusai**
Named by Collingwood Ingram in memory of the artist Katsushika Hokusai

**Horinji (Horin-ji)**
Is a temple in Kyoto

**Shirofugen**
A whiter form of the original 'Fugenzo'

**Shirotae**
Is the white paper made from the 'paper mulberry tree' Broussonetia papyrifera

## -'Shirotae' (Mount Fuji)

This is one of the most beautiful and classic of Japanese cherries, with horizontal to slightly pendulous branches. Very large single or semi-double, fragrant, white flowers burst from soft green foliage in drooping clusters. The flowers contrast spectacularly with the dark almost black bark of the trunk and main branches.

## -'Shizuka' FRAGRANT CLOUD

A spectacular vigorous grower with a spreading, slightly ascending habit. The huge clusters of large, white, semi-double flowers are borne in profusion in May and turn pinkish as they age. They are also slightly scented, an unusual feature for a flowering cherry. Soft tones of orange leaves persist well into the autumn.

## -'Shogetsu' Syn: P. 'Shimidsu', P. 'Shimidsu-zakura', P. 'Longipes' BLUSHING BRIDE

A tree of graceful spreading habit. Large semi-double flowers, pink tinted in bud opening to pure white, hang all along the branches on long stalked clusters. One of the loveliest of all cherries.

## -'Sunset Boulevard'

## -'Ukon'

 A stunning fastigiate tree with bold large single white flowers containing a distinctive pink centre. Although used as a street tree it should have wider garden use.

Young foliage brownish-bronze. Very unusual semi-double pale yellow or sulphur flowers and brownish-bronze foliage. A beautiful cherry with similarities to P. 'Gyoikō'.

## -'Taihaku' (Great White Cherry)

Known as the 'Great White', this is a classic cherry. The flowers are very large, single white and stunning when seen against copper coloured young foliage. A sight to take your breath away. Re-introduced from the UK to Japan in 1932 by Collingwood Ingram.

# PSEUDOLARIX

An interesting genus, related to the larches, containing only one species. Prefers neutral or limefree soil.

## -*amabilis* (**Golden Larch**)

 A very good slow growing deciduous conifer with long, soft, light green leaves turning a rich yellow in autumn. Cones appear as pale green artichokes along the branches. (E. China)

## BEWARE OF STRIMMERS!

Strimmers have been responsible for the deaths of thousands of trees in the landscape since they were invented. The picture here shows typical damage. Although this tree has struggled to survive and the wounds are healing, very few fulfil their potential.

Help trees by banning strimmers, at least in the hands of the untrained and irresponsible.

# PTEROCARYA

Related to the walnut family (Juglandaceae) the 'wingnuts' are rapidly becoming popular for their ornamental leaves, long catkins and ability to thrive on all fertile soils.

## -*fraxinifolia*

 A widespreading, suckering tree with deeply furrowed bark and deeply divided pinnate leaves. Long green catkins up to 50cm long are produced in summer, followed by winged fruits and butter-yellow leaves in autumn. A lovely hardy tree. (Caucasus and N. Iran)

# PYRUS

## (Pear)

An attractive and varied range of trees for foliage, snowy white flowers, ornamental fruit and good autumn colour. Suitable for most soils, tolerant of drought and very hardy.

## -*calleryana* '**Chanticleer**'

 A classic street tree with narrow pyramidal habit, white flowers and glossy leaves turning purple and claret in autumn. The leaves stay on late and the flower is early so a good value tree for all seasons. (USA)

*-elaeagnifolia var. kotschyana* **'Silver Sail'**

This excellent silver foliage tree is a good alternative to P. salicifolia 'Pendula' being a better flowering form and producing small ornamental fruit in the autumn. The green-silver leaves are shaped like boat sails. The flowers are large, pure white with red anthers in March. (Europe and Turkey)

*-nivalis*

A small, classic, silver leaved tree with stout ascending branches and abundant pure white flowers in April. A bonus is the crop of small sweet edible fruit. (S. Europe)

*-nivalis* **'Catalia'**

A small compact form with large succulent, silky grey leaves and larger white flowers. A good crop of attractive russet pears are produced in early autumn.

*-pashia*

Round-headed compact tree with ovate, finely toothed leaves, attractive white flowers with red anthers and small pear-like fruits. Its most stunning feature is the intense crimson leaf colour in autumn.
(Himalaya and W. China)

## *-salicifolia var. orientalis* **'Pendula'** (Weeping Willow Leaved Pear)

 Elegant, small tree of weeping habit forming a dense mound. Silver willow-like leaves on weeping branches. Attractive small creamy white flowers in April.

### Tree shaping and topiary

With a little imagination and a sharp pair of shears it is quite possible to change and train a tree or shrub into something completely different.

The tree shown here is an ornamental weeping pear Pyrus salicifolia Pendula and having been left to grow naturally is of untidy appearance, becomes woody and tangled and takes increasing space in the garden as it gets older. The owner of the same tree shown above has enhanced their garden with imaginative pruning to suit the situation. It still flowers and provides the silver foil for so many other dynamic colours without shading and dominating other plant life.

For more on ornamental tree pruning see page 198.

# QUERCUS

## The Oaks

Although mostly woodland trees, there are several very interesting varieties with ornamental value. The few mentioned here do no justice to the oaks which number over 500 species and varieties and for this we offer apologies to the reader.

## *-cerris* **'Argenteovariegata'** (Variegated Turkey Oak)

The leaves have a conspicuous creamy-white margin. Acorns are half enclosed in cups with long slender scales. This most effective variegated tree grows best in deep fertile soil. Tolerant of chalk, semi-shade and coastal sites.

### Truffle Oaks

It is possible to purchase oak trees inoculated with Black Truffle mycorrhiza spores Tuber melanosporum. This highly prized truffle is naturally found in the Perigord region of France and only on oak trees. There are several interesting facts to consider when establishing inoculated trees.

- The survival of the fungi will probably only be guaranteed for one season.

- Success can only be achieved when the site conditions are similar to Perigord both climatically and soil type which in this case is calcareous (high pH).

- You will need to train a dog or pig to find them – which could be rather expensive.

## *-frainetto* (The Hungarian Oak)

 An exotic, large, majestic, wide spreading tree with fissured bark. Large leaves with oblong lobes. Fast growing and suitable for all soils. (SE Europe)

## *-ilex* (Evergreen or Holm Oak)

A versatile evergreen eventually becoming a dome-shaped specimen parkland tree. Its dark grey bark and narrow oval leaves are dark green above, silver grey and hairy underneath. Yellow catkins in June give rise to acorns one third enclosed. Grows best in deep fertile soil in mild areas, but will tolerate both dry and chalky soil and a coastal location. Excellent as a hedging plant.

## Looking to the past and the future

Planting trees to commemorate people and events has been part of our way of life for years. The opening of village halls, new hospitals and schools, churches and parish rooms, the ending of wars, the valour of heroes and the more ordinary lives of lesser mortals have all been marked for the better by the planting of a tree. Many local authorities have spaces available for such planting whilst the National Memorial Arboretum in Staffordshire is our nation's living memorial to commemorate and celebrate those who have given their lives in the service of their country, all who have served and those who have suffered as a result of conflict, and others who are commemorated there. The tree planting pictured here is to commemorate the centenary of an agricultural society in a small town in Worcestershire.

*The Stag Horn Oak below is a reminder for us to plant more often*

153

## *-palustris* **(Pin Oak)**

 A fast growing, large, dense-headed tree with slender drooping branches. The smooth bark is grey-brown. Large rich scarlet coloured leaves in autumn. (SE Canada and USA)

## *-palustris* **'Swamp Pigmy'**

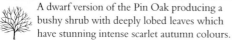 A dwarf version of the Pin Oak producing a bushy shrub with deeply lobed leaves which have stunning intense scarlet autumn colours.

## *-rhysophylla*

 A very unusual and remarkable evergreen tree with glossy dark green ridged leaves that begin chocolate brown in colour while the young shoots are extending growth. Each growth phase produces this two toned effect through the spring and early summer. (Mexico)

## *-robur*
## **(English or Pedunculate Oak)**

The long lived, broad, dome-headed tree is the more common of the two native oaks, the other being Q. petraea. The lobed leaves are dark green above, paler underneath, turning orange or rusty brown in autumn. Acorns are produced in abundance. Adaptable to most soils even heavy clay.
(Europe, Caucasus, SW Asia, N Africa)

## -robur 'Concordia' (Golden Oak)

A small, eventually medium rounded tree of very slow growth. Leaves suffused golden-yellow throughout spring and summer. (Belgium)

### The Dunkirk Oaks

Thirty six British Oak trees are planted in a field at Esquelbecq near Dunkirk to commemorate the thirty six men murdered in the Barn Massacre. The men, from the 2nd Battalion Royal Warwickshire Regiment, the Cheshire Regiment, and the Royal Artillery, and a single French man, were in retreat to Dunkirk in 1940 when, after an engagement with the SS Liebstandarte Adolf Hitler Division, they were herded into a barn into which the German soldiers threw hand grenades.

## -rubra (Red Oak)

Fast growing broad-headed tree. Stunning crimson foliage colours in autumn. Will tolerate urban pollution and almost any well drained soil, including chalky. (E. and N. America)

## -rubra 'Magic Fire'

An excellent form of the red oak with golden leaves in spring and stunning autumn colours of yellow, orange and red. More compact than other Q. rubra forms.

# ROBINIA

This variable group, containing majestic large specimens to small, ornate, shrubby, flowering trees, all have attractive pinnate leaves, pea-like flowers and are hardy and suitable for most soils. Some forms are brittle so are best in more sheltered areas.

## -x ambigua

 A small, manageable tree with slightly viscid (sticky) shoots and short racemes of pale pink flowers appearing in June and in good summers often again in the autumn.

## -x margaretta 'Pink Cascade'
Syn: R. x margaretta 'Casque Rouge'

 A very profuse and exotic rich pink flowering form of the false acacia tree. The lovely flowers appear in June and the dark green pinnate leaves are particularly attractive. (USA)

## -pseudoacacia (Common Acacia)

Also known as the **false acacia** or **black locust**, this tree is well naturalised in Europe. The scented white flowers in June attract bees to make sublime acacia honey. The timber is hard and valued for many uses. (E. USA)

## Robinia facts

- Robinia pseudoacacia 'Frisia' occasionally succumbs to premature leaf fall where the leaf rib remains on the tree, caused by a fungal leaf spot. This does not appear to effect other varieties. It remains certain that wet, cool summers can increase this problem.

- Robinia flowers are a very important source of nectar for bees for acacia honey.

- Robinia is nitrogen fixing and is suitable for poor, dry soils particularly over chalk.

- Robinia timber is very hard, rot resistant and ideal for posts, boats, posts and rails for splitting. The logs burn hot and long. It can be coppiced right back to the roots and will grow again.

- Robinia seeds or pods are poisonous and most other tree parts are toxic apart from the flowers.

*-pseudoacacia* **'Frisia'**

A beautiful tree renowned for its bright golden pinnate leaves throughout the summer. Pendent clusters of small fragrant pea-like white flowers in mid summer. Although prone to wind damage as a young vigorous tree, it grows in any soil. (Holland)

*-pseudoacacia* **'Lace Lady'**
Syn: R. *pseudoacacia* 'TWISTY BABE'

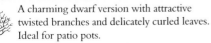 A charming dwarf version with attractive twisted branches and delicately curled leaves. Ideal for patio pots.

# SALIX

## (Willow)

A hugely diverse range: from very vigorous to very dwarf, with catkins, stem colour and variegated foliage. Most are quick and easy to grow and are very hardy. Hard pruning in early spring is recommended of those grown for their winter stem colour.

*-alba* **'Hutchinson's Yellow'**

 A selected clone for its intense winter yellow colour.

*-alba var. vitellina* **'Britzensis'**
Syn: S. *alba* 'Chermesina' **(Scarlet Willow)**

A classic for the scarlet-orange winter colours.

## -*alba var. vitellina* 'Yelverton'

 A rich bronze-red stem colour makes this form particularly worthwhile.

 M ·⚘· B ⓒ ⊖ 🐸 🍂 🎋 ▷

One of many of the 'winter' willows that can be so effective. This picture is at the end of the second year after pruning just before it is due again.

## -'Erythroflexuosa' GOLDEN CURLS

 A charming pendulous tree with golden twisted stems and leaves. The young vigorous shoots are ideal for flower arrangements. (Argentina)

S B 🍁 ⓒ ⊖ 🐸 🍂 🎋 ▷

## -*exigua* (Coyote Willow)

 Beautiful, large, erect shrub or small tree with long slender greyish-brown branches clothed with linear, silvery-silky, minutely toothed leaves and slender catkins. (N. America and Mexico)

 S  B 🍁 ⓒ ⊖ 🐸 🍂  ▷

## -irrorata

 The young green shoots turn purple as they age with a striking white bloom. The male catkins have red anthers that turn yellow as they mature. (SW USA)

M 🐎 B Ⓒ ⊖ 🐸 🌲 ⬆ ➤

## -magnifica

Large shrub or small tree with large oval, magnolia-like leaves and very large female catkins. (China)

S 🐌 🍁 ⊖ 🐸 🌲 ⬆ ➤ 🏆

## -x sepulcratis var. chrysocoma
Syn: *S. alba* 'Tristis'
**(Golden Weeping Willow)**

Fast growing tree with a broadly domed shape, graceful arching, weeping branches and golden yellow shoots. Narrow, lance-shaped leaves. Ideal for waterside planting and tolerant of most soils.

M 🐎 B Ⓒ ⊖ 🐸 🌲 ⬆ ➤

# SAMBUCUS

## (Elder)

These very hardy small trees or large shrubs will tolerate almost any soil and site. S. nigra the common hedgerow elder is so useful for its perfumed flowers, for making cordials and its fruit for autumn jellies.

Apart from its flowers and fruit for wine it is a major contributor to western herbal medicine and to folklore. According to Mrs. Grieve in *The Modern Herbal*, the wine has potent anti-viral properties.

### -*nigra porphyrophylla* BLACK BEAUTY (S. *nigra* 'Gerda')

 A selection bred in the UK with attractive dark purple ornamental leaves and large pink-white flower bracts. (Kent)

### -*nigra porphyrophylla* 'BLACK LACE' (S. *nigra* 'Eva')

 The second introduction from the same breeding programme as S. 'BLACK BEAUTY', particularly ornamental with distinctive, delicate, dark purple finely cut leaves which resemble the Japanese maples. (Kent)

# SEQUOIA & SEQUOIADENDRON

These two species include the Californian Redwood (Sequoia sempervirens) and the Wellingtonia (Sequoiadendron giganteum). The former being the world's tallest tree currently recorded at 371 feet, living up to 700 years old. The latter will achieve a greater girth although not as tall. Obviously not trees for the average garden but special all the same. Both are lime tolerant although the Sequoia more so.

*Benmore Botanic Gardens*
*(Part of the Royal Botanic Garden Edinburgh)*
*This avenue of trees are the famous Sierra Redwoods*
*(Sequoiadendron giganteum) planted in 1863*

# SOPHORA

Attractive, oriental looking trees thriving best on well drained soil and in full sun. Large terminal panicles of pea flowers are one of their features.

## *-japonica* **(The Japanese Pagoda Tree)**

 A strong growing, rounded, spreading tree with rich green pinnate leaves composed of nine-fifteen leaflets on green barked shoots. White flowers appear on mature trees. (China)

## *-japonica* **'Pendula'**

 A picturesque, small weeping tree with stiff drooping branches. Good as a lawn specimen.

## Using water wisely

It seems to be feast or famine these days: even when it rains on our gardens it dries up quickly. The trend in 'patio pot gardening' increases water consumption dramatically, whilst hard landscaping loses valuable water quickly.

Here are some things you can do to help:

- Mulch your trees and plants with gravel (lighter forms reflect light and keep the soil cool), slate, bark chippings, composted green waste, cardboard, old carpet... the list is endless.
- Lay gravel paths and drives rather than concrete and tarmac.
- Leave autumn leaves on the ground as a mulch, feed the worms, provide worms for birds and increase organic matter in the soil to increase water retention.
- Water at dusk or dawn: dawn reduces the incidence of fungal infections, dusk reduces evaporation.
- When planting large trees place a perforated pipe in the planting hole and water down the pipe to reduce evaporation. This also discourages weed growth by keeping the surface dry.
- Wash and peel fruit and veg in a washing up bowl and use the water for your plants afterwards thus adding nutrients at the same time.
- Install water butts on gutter downpipes.
- Use naturally dry areas in the garden for drought tolerant trees. See the Camel symbol in this book.
- Lift the blade of your mower, cut the lawn less often: this will also please the neighbours.
- Use ground cover plants under trees and in borders.
- Slightly under-water trees after the first year to minimise shallow feeding roots and make the tree more anchored and drought resistant. Stress forms flower buds more readily so with fruit trees there is even more benefit with this approach.
- Use large droplet roses on hose and watering cans to reduce evaporation.
- Don't over-water, the symptoms will be virtually identical to under watering!

*Our thanks to Andrew Forsyth of Weasdale Nurseries in Cumbria, the main contributor to this useful advice.*

# SORBUS

## Mountain Ash and Whitebeam

White, pink, yellow and red berries, delicate leaves and stunning autumn colours. Easy to grow in almost any soil, and are generally small trees. They are hardy and tolerant of urban pollution and coastal conditions. One of the most diverse, interesting and rewarding of tree groups for gardens.

*-alnifolia*

 An interesting species with hornbeam-like leaves, rich scarlet and orange-red autumn colours and small bright red fruits. (Japan, Korea, China)

*-aria* **(Whitebeam)**

A neat, compact, round-headed, native tree with leaves greyish-white then bright green and white underneath. Gold and russet autumn colours and deep crimson fruits in autumn. (Europe)

*-aria* **'Lutescens'**

 A healthy, attractive, robust tree for all landscape and garden situations. The young creamy-white leaves appear as candles as they emerge and turn grey-green in summer, russet and gold in autumn. Clusters of orange-red berries in autumn.

## Sorbus Facts

- Sorbus berries (particularly aucuparia) make delicious jellies similar to crab apples (see page 165).
- Why mountain ash? As its pinnate leaves are similar to the common ash (Fraxinus excelsior).
- Most Sorbus grow fairly true from seed. A yellow berry mostly will produce yellow berried offspring and the same with red, white and pink. Seed germinates readily.
- The birds will take the red berries first leaving the obviously less appetising other colours until later. This way a collection of Sorbus can attract a wide variety of birds over several months.
- Sorbus aucuparia and its many varieties are good host trees for mistletoe.
- For a full account of the Sorbus tree and particularly its many species it is worth acquiring Hugh McAllister's *The Genus Sorbus Mountain Ash and other Rowans* ISBN 1 84246 088 9 published by Royal Botanic Gardens Kew. A comprehensive and enjoyable read.

### -*aucuparia* (**Rowan or Mountain Ash**)

A native tree widespread in the UK. The lance-shaped leaves are dark green above, blue-green underneath, turning red in autumn. Very distinctive for its generally large bunches of bright red fruit so attractive to birds in the early autumn. The parent of many hybrids listed here. (Europe)

### -*aucuparia* '**Aspleniifolia**'

Very attractive and elegant tree with fern-like leaves, a stiff, neat, upright habit. Large bunches of red berries.

### -*aucuparia* '**Croft Coral**'

Included here as one of the few true orange fruited mountain ash. A neat tree with delicate leaves.

### -*aucuparia* '**Ember Glow**'

The fruits of this distinctive tree remain red deep into the winter instead of turning whitish as in most forms of this species. Handsome bluish-green leaves provide good autumn tints.
(Liverpool University Botanic Gardens, Ness)

Sorbus 'Autumn Spire'

## -'Autumn Spire' (S. 'Flanrock')

An exceptionally handsome, upright seedling of S. 'Joseph Rock' with a distinctive, compact, columnar habit. A profusion of yellow berries with reddish centres contrasts well with the excellent reddish-yellow autumn leaves. (Ireland)

## -*cashmiriana*

An excellent small tree of open and spreading habit. Leaves are dark green above and grey-green underneath, orange and yellow in autumn. Large marble-like persistent fruits. One of the few sorbus whose flowers can impress. A classic small garden tree. (Kashmir)

### Rowan Jelly

Rowan jelly is mainly encountered where there is a Scottish influence in the household and is considered very fine indeed with a slightly piquant, aromatic flavour and a beautiful amber colour. It goes particularly well with venison, lamb or ham.

**Recipe:** Fill a large pan half and half with ripe rowan berries (ie late August), stalks and all, and roughtly chopped cooking apples or crab apples, such as Jelly King, Laura or Harry Baker (no need to peel). Cover with water and bring to the boil and simmer until soft. Strain overnight through a jelly bag (do not push pulp through the bag).

Measure the liquid and bring to the boil. When hot, add 1lb sugar to 1 pint of liquid. Boil until setting point-usually 25 minutes, but you may need to check earlier. When a good 'wrinkle' can be achieved on the cold saucer, put into clean hot jars.

*Thanks to Keith Atkey*

## -'Chinese Lace'

A very healthy, round-headed small tree with unusually attractive deeply cut foliage turning red-purple in autumn. Dark red fruits are abundant in large bunches.

## -'Copper Kettle'

A compact, small, healthy tree with heavy clusters of dynamic copper coloured fruit that often persist well into winter. Reliable autumn leaf colours of red and orange. Most likely to be a seedling of S. 'Joseph Rock'.

Sorbus 'Dodong' OLYMPIC FLAME

## -'Dodong' OLYMPIC FLAME

A superb selection of S. Dodong. A stiff, columnar tree when young, leaves green, coppery in the spring with stunning orange and red tints in autumn. The fruits are bright orange-red and not persistent. See picture opposite. (Island of Ulleung and Korea)

## -*domestica*
## (Service Tree or True Service Tree)

To be distinguished from the Wild Service tree (S. torminalis) described on page 171.

This tree is best recognised by its shining, sticky winter buds and pinnate leaves turning orange-red and yellow shades in autumn with red blushed fruits. Because this tree is usually raised from seed the fruits can vary in colour and form being either apple or pear shaped. See Whitty Pear in fruit section page 270. (S and E Europe)

## -'Eastern Promise'

A small, upright, spreading tree of many lovely features. Fern-like leaves producing excellent autumn colours and large bunches of deep rose-pink fruit. Raised by Hillier Nursery, Hampshire.

## -*folgneri* 'Lemon Drop'

A small graceful tree with slender arching branches. Leaves are deep green and white beneath with small bright yellow fruits. Raised at Hillier Nursery, Hampshire.

## -*gonggashanica*

An attractive tree with a neat habit and heavy crops of pinkish-white fruits. In twenty years at Ness Gardens it only reached 3.5 metres so ideal for the small garden.
(Gongga Shan Mountain, Sichuan, China)

## -*hedlundii*

Probably the most handsome of the whitebeams having large silvery-white leaves with pronounced midribs and veins. Worthy of wider planting. (E. Himalaya)

## -hemsleyi 'John Bond'

 A stunning little tree with heavily veined grey-green leaves that appear to weep and twist to reveal their striking white undersides throughout the growing season. Small brown fruits appear in autumn. This particular form is a slight improvement on the species. (China)

## -hupehensis 'Pink Pagoda'

An outstanding form of S. hupehensis with blue-green large pinnate compound leaves, red twigs and petioles and white flower clusters in spring. The fruit, persistent and borne in profusion, are a vivid pink slowly turning white by mid winter. (Vancouver, Canada)

## -hybrida 'Gibbsii'

An improvement on S. hydrida 'Fastigiata' with a more compact habit and even larger bunches of luscious red fruits and good autumn colour.

## -japonica

An attractive naturally upright rare tree with large oval leaves and young shoots beneath covered in white downy film. It produces red fruits with brown speckles and good autumn tints. (Japan)

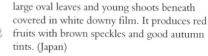

## -'Joseph Rock'

An outstanding little tree with an upright compact shape renowned for its clusters of persistent, round, creamy yellow fruit, becoming orange-yellow as they ripen. The leaves turn shades of red, orange and purple in the autumn. (China)

## -'Leonard Messel'

A superb, small, oval-shaped tree with upright branches. The winter buds are red and the leaves unusually large with many leaflets achieving excellent autumn colours. Distinctive, attractive, bright pink fruits hang in large clusters.

## -'Pink-Ness'

Broadly pyramidal with glaucous grey-green leaves and unusual small mauve-pink fruit. (Liverpool University Botanic Gardens, Ness)

## -*pseudovilmorinii*

An exquisite little tree similar to S. vilmorinii but less vigorous. The leaves are finer and more delicate, the fruit a similar attractive deep rose-red and the fruiting habit is more abundant. Raised at Ness from seed collected in Yunnan, China.

## -'Ravensbill'

A small to medium sized tree with an upright, oval shape. The leaves are made up of long, elegant leaflets that turn yellow-orange in the autumn. Large clusters of small orange fruit. The most distinguishing feature is the long curved, blue-black winter buds from which it gets its name. (South Korea)

## -rosea 'Rosiness'

Originally considered to be a form of S. cashmiriana, with which it has much in common, it has now been given separate specific status. It has the largest pink berries of any Sorbus, deepening and intensifying in colour as the season progresses.

## -sargentiana

The large pinnate leaves and sticky winter buds make this a most unusual and special tree. The large plume-like red stalked leaves are downy underneath turning rich red in autumn. Huge clusters of small scarlet fruit. (W. China)

## -scalaris

A pretty small tree with a neat spreading habit. Attractive frond-like rich green leaves in summer turn purple-red in late autumn. Small red fruits come in large bunches. (W. China)

*-thibetica* **'John Mitchell'**
Syn: S. *aria* 'Mitchellii'

*-torminalis*
**(Wild Service or Chequer Tree)**

 This classic tree is strong growing becoming round-headed. Very large, round, robust leaves, green above and white beneath. Russet-brown apple-shaped fruit appear in late summer.

 This important native tree is distinctive with sharply lobed maple-like leaves, shiny green turning crimson or yellow in autumn. Russet brown oval or round fruits.
(Europe, Asia Minor, N. Africa)

## The Rowan Tree

Some experts in the history of language believe that rowan might come from an old Germanic word 'raudnian' meaning "getting red", referring to the tree's red foliage and red berries in the autumn. Rowan is certainly one of the most familiar wild trees in the British Isles, and has acquired numerous folk names among which are recorded Mountain ash, Quickbane, Quickbeam, Quicken tree, Quickenbeam, Ran tree, Roan tree, Roden-quicken, Roden-quicken-royan, Round wood, Round tree, Royne tree, Rune tree (sticks of the Rowan were used to carve runes on), Sorb apple, Thor's helper, Whispering tree, Whitty, Wicken-tree, Wiggin, Wiggy, Wiky, Witch wood, Witchbane, Witchen, Witchen Wittern tree. These names can be linked to the folklore surrounding the tree such as placing a branch in a house on Good Friday or in a bed to ward off evil

forces; wearing a sprig of Rowan to protect against charms; planting the tree in churchyards to protect against evil.

The Rowan tree was known for aid and protection against enchantment. It was also used in the art of metal divining. Rowan crosses were placed over cattle in pens and over homes for protection (the Celts would use charms and spells involving Rowan to protect their cattle). The tree was also said to possess the power to heal and if carried, Rowan wood will increase one's psychic powers. This tree has been associated with magic and witchcraft and its branches were used for warding off evil. In Celtic legend, it is always connected with either Druids or other practitioners of magic. One way of delivering yourself from witches was to try and touch a witch with a branch of the Rowan tree.

*-vilmorinii*

Small elegant spreading tree with dark green fern-like leaves that turn orange or bronze in autumn. The pink fruit turn white as they age. (W. China)

-'Wisley Gold'

A good form of the yellow fruited mountain ash, with impressive heavy bunches of golden fruit. Introduced by the RHS from a seedling on Battleston Hill at Wisley with a likelihood of S. 'Ethel's Gold' as its parent.

# STEWARTIA

Related to the Camellia, Stewartias are striking flowering trees with attractive autumn foliage. They require moist well drained lime-free soil and a sunny position.

*-pseudocamellia*

© Ronald Houtman

A broadly columnar tree with very attractive flaking bark, which is red-brown and grey-pink underneath. Glistening white flowers with bright yellow anthers in July. Oval dark green leaves turn yellow and red in autumn. Prefers some shelter from cold winds. (Japan)

### Stewartia: a case of mistaken identity?

Originally recorded in America in the 17th Century, this tree was introduced into cultivation in the 1730s with plants eventually passing to John Stuart, the 3rd Earl of Bute, a leading light in the foundation of the botanical garden at Kew.

Linnaeus, a founding father of the science of naming plants, later acquired specimens and named the tree after John Stuart but, being mistaken about the spelling of the name, published it as Stewartia rather than Stuartia.

# STYRAX

Beautiful elegant trees grown for their flowers and foliage colour. They will grow best in moist, well drained neutral to acid soil, with shelter from cold winds.

## -hemsleyanus

A delightful small tree with open branches and broad, large elliptic leaves. The pure white flowers with pretty long yellow anthers are borne in long racemes in June. (Central and west China)

## Styrax: the sweet smell of success

Styrax resin has been used in perfumes, some kinds of incense, and in medicines by Phoenicians, Arabs, Turks, Greeks and Romans and is still in use today. Styrax incense is used in the Middle East and adjacent regions as an air freshener. Styrax was also important in Islamic medicine with early experts indicating that styrax resin mixed with other antibiotic substances gives a good dental restorative, whilst today a tincture of the resin that comes from Styrax is often used in first aid for small injuries as it acts as a disinfectant and local anaesthetic and seems to promote healing. It is also added to boiling water to produce fumes which have a soothing effect on the lungs and bronchial tubes, helping recovery from the common cold, bronchitis, or asthma.

## -japonicus **Benibana Group 'Pink Chimes'**

A beautiful slightly weeping small tree with glossy green oval leaves turning yellow or red. Fragrant pale pink flowers. The species japonica is similarly worthy with white flowers. (Japan)

## -obassia

A small rounded tree with bark which becomes chestnut coloured and exfoliating when young. Distinctive large rounded leaves. Fragrant bell-shaped flowers in June. (Japan)

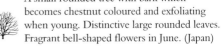

# SYRINGA (Lilac)

For flower and particularly scent there is little to
surpass these lovely small trees or shrubs. Although
they will grow in just about any soil, they especially like
chalky clay. They will tolerate some shade but prefer
full sun.

This picture shows a 'family' lilac of several varieties on
one tree.

## *-pekinensis* 'Beijing Gold'

 Closely related to the S. reticulata species, this less vigorous form has trusses of highly fragrant yellow blooms and cinnamon bark. (Beijing Botanic Gardens, China)

### Lilac species

Most of the lilacs mentioned here are single and double cultivars of the common lilac S. vulgaris that originated in Eastern Europe. It has been the focus of breeders for many years and there are over 500 varieties in circulation.

However, there are also some delightful species and S. tomentella shown here is one of many that have their origins in a different part of the world predominantly China (in the case of S. tomentella) but also a few from India, Japan and Korea. Invariably, these species are stronger scented and have a capacity for a longer flowering period.

Other species worthy of consideration are:

- **josikaea**
  Glossy dark green leaves, deep violet-mauve flowers in June.

- **meyeri**
  Violet-purple flowers in May and possibly also in September.

- **villosa**
  Erect panicles of lilac-rose flowers in May and June.

## *-reticulata* 'Ivory Silk'

A beautiful, compact, Japanese Tree Lilac. Very large cream coloured highly scented panicles almost resembling the flower of Fraxinus ornus 'Manna Ash'. These are freely borne in May and long lasting for several weeks. (Canada)

## *-tomentella*

A species lilac and one of the most delightful. Sweetly scented with deep lilac pink flowers borne in terminal panicles. (SW China)

### -*vulgaris* 'Charles Joly'

A round-shaped small tree or large shrub with a typical erect habit. One of the classic lilacs with single very dark red-purple flower panicles which are highly scented.

### -*vulgaris* 'Katherine Havemeyer'

One of the favourites, with large dense bunches of highly fragrant double purple-lavender flowers in May, fading to pale lilac in mid summer.

### -*vulgaris* 'Krasavitsa Moskvy'
Syn: S. *vulgaris* 'Beauty of Moscow'

A 'Queen' among lilacs. A double white with pale lavender tinted buds. An extremely fine and heavy bloomer with a strong habit.

### -*vulgaris* 'Madame Lemoine'

Dense bunches of large, highly fragrant, double white flowers make this a superb lilac. The flowers begin green-yellow but open pure white. Of broad spreading habit.

## -vulgaris 'Michel Buchner'

A less well known variety deserving wider planting. Dense double, pale rosy-lilac flowers.

## -vulgaris 'Primrose'

An unusual and unique variety with small panicles of single pale primrose yellow blooms. (Holland)

## -vulgaris 'Sensation'

A unique and lovely lilac with single large purplish-red florets edged with distinctive white margins to each petal. Highly scented.

## -vulgaris 'Souvenir de Louis Spaeth'
Syn: S. *vulgaris* 'Andenken an Ludwig Späth'

Single pure wine red flowers. One of the most consistent and reliable of the lilacs and well scented as expected.

## -vulgaris 'Sweetheart'

Very large, highly scented flower bracts lasting over several weeks. Not all the single flowers appear to mature at the same time creating a pretty light pink and mauve contrast of colours.

# TAXODIUM

These tall growing deciduous conifers, although suited to wet sites, will grow in all but the very driest of conditions.

## -distichum (Swamp Cypress)

A broadly conical large tree with reddish-brown bark, leaves grass-green, turning bronze yellow in autumn. Small green cones turning brown when ripe. A classic for waterside planting. (S. USA)

**L B** 🍂 ⬤ 🐸 ✖ 🏆 🌳

### Taxodium: A tall story

The tallest known specimen of Taxodium distichum growing near Williamsburg, Virginia, is 44m tall. The largest, known as "The Senator" growing near Longwood, Florida is 35m tall with diameter of 344cm

## -distichum 'Cascade Falls'

© Ronald Houtman

A very elegant weeping form with arching branches. (USA)

**M B** 🍂 ⬤ 🐸 ✖

## -distichum var. imbricatum 'Nutans'

A beautiful columnar form of the 'Swamp Cypress' with shortly spreading or ascending branches. Originally introduced in 1789.

**L B** 🍂 ⬤ 🐸 ✖ 🏆 🌳

*-distichum* **'Peve Minaret'**

 A very slow-growing, slender column. Would look well in rock gardens and around other dwarf conifers and heathers.

### The pruning of conifers

Most conifers in this book have the 'do not prune' symbol. This is because when pruning into wood older than two years old the tree is unable to initiate new buds, unlike most deciduous trees. Exceptions would include Taxodium, Taxus and Thuja plicata. See the pruning of conifers on page 199.

### Medicine from a poisonous tree

Even with all its sacred and symbolic representations, the Yew also provides modern medicinal uses. Its production of taxol, so effective for the fight against cancer, makes this tree very special indeed.

# TAXUS

## (Yew)

The yew plays a very special part in British history as it was used for the manufacture of bows and arrows. They are of great garden value with a variety of functions and are tolerant of most soils and situations. However, they do require good drainage. Toxic if eaten, they are well established in churchyards where animals are forbidden. Amongst our oldest living trees.

*-baccata* **(Common Yew)**

 Slow growing, small to medium size tree or large shrub with very small dark green leaves and red fruits. Suitable for hedging and topiary, trimming is best carried out in May and September for the best result.
(Europe. W. Asia and N. Africa)

### -*baccata* 'Fastigiata' (Irish Yew)

A dense compact tree with a slender erect habit. Dark green leaves and bright red fruits. Tolerant of very dry and shady conditions. An ideal formal feature tree.

### -*baccata* 'Fastigiata Aureomarginata' (Golden Irish Yew)

A golden-leaved variety of the above, broader but still erect.

### -*baccata* 'Standishii'

Slower growing and a brighter gold, with a tight, columnar habit.

### -*x media* 'Hicksii'

A broadly columnar form which makes a natural hedge needing little attention, reducing the painstaking work of hedge trimming considerably.

## Taxus

Much has been written about the planting of Yew trees in churchyards. However, recent research indicates that - in some cases – so long lived are these trees, churches might in fact have been planted in Yew groves!

# TETRADIUM

Natives of the Himalaya, these interesting and unusual trees have attractive pinnate leaves and thrive in any reasonably well-drained, fertile soil.

## -daniellii

An interesting, fast-growing tree, with large, handsome leaves and clusters of small, pungently scented white flowers in late summer, followed by glossy black fruits on female trees in autumn. (China and Korea)

# THUJA

These evergreen conifers can be grown as specimen trees or hedges. They prefer well drained but not too dry soil, sun or partial shade.

## -occidentalis 'Degroots Spire'

A slow growing, compact version forming a narrow spire with its leaves giving an attractive crinkled look.

## -plicata (Western Red Cedar)

A large, upright, fast growing conifer of conical habit and shredding bark. The bright glossy green leaves are glaucous underneath and aromatic when crushed giving a scent of apple or pineapple. Makes an excellent hedge. (NW America)

181

# TILIA

## (Lime or Linden)

These noble trees with their handsome, glossy green foliage are ideal for large gardens, parks and avenues. Particularly suited to pollarding and pleaching due to their flexible and soft shoots. They will thrive in almost any soil except the extremes of wet and dry.

### -chingiana

 A rare and beautiful tree with attractive smallish leaves which are offset at the base and unusually shaped with a paler underside. Flowers in July. (China)

### -cordata (Small Leaved Lime)

©Archie Miles

 A native tree of rounded habit. The heart-shaped leaves are leathery, glossy green above and paler underneath. White or ivory star-shaped sweetly scented flowers in summer. Less prone to aphid honeydew than most species. (Europe)

### -cordata 'Winter Orange'

 A compact Lime with orange-red stems in winter. Recommended for the winter garden. Prune hard in March or April.

©Nathan Matthews

*A pleached Lime*

## Tilia

The scent of the flowers is said to have mythical hallucinary effects for those who fall asleep as they may find themselves in fairyland. Quality bee honey and tea are just two bi-products. Its pale wood contributes in the making of many musical instruments.

## -x europaea 'Pallida'

A large tree of broadly conical habit. Branches are reddish-brown in winter. Leaves are yellowish-green underneath.

## -x europaea 'Wratislaviensis' (Golden Lime)

Soft, mellow, golden-yellow leaves when young, becoming green with age. Ideal for coppicing to show off the golden shoots in winter.

## -henryana

A rare and lovely tree with bristle margined leaves almost 'venus fly trap' like in appearance. The young growing tips are also an attractive downy pink in colour. (China)

## -oliveri

An elegant medium to large tree with pendant glabrous shoots. Broad finely toothed leaves are silvery white beneath. A lovely form of Lime, also free from aphids. (C. China)

## -platyphyllos 'Pendula' (Weeping Silver Lime) Syn: T. 'Petiolaris'

A round-headed tree with graceful downward sweeping branches. Dark green leaves are white felted underneath. The cup-shaped, creamy-yellow, richly scented flowers are narcotic to bees.

# TOONA

Once established these interesting trees will grow in almost any fertile soil.

## -sinensis 'Flamingo'

 In the UK this is a slow growing, large shrub or small tree with handsome large pinnate leaves that are spectacular brilliant pink in spring turning quickly cream to green. (Australia)

# TRACHYCARPUS

These evergreen palms are hardy just about anywhere in Britain and grow in a wide range of soils.

## -fortunei (Chusan Palm)

The tall, single trunk is thickly clothed with fibrous remains of old leaf bases. Fan-shaped dark green leaves are blue-green underneath. Small yellow flowers in summer followed by marble-like bluish-black fruits.

# TSUGA

These worthy evergreen trees are very elegant in their structure producing wide arching branches that droop at the edges. There are many dwarf forms of T. canadensis (Eastern Hemlock) ideal for rock gardens and stone troughs.

## -heterophylla (Western Hemlock)

 A fast growing tree with graceful spreading branches and fine needles and small attractive cones developing into a symmetrical spire, making a beautiful specimen tree for those who have room. An important timber tree in N. America but also suitable for most areas of the British Isles. (W. North America)

The name Tsuga comes from an anglicised version of this Japanese word. This reminds us yet again how our gardens are stocked with plants from every part of the world bringing with them not only horticultural pleasure but connections with cultures very different to our own.

# ULMUS

## (Elm)

Although they are suitable for most soil conditions, the Elm prefers moist sites. We describe some of the interesting forms which are resistant to Dutch Elm disease.

## -glabra 'Camperdownii' (Camperdown Elm)

A visually strong, compact, neatly-shaped tree with steep pendant branches forming a dome.

## -glabra 'Lutescens'

A round-shaped tree with spreading branches. Leaves soft cream-yellow in spring, becoming yellowish-green. Good for pollarding.

## -x hollandica 'Dampieri Aurea'
Syn: U. x hollandica 'Wredei'

A narrowly conical tree with broad leaves that are bright yellow where exposed to the sun and greener in the shaded parts giving a suffused appearance.

## DUTCH ELM DISEASE RESISTANT HYBRIDS

There are several recently introduced hybrids that have been bred to survive dutch elm disease. The complex parentage of these hybrids (with species such as U. parviflora, U. japonica and U. americana being involved) provides this strong natural resistance. Some of those available include U. 'Accolade', U. 'New Horizon', U. 'Cathedral', U. 'Prospector' and U. 'Triumph' from the USA and U. 'Homestead' from Holland and an impressive upright form for restricted spaces, U. 'Wanoux' VADA also raised in Holland. One of the most promising of all these hybrids is Ulmus LUTECE 'Nanguen' produced by a French/Dutch collaborative selection programme being of essentially European parentage. There are many others.

Since the devastating decline of the 'English Elm' (Ulmus pocera) careful observations and selection of a few surviving specimens have taken place. These have been propagated by the modern method of 'tissue culture'. Perhaps this will be the beginning of the rise of the true native in years to come. 'Epitaph of the Elm' by Gerald Wilkinson is a moving and fascinating story of the decline of these great trees.

# WISTERIA

These twining climbers are best grown in full sun and trained over walls, pergolas and trees and can be made into ornamental trees themselves.

## -'Burford'

Originally propagated from the unrivalled Wisteria at Burford House, Tenbury Wells. The flower racemes combining lilac-blue and purple are up to 1m in length and heavily scented. A very vigorous form suitable for any situation including specimen standards.

*Wisteria at Burford House*

## -'Caroline'

 The deep violet-blue flowers contrast well against the emerging copper leaves. One of the most highly scented varieties, slow growing (clockwise turning) and ideal for patio or bonsai use.

## -*floribunda* **'Hon-beni'** Syn: W. *floribunda* 'Rosea'

 A charming pale rose form with purple tips and very long racemes. Also known as W. 'Rosea Plena'.

## -*floribunda* **'Shiro-noda'**
Syn: W. *floribunda 'Longissimia Alba' /*
W. *floribunda* 'Snow Shower'

 The white Wisteria is very dramatic and
contrasts well with other coloured forms.
This particular form has very long racemes.

Wisteria is named after Daniel Wister (1738-1805)
son of notable Quaker and businessman John
Wister of Philadelphia. Daniel Wister joined with
Samuel Miles and Robert Morris to underwrite the
voyage of the American commercial vessel Empress
of China – the first ship to trade between the
United States and China which had previously been
closed to most foreigners.

## -*floribunda* **'Violacea Plena'**
Syn: W. *floribunda* 'Black Dragon'

This lovely double purple-blue form is
generally the most widely accepted as Black
 Dragon although the experts correctly list this
variety as a single flower and the double form
as Violacea Plena.

## -**'Showa-beni'**

A beautiful variety with intense bronze almost
 chocolate coloured leaves in spring,
contrasting with the short, luscious, highly
scented, true pink racemes.

## *-sinensis* 'Prolific'

 Mauve-blue flowers on short racemes are very well scented. Flowers as a young plant. A good all round performer.

# ZELKOVA

Members of the Elm family, these elegant trees are ideal for large gardens. Best grown with shelter from strong wind.

## -'Kiwi Sunset'

 This is a beautiful recent introduction. A vigorous umbrella-shaped tree, lush, golden, serrated leaves with pink growing tips that maintain their colour throughout the season. A graceful specimen where space is offered. (New Zealand)

## Cultural tips for Wisteria

### Pruning

Due to their exotic delicate looks and their initial need of support Wisteria appear delicate creatures but they are actually tough and hardy and can be treated as such. They are triffid-like in their growth habit and need a firm hand to keep them in check. Their rampant growth can be cut back hard at any time of year – each shoot to only 2 or even 1 bud of the current season's growth and they will still flower strongly the following spring. Prune back strong annual growth in July to three buds which will assist the onset of flower buds and prune the remaining shoots in the same way in February. In some cases a hedge cutter needs to be used on the more rampant forms! The pictures here show before and after to illustrate the need to cut as hard as possible.

### Growing in pots

They are ideal for growing in pots. A stout cane or small stake will soon disappear beneath the torturous stranglehold of thick twining stems forming its own main trunk from which you can develop any shape of head to suit the situation. One technique is to initially allow the plant to twine up string to create an attractive bent stem eventually thickening to become free standing trees when planted out.

### Pest and disease

Wisteria are relatively clean and suffer few disorders. Aphids and scale insects are sometimes seen but rarely trouble for long.

### Buying tips

When buying Wisteria always check that they are true to their name. If they are grafted they are sure to be a known good flowering variety. If they are not they could be propagated from cuttings or seed, the latter being a species may be slow to flower and inferior in quality.

# The shape of leaves

Being able to recognise the different leaf shapes that occur in garden trees will help you correctly identify and describe them – and will certainly impress your family and friends.

However, such knowledge is far from necessary to enjoy the sheer variety and intricacy of shapes and forms that exist.

## Leaf shapes

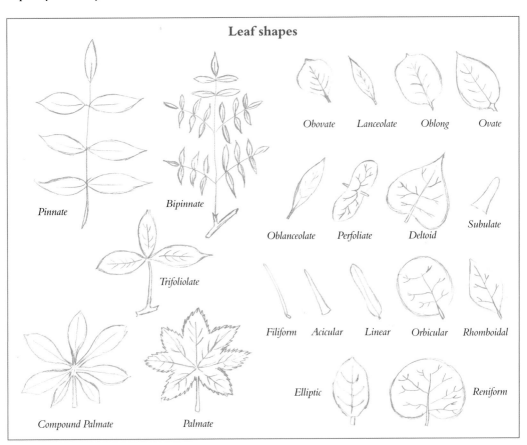

Pinnate

Bipinnate

Trifoliolate

Compound Palmate

Palmate

Obovate    Lanceolate    Oblong    Ovate

Oblanceolate    Perfoliate    Deltoid    Subulate

Filiform    Acicular    Linear    Orbicular    Rhomboidal

Elliptic    Reniform

## Leaf tips

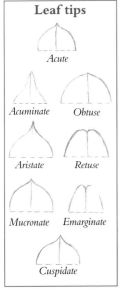

Acute

Acuminate    Obtuse

Aristate    Retuse

Mucronate    Emarginate

Cuspidate

## Leaf bases

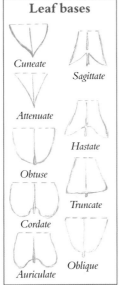

Cuneate

Sagittate

Attenuate

Hastate

Obtuse

Truncate

Cordate

Oblique

Auriculate

## Leaf margins

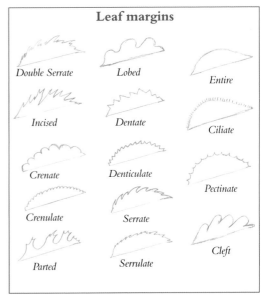

Double Serrate    Lobed    Entire

Incised    Dentate    Ciliate

Crenate    Denticulate    Pectinate

Crenulate    Serrate

Parted    Serrulate    Cleft

# English common names to Latin

## Why use Latin to name plants?

Botanical Latin is the language used throughout the world for naming and describing plants. Some of the very first writing about plants was in Latin and the Swedish botanist Linnaeus, who lived in the 18th Century, formally established the tradition that all plants should be given Latin names (or names of Latin form) and also that works relating to them should also be in Latin. Thankfully, whilst we still name plants in Latin we are no longer compelled to use it whilst writing about them!

This tradition of using Latin has continued for many good reasons not least that it has an abundance of words to describe the characteristics of plants such as colour, texture, size, and form. Also, since Latin is no longer spoken in an everyday sense the meanings of words in Latin do not change. (Remember, in English, a *computer* once referred to *a person who adds up*.) The other major advantage of using Latin is that the words mean the same to people wherever they are in the world and whatever their mother tongue.

Below is an A – Z of common names of trees with a reference to their Latin names and where they can be found in this book. Mostly it is genera and species that have common names but occasionally a variety has attracted a descriptive term, but this is rare.

In the case of genera and species the page number is approximate and may only refer to the beginning of the section where they are to be found.

# A glossary of horticultural terms

Following on from our section on Latin to English common names and the Naming of plants (see page 15) we include below a glossary of horticultural terms – themselves in Latin. Most of these are included in the ornamental section of this book either replicating the 'species' or used within the description text.

There are some additional logical terms that could also be useful to the reader. Please note that in some cases the glossary terms can vary, for example aucuparius would mean the same as aucuparia as used in this book.

## A

acerifolius ............................leaves like those of maples

aconitifolius ................................aconite-like leaves

alatus (um) (a) ..........................................winged

alba (us) (um) ..............................................white

alnifolius.............................with leaves like alders

alternifolius ..................................alternate leaves

altissimus ..............................................very high

amabilis ..........................................sweet, lovely

americanus ....................................from America

angustifolia (um) (us) ....................narrow-leafed

aquifolius...................................needle- leafed

arborescens .........................................tree-like

arbutifolius ...................................arbutus-leafed

argentea (us) (um) ..................................silvery

aromatica (us) (um) .....................spicy, aromatic

atlantica (um) (us).................of the Atlas Mountains (N.Africa)

atropurpureus ..............................dark purple

atrovirens ......................................dark green

aucuparius ..........................used for catching birds

aurea (us) (um)..............................golden yellow

autumnalis ........................................autumnal

avium......................................of birds, eaten by birds

## B

baccatus.........................................has berries

betulifolius ................leaves like birches, birch-leafed

betulus.......................................like birches

bicolor ................................two-coloured/toned

brachybotrys..............................short racemes

## C

californicum (us) (a) ..................of California

calocarpus...............................with pretty fruits

campanulatum (us) (a) ........................bell-shaped

campestris, campestre .................of plains or flat areas

canadensis.................................from Canada

candicans ....................................turning white

canescens...........................turning white grey, greying

carnea (us) (um) ..........................flesh-coloured

carpinifolius ..................with leaves like hornbeams

cerasifera ..................................bearing cherries

cerasus..............................................cherry

chamaecyparissus ............................like Chamaecyparis

chinensis ..........................................Chinese

circinatus..............................................circular

coccinea (us) (um) ................................scarlet

coggygria ....................specific name of the Smoke Tree

columnaris..............................................columnar

communis .............................................common

compactus ...............................................dense

concordius.......................................harmonious

conspicuus ....................................conspicuous

contortus .........................................contorted

cordatus .............................................cordate

cornutus ......................................with horns

crataegifolius ......................leaves like Hawthorn

## D

decidua (um) (us)........................deciduous, dropping

dissectus ..........................finely slit, dissected

dulcis ..................................................sweet

## E

elaeagnos............................ancient name for Elaeagnus

elatus ..........................................lofty, sublime

elegans ........................................fine, delicate

erectus ............................................upright

euchlorus....................................pretty colours

europaeus (um) (a) ..........................European

excelsior ..............................more lofty, sublime

## F

fastigiata (um) (us)...............branches growing pointed, erect

floribunda (us) (um) ..........having many flowers, free-flowering

florida (us) (um) .....................having many flowers, floriferous

fragrans ...........................................fragrant

fraxinifolius..............................with leaves like the Ash

## G

glabra, (um)(us) .......................................not hairy

glauca (us) (um)....................blue-green or sea-green

glutinosus..........................................glutinous, sticky

grandifolius .............................having large leaves

griseus.................................................grey

## H

henryana (um) (us) ............................after Dr. Augustine Henry

himalaicus (um) (a)..............................of the Himalayas

hippocastanum ......................................Horse Chesnut

hispanica (um) (us)......................................of Spain

horizontalis ..................................horizontally spreading

hybrida (us) (um) ....................................hybrid

## I

incana (us) (um) ..............................grey-downy

intermedia (us) (um)......................intermediate

## J

japonica (us) (um)........................................of Japan

**K**

kewensis .................................................from Kew Gardens

**L**

latifolia (um) (us)..................................broad-leafed

laurocerasus .........................................Cherry Laurel

ligustrinus ............................................like privets

linearifolius.........................................with linear leaves

lucidus ..................................................very shiny

lusitanica (um) (us) ..............................of Portugal

lutescens ..............................................yellowish

lutea (um) (us) .....................................yellow

**M**

macranthus ..........................................having large flowers

major .....................................................larger, greater

marginata (us) (um)..............................margined

maritima (um) (us) ...............................by the sea

mas.........................................................male

maximus ................................................largest

melanocarpus .......................................with black fruits

micranthus ...........................................small flowers

microphylla (us) (um) ..........................small leaves

minor.....................................................smaller, lesser

mollis ....................................................soft

montana (us) (um) ................................of mountains

mutabilis................................................changeable

**N**

nana (um) (us)......................................dwarf

nigra .....................................................black

nipponica (us) (um) ..............from the island of Nippon (Japan)

nitida (um) (us) ....................................shiny

nivalis ...................................................snow-white

nutans ..................................................nodding

**O**

officinalis..............................................used in medicine, herbal

orientalis ..............................................oriental/eastern

oxyacanthus..........................................with acute prickles

**P**

palmatus................................................hand shaped

paniculata (us) (um) ............................flowers in panicles

papyrifera .............................................providing paper

parviflora (um) (us) ..............................with small flowers

patulus...................................................spread out, extended

pendula (us) (um) ................................pendulous, weeping

petiolaris ..............................................petrioled

platanoides ...........................................like planes

platyphyllos (a) (um) (us)......................broad leafed

plenus....................................................double

plicatus.................................................folded

praecox..................................................early

procera (um) (us) .................................very tall, slender

prunifolius.............................................with leaves like plums

pseudoacacia.........................................false acacia

pseudo-cerasus .....................................cherry-like, false cherry

pubescens ............................................with downy fuzz

pungens .................................................pungent

purpurea (us) (um) ..............................purple-red

pyramidalis...........................................pyramidal

pyrifolius ..............................................leaves like pears

**Q**

quercifolius ..........................................leaves like oaks

quinquefolius ........................................five leafed

**R**

radiatus .................................................radiate

reflexus .................................................bent down

repens ...................................................creeping

reticulata (um) (us) ..............................net veined

robur .....................................strength, literally oak wood

rosea (um) (us) .....................................rose-coloured

rotundifolius..........................................with round leaves

rubra (um) (us) .....................................red

**S**

saccharinus ...........................................provides sugar

salicifolius (um)(a)................................willow-like leaves

sanguineum (us) (a) ..............................blood-red

sativa (um)(us) .....................................planted or sown

sempervirens.........................................evergreen

serotinus ...............................................late

serratus .................................................serrated

serrulatus...............................................slightly serrated

sibiricus.................................................from Siberia

sinensis..................................................Chinese

sorbifolius..............................................Rowan-like leaves

spectabilis .............................................attractive

spinosus.................................................thorny, prickly

splendens ..............................................glittering, shining

stellata (um)(us) ..................................star-like

striatus..................................................stripes

sylvatica (um) (us) ...............................living in forests

**T**

terminalis...............................................terminal

tomentosa (um)(us)........covered with a short dense pubescence

tremulus ................................................trembling

triacanthus ...........................................three thorned

tricolor...................................................three coloured

trifoliate................................................three leafed

tristis ....................................................sad

**U**

ulmoides ...............................................like Elms

**V**

variegata (um)(us).................................variegated, two coloured

velutina (um)(us) .................................velvety

versicolor .........................variously coloured or changing colour

violacea (um)(us) .................................violet

viridis ...................................................turning green

vulgaris .................................................common

**W**

wilsoniae................................................after Mrs EH Wilson

# The right ornamental trees for you and your garden

Ornamental trees are grown for the beauty of their foliage, bark, spring flowers, berries, or autumn colour. Their ability to give of their best in your garden will be affected by the suitability or otherwise of the situation in which they are planted and the characteristics of your soil.

The following section is a guide to trees suitable for a range of situations, one or more of which will probably match your garden. It is far from exhaustive and it must be remembered that many trees will grow happily in a wide variety of situations. Symbols next to the selections will help you find them quickly in the book.

## Trees with aromatic foliage

Plants with scented foliage or wood often give off their aroma as a result of gentle bruising. Plant them near paths or heavily used areas, thinking about the direction of the prevailing wind.

Cercidiphyllum ............................japonicum – in autumn
Eucalyptus ..............................................................(all)
Juglans....................................................................(all)
Populus................................................................(most)
Thuja.....................................................................(all)

## Trees for clay soils

Clay soil is sticky and unworkable when it is wet and as hard as concrete when dry. However, clay is often fertile and if properly worked can provide an excellent home. Care should be given to providing good drainage.

Acer .......................................................................(all)
Aesculus..................................................................(all)
Alnus......................................................................(all)
Aronia ....................................................................(all)
Betula .....................................................................(all)
Carpinus..................................................................(all)
Cornus ....................................................................(all)
Corylus ...................................................................(all)
Cotinus ...................................................................(all)
Cotoneaster .............................................................(all)
Crataegus ................................................................(all)
Cytisus ....................................................................(all)
Eucalyptus ...............................................................(all)
Fraxinus ..................................................................(all)
Hamamelis...............................................................(all)
Ilex.........................................................................(all)
Laburnum................................................................(all)
Larix .......................................................................(all)
Magnolia .................................................................(all)
Malus ......................................................................(all)
Pinus ......................................................................(all)
Platanus...................................................................(all)
Populus ...................................................................(all)
Prunus.....................................................................(all)
Quercus ...................................................................(all)
Salix........................................................................(all)
Sorbus.....................................................................(all)
Taxodium ................................................................(all)
Taxus ......................................................................(all)
Thuja.......................................................................(all)
Tilia ........................................................................(all)

## Trees adapted to acid soils

Many plants are well adapted to acid soil which is usually easy to work and has the advantage of being quick to warm up early in the year. The fertility of acid soils can be improved with the addition of organic matter, so if you are starting a new garden in these conditions, select plants from the list below at the outset then include other trees after a few seasons of soil improvement. Remember to water trees in well and mulch heavily.

Acer ...............................................ginnala • negundo & cultivars
Betula .....................................................................(all)
Castanea .................................................................(all)
Cercis .....................................................................(all)
Cotoneaster .............................................................(all)
Enkianthus...............................................................(all)
Fothergilla................................................................(all)
Gleditsia ..................................................................(all)
Halesia ....................................................................(all)
Hamamelis...............................................................(all)
Ilex...............................................aquifolium & cultivars
Nyssa......................................................................(all)
Pinus ......................................................................(all)
Populus ...................................................................(all)
Pseudolarix ..............................................................(all)
Robinia ...................................................................(all)
Stewartia .................................................................(all)

## Trees for chalk soils

Chalk soils have a very high lime content so can be harmful to many trees. That being said, calcium and magnesium limestone in the wild supports a very diverse range of plants so the gardener need not be entirely defeated by these conditions. Chalk is more difficult when there is only a shallow layer of soil above the rock since this leads to soils drying out quickly. Attempts to fight nature by planting your favourites will almost certainly fail. The best advice is to go with the flow by choosing from the list below of varieties known to be happy in these situations.

Acer......................................................................(most)
Aesculus..................................................................(all)
Carpinus.............................................betulus & cultivars
Cercis ....................................................siliquastrum
Cornus ...............................................mas & cultivars
Cotoneaster .............................................................(all)
Crataegus ................................................................(all)
Euonymus................................................................(all)
Fagus ...............................................sylvatica & cultivars
Fraxinus ...........................................excelsior & cultivars
Prunus...................................................................(most)
Sambucus.................................................................(all)
Sorbus.................................................aria & cultivars
Sorbus...............................................hybrida & cultivars
Syringa ...................................................................(all)
Taxus ................................................baccata & cultivars
Thuja.....................................................................plicata

## Trees for damp sites

Trees in general require good drainage and locations where the soil is not waterlogged. However, there are some which are perfectly adapted to thriving in permanent dampness or even wetness. Trees such as the Swamp Cypress (Taxodium distichum) can survive wet for many months. However, trees without special adaptations to such environmental conditions might die within a few weeks if they are flooded during the growing season.

Alnus ...................................................................(all)
Amelanchier ........................................................(all)
Aronia .................................................................(all)
Betula .................................................................(all)
Crataegus ...........................................................(all)
Metasequoia ........................................................(all)
Populus ...............................................................(all)
Quercus ......................................................palustris
Salix ...................................................................(all)
Sambucus ............................................................(all)
Sorbus ..........................................aucuparia & cultivars
Taxodium ......................................................distichum

## Trees for cold exposed areas

Many of us have become familiar with the idea of a wind chill factor. This affects trees as much as it does us, so finding trees that can withstand icy blasts is important, not least because the soil in such spots is also often very cold or even frozen, leaving the tree to struggle for moisture from the ground as it loses extra moisture through its leaves. Thankfully a good selection of evergreens and many deciduous trees come to our rescue.

Acer .................................pseudoplatanus & cultivars
Betula ..............................................................(most)
Cotinus .....................................coggygria & cultivars
Crataegus ..............................monogyna & cultivars
Fagus .................................................................(all)
Fraxinus ...........................................excelsior & cultivars
Ginkgo ...........................................................biloba
Laburnum ...........................................................(all)
Populus ..........................................................tremula
Quercus .......................................robur & cultivars
Salix ...................................................................(all)
Sorbus .........................aria & cultivars • aucuparia & cultivars
Taxus ...........................................baccata & cultivars
Tilia ............................................cordata & cultivars

## Trees for planting by the seaside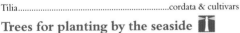

As well as coping with more wind and higher average temperatures than those inland, seaside gardens need to cope with the high salt content of the air and soil. Plants with tough, waxy leaves and grey foliage often withstand seaside conditions well.

Acer ....................................................pseudoplatanus
Arbutus ......................................unedo & cultivars
Castanea ..........................................................sativa
Cotoneaster ...................................................(many)
Crataegus ...........................................................(all)
Cytisus ...............................................................(all)
Eucalyptus ..........................................................(all)
Fraxinus ......................................excelsior & cultivars
Ilex .........................................aquifolium & cultivars
Pinus ..............................................................radiata
Populus ..........................................................tremula
Quercus ..........................................cerris • ilex • robur
Salix ................................................................(most)
Sorbus .........................aria & cultivars • aucuparia & cultivars

## Trees for shady spots

There are very few trees which will tolerate deep shade since their instincts are to grow up to the light. However, since most gardens have shady spots the trees which will thrive there are especially valuable.

Acer .......................................palmatum & cultivars
Cedrela ....................................sinensis 'Flamingo'
Cornus ............................................................(most)
Corylus ...............................................................(all)
Crataegus ...........................................................(all)
Dicksonia ...........................................................(all)
Exochorda ...........................................................(all)
Halesia ...............................................................(all)
Hamamelis ..........................................................(all)
Ilex .........................................aquifolium & cultivars
Prunus ...............laurocerasus & cultivars • lusitanica & cultivars
Taxus ..................................................................(all)

## Trees of weeping or pendulous habit

When planning a garden we often seek as much variety as possible. So, whilst many trees are characterised by a form which has branches reaching upwards, it is pleasing to find others which depart from this to provide the contrast we need.

Betula .................ermanii 'Pendula' • nigra 'Summer Cascade'
                        pendula 'Tristis' 'Youngii' • 'Long Trunk'
Cedrus ...........................atlantica 'Glauca Pendula'
Cercidiphyllum ...................japonicum 'Pendulum'
Cotoneaster ..............................'Hybridus Pendulus'
Fagus ...................sylvatica 'Black Swan' • 'Purple Fountain'
                                            'Purpurea Pendula'
Fraxinus ..................excelsior 'Aurea Pendula' • 'Pendula'
Larix ...............................................................'Puli'
Malus .......................'Louisa' • 'Royal Beauty' • 'Sun Rival'
Morus ....................................................alba 'Pendula'
Prunus ...................incisa 'Pendula' • 'Kiku Shidare Zakura'
                            'Snow Showers' • 'Weeping Yoshino'
Prunus ...........................................pendula 'Rubra'
Pyrus .....................................salicifolia 'Pendula'
Salix ...............x sepulcratis 'Chrysocoma' • caprea 'Pendula'
Tilia .............................................................'Petiolaris'

## Trees of upright or fastigiate habit

Trees of this shape are especially useful in the smaller garden since they take up less space and cast a smaller shadow. They also form an excellent contrast with other trees.

Amelanchier ......................................alnifolia 'Obelisk'
Betula .................pendula 'Dalecarlica' • 'Edinburgh'
                            platyphylla 'Dakota Pinnacle'
Carpinus ............................betulus 'Frans Fontaine'
Fagus ...................sylvatica 'Dawyck Gold' • 'Dawyck Purple'
Liriodendron ........................tulipifera 'Fastigiatum'
Malus ...............'Admiration' 'Laura' • trilobata 'Guardsman'
Populus ............................................tremula 'Erecta'
Prunus .................'Amanogawa' • nipponica 'Brilliant'
                            'Shosar' • 'Snowgoose'
Sorbus .................'Autumn Spire' • hemsleyi • japonica
Taxus ............baccata 'Fastigiata' 'Standishii' • 'Fastigiata Aurea'
Ulmus .............................minor Dampieri 'Wredei'
                            prunifolia 'Splendens'

## Trees with ornamental bark 🅱 and twigs

We are used to thinking of planting trees for their flower or foliage, but many have attractively coloured or peeling or patterned bark, or throw out particularly colourful new growth.

Acer .....................capillipes • davidii 'George Forrest' • griseum
hersii • palmatum 'Sangu Kaku' • rufinerve
Betula................................................................(most)
Castanea................................................................sativa
Eucalyptus ...........................................................(most)
Fraxinus ..........................excelsior 'Aurea Pendula' • 'Jaspidea'
pennsylvanica 'Cimmzam'
Metasequoia........................................................(all)
Parrotia...............................................................persica
Platanus...............................................................(all)
Prunus ...........................himalaica • rufa • serrula
Salix...........................x sepulcratis 'Chrysocoma'
x erythroflexuosa 'Golden Curls'
Sequoia...............................................sempervirens
Sophora...............................................japonica
Stewartia.............................................(most)
Taxodium.............................................(all)
Tilia.................................cordata 'Winter Orange'

## Trees grown for their foliage 🍁 (large or shaped)

After the form of the tree, it is perhaps through foliage that we can best create the design feel we seek in our gardens. Large or interestingly shaped leaves create new points of interest and emphasis in the following :

Acer.........................japonicum 'Aconitifolium' • pentaphyllum
• saccharinum
Betula..................................pendula 'Dalecarlica'
Catalpa .................................................(all)
Crataegus .............................................arnoldiana
Crataegus .............................................laciniata • orientalis
Ginkgo ..................................................(all)
Liriodendron .........................................(all)
Malus..................................'Profusion Improved' • transitoria
toringoides • trilobata 'Guardsman'
Paulownia .............................................(all)
Platanus.................................................(all)
Quercus...........................palustris • rubra • rubra 'Magic Fire'
Sorbus ................'Chinese Lace' • dodong 'OLYMPIC FLAME
folgneri 'Lemon Drop' • scalaris
thibetica 'John Mitchell' • hedlundi
Tilia ............................................tomentosa 'Petiolaris'

## Trees for autumn colour 🍁

Autumn foliage is especially important in the garden. In all varieties the richness of the colours will be better on some soils than others and will vary from year to year. With a bit of forward planning, medium and larger gardens can enjoy a spectacular display of reds, yellows and oranges lasting several weeks.

Acer..........................................................(many)
Aesculus..........................x neglecta 'Autumn Fire' • parviflora
Amelanchier ...............................................(most)
Betula..........................................................(most)

Carpinus ............................................................(all)
Cercidiphyllum.................................................japonicum
Cornus...............................................florida & cultivars
Cotinus ...............................................(all)
Crataegus ..................................lavalleei 'Carrierei' • pedicellata
prunifolia 'Splendens'
Euonymus ...........................................(most)
Fagus.......................sylvatica • sylvatica 'Aspleniifolia'
Fraxinus ...............................................(all)
Fothergilla..........................................(all)
Ginkgo ..................................................(all)
Hamamelis.............................................(all)
Larix......................................................(all)
Liquidambar .........................................(all)
Malus.....................................coronaria 'Elk River' • toringoides
transitoria • trilobata 'Guardsman'
Metasequoia........................................(all)
Morus...............................................alba pendula
Nyssa....................................................(all)
Parrotia...............................................persica (all)
Populus.............................................tremula
Prunus ..........all incisa forms, many cultivars including Japanese
Prunus .................................................sargentii
Pyrus ...............................'Chanticleer' • pashia
Quercus.......................palustris 'Swamp Pygmy'
Quercus...............................................rubra
Robinia.........................pseudoacacia 'Frisia'
Sorbus..................................................(most)
Stewartia..............................................(all)
Taxodium..............................................(all)

## Trees with red or purple foliage 🍁

The rich colours of these trees can make a striking contribution to any garden. However, in small gardens the temptation should be resisted to plant more than one. These coloured leaves are often seen at their best with the sun behind them so it is worth trying to find a site for them where they will be between you and the sun as you walk along a path, relax, or potter.

Acer.......palmatum 'Crimson Queen' • 'Garnet' • 'Purpureum'
'Sumi nagishi' • 'Tamukeyama' • platanoides 'Crimson King'
Betula....................................................'Royal Frost'
Catalpa .....................................x erubescens 'Purpurea'
Cercidiphyllum.............................japonicum 'Rotfuchs'
Cercis...................................................'Forest Pansy'
Corylus .........................maxima 'Purpurea' (Red Filbert)
Cotinus ...........................coggygria 'Royal Purple'
Fagus .........................sylvatica 'Black Swan' • 'Dawyck Purple'
'Purple Fountain' • 'Purpurea Tricolor
sylvatica Purpurea Group • sylvatica 'Riversii'
Gleditsia................................triacanthos 'Ruby Lace'
Liquidambar ............................................acalycina
Malus...................'Liset' • 'Royal Beauty' • 'Royalty' • 'Rudolf'
Photinia ..................................................'Red Robin'
Prunus ............................x blireana • cerasifera 'Nigra'
x cistena 'Crimson Dwarf' • 'Royal Burgundy'
Sambucus..................nigra 'BLACK BEAUTY' 'BLACK LACE'

## Trees with golden or yellow foliage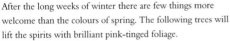

One or two well-placed, well chosen trees from this group, especially in a dull corner, can transform a garden by suffusing it with a different kind of light. However, as with purple foliage, resist the temptation to overdo it.

Acer ............ cappadocicum 'Aureum' • negundo 'Kelly's Gold' platanoides 'Princeton Gold' • pseudoplatanus 'Worley'
Betula ................................................... pendula 'Golden Beauty'
Catalpa .................................................. bignonioides 'Aurea'
Corylus ................................................... avellana 'Aurea'
Cotinus ................................................ coggygria 'Golden Spirit'
Fagus ..................................................... sylvatica 'Dawyck Gold'
Fraxinus ................................................ excelsior 'Aurea Pendula'
Gleditsia ................... triacanthos 'Spectrum' • 'Sunburst'
Metasequoia .......................... glyptostroboides 'Goldrush'
Pinus ................................................................ radiata 'Aurea'
Populus .............................................................. alba 'Richardii'
Quercus ........................................................ robur 'Concordia'
Robinia ............................................... pseudoacacia 'Frisia'
Taxus ................ baccata 'Fastigiata Aurea' • 'Standishii'
Tilia ................................................ 'Wratislaviensis' (Golden)
Ulmus ............ glabra 'Lutescens' • minor Dampieri 'Wredei'

## Trees with grey or silver foliage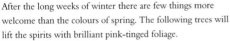

Grey, silver and blue foliage makes for a subtle range of tones and contrasts. Many trees with silver or grey foliage are able to withstand dry conditions, as the hairs or waxy coatings which give them their colour are usually there to help minimise water loss.

Acacia ...................................................................... dealbata
Cedrus .......................................... atlantica 'Glauca' group
Cytisus ..................................................................... battandierii
Eucalyptus ................................... gunnii • niphophila
Pyrus ...................................................................... (most)
Salix ......................................................................... exigua
Sorbus ............................................... most whitebeam forms

## Trees with dramatic pink foliage in spring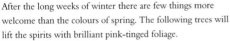

After the long weeks of winter there are few things more welcome than the colours of spring. The following trees will lift the spirits with brilliant pink-tinged foliage.

Acer ........ pseudoplatanus 'Brilliantissimum' • 'Prinz Handjery'
Aesculus .............................. x neglecta 'Erythroblastos'
Toona ............................................ sinensis 'Flamingo'

## Trees with variegated foliage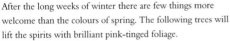

As with strong foliage colours, trees with variegated foliage work best in the garden when there are few of them. They are at their most effective when grown apart from others so that their canopies are low and not too far from eye level.

Acer ............................ negundo 'Elegans' • 'Flamingo' palmatum 'Butterfly' • platanoides 'Drummondii' pseudoplatanus 'Gadsby' • 'Simon-Louis Freres'
Castanea ............................ sativa 'Albomarginata' • 'Variegata'
Cornus ................. controversa 'Variegata' • florida 'Rainbow' 'Sunset'
Fagus ........................................ sylvatica 'Purpurea Tricolor'
Ilex ........................................................................... (many)

Liriodendron ................................ tulipifera 'Aureomarginatum'
Photinia ................................................ davidiana 'Palette
Populus ............................................... candicans 'Aurora'
Quercus ................................................ cerris 'Variegata'

## Trees with fruit to attract wild life

Fruit of this kind is often not only very pleasing to look at but forms the attraction for a wide variety of wild life. Yellow or amber berries often last longer than red ones, as they are not as attractive to birds. White fruits, such as those of Sorbus hupehensis, are often the longest lasting of all.

Arbutus ...................................................................... (all)
Aronia ................................................ arbutifolia 'Brilliant'
Castanea ........................ sativa • sativa 'Albomarginata'
Catalpa ...................................................... bignonioides
Cercis ....................................................... siliquastrum
Cornus ................................... kousa chinensis • mas
Cotoneaster ............................................................... (all)
Crataegus ................................................................ (most)
Davidia ................................................................ involucrata
Euonymus .................................................................. (most)
Halesia ...................................................................... (all)
Ilex ......................................................................... (most)
Juglans ..................................................................... nigra
Juglans ...................................................................... regia
Koelreuteria ........................................................ paniculata
Malus ........................................................................ (most)
Morus ................................................................. alba pendula
Prunus ............................................... padus 'Watereri'
Sorbus ...................................................................... (most)

## Trees with scented flowers

The best gardens feed all of the senses and choosing trees with scented flowers can make a huge contribution to this process. It is worth noting that a high proportion of those that flower in winter are scented, so if you plan to have flowers in winter, you will enjoy scent as well. Plant them near paths or sitting areas or the boundaries of the garden from which the prevailing wind comes.

Acacia ...................................................................... dealbata
Aesculus .......................................... hippocastanum
Cytisus ..................................................... battandierii
Hamamelis .................................................................. (most)
Laburnum .................................................................. 'Vossii'
Magnolia .................................................................... (most)
Malus ........................................................................ (all)
Prunus ............................... 'Amanogawa' • 'Fragrant Cloud' lusitanica & cultivars • mume & cultivars padus 'Waterii' • x yedoensis & cultivars
Robinia .................... pseudoacacia • x margarette 'Pink Cascade'
Styrax ...................................................................... japonica
Syringa ...................................................................... (all)
Tilia ......................................... platyphyllos • 'Petiolaris'
Wisteria ...................................................................... (all)

# The pruning of ornamental trees

It is a common misconception that once we have planted an ornamental tree it should remain untouched. If this was the case then we would miss some wonderful opportunities to explore the full potential of a tree's characteristics. Another mistaken belief is that pruning is only needed to solve problems. The fact is that it is also creative and artistic. Pleached Limes, trimmed Yews and archways and pagodas of Laburnum and Wisteria are a few of the accepted forms of ornamental tree pruning, but there are many more reasons to prune trees.

An imaginative approach to pruning can turn trees into shrubs and shrubs into trees. Fan trained trees such as Malus crab apples and Forsythia are just a couple of examples of what is possible with regular formative pruning. For those who wish to research this subject thoroughly, 'The Pruning of Trees, Shrubs and Conifers' by George E Brown (ISBN 0-88192-319-2) is an excellent book.

Here are two instances where the pleaching of Hornbeam (Carpinus betulus) (above) and the shaping of London Plane (Platanus x hispanica) (below) are created with hard pruning in a garden situation. If left untouched they would become large majestic trees but here they are easily tamed to do with as we please.

## The 4 pruning techniques

Four (4) pruning technique options are suggested and represented with separate symbols in the A – Z of Ornamental Trees. These are now explained further.

### 1 Hard prune

These trees can be pruned severely at any time without causing any harm to the tree. There are several terms used for this technique such as 'Coppicing' (ground level) and 'Pollarding' (above ground). After severe cutting of the main branches the tree will respond by growing very vigorous young growth. This strong growth will provide spectacular results with large succulent leaves and more intense autumn and winter shoot colour. What happens above ground will also be mirrored below with a restricted root system.

The pictures below (taken in June) show two trees that are both over 15 years old and no more than 2.5 metres tall, that have superb summer foliage.

*Catalpa bignonioides 'Aurea'*

*Tilia 'Wratislaviensis' (Golden Lime)*

All these trees were hard pruned in the winter by removing all the previous season's growth. These techniques will allow trees to be grown in restricted space as large shrubs!

The pictures below show the heavy saw cut on a coppiced purple nut made in March and the dramatic result in late April and mid June.

*Late April*                     *Mid June*

## 2 Prune after flowering

These varieties can be pruned hard after flowering to promote even better bloom the following year. In the A-Z lists this symbol is used for non fruiting trees that flower on one year wood. By hard pruning all the shoots after flowering the resulting growth produces healthy flower bud for the following spring.

The picture above is of Prunus 'Snow Showers' as a small weeping tree where all the flower is produced on last season's growth, following hard pruning.

## 3 Replacement prune

An occasional thinning out of some of the branches can be undertaken to encourage fresh replacement growth. Most trees in this category flower on older than one year wood and would benefit from air and light being introduced to the canopy encouraging healthy replacement growth. Up to a maximum of 1/4 of all branches can be removed each year. Pruning in the summer is often advisable as less disease would enter pruning cuts and the pruner can see the full effect of the foliage result. This technique is useful where trees are used for supports for climbers such as clematis and vines.

## 4 No pruning

These varieties prefer to be left alone and would not benefit from any regular or structured pruning. This refers to many conifers which do not easily produce new growth from heavy cuts into old wood and where excessive sap loss or bacterial infection can result if pruned too often.

## Tree bough pruning

Where larger trees need an isolated bough removed then it is worth following the correct method. When a large bough is cut from a tree more damage can occur if done the wrong way. The illustration identifies the branch collar (shaded area) and shows where not to cut and the correct cutting position. If the sequence of cuts 1, 2 and 3 are followed no damage will occur. This method is also the safest.

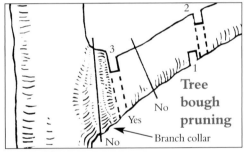

## Large Trees

When dealing with large trees that need professional skills and equipment it is advisable to ask a qualified tree surgeon.

## Pruning conifers

It is generally not advisable to prune conifers without establishing a few principles first. Those that can be pruned successfully into old wood from which re-growth would be successful are Larix, Taxodium, Taxus and Thuja, the first two being the deciduous conifers.

All other conifers can be pruned in two ways: the first is clipping annually but restricting this to the foliage only as one would do with hedging, and secondly by pruning off lower branches or 'crown lifting', a technique quite effective with dwarf pines to show off their attractive bark. It is important to remember to be bold and remove the branch entirely with a clean cut back to the main trunk. The illustration above under Tree bough pruning is particularly appropriate in this case.

# Fruit trees

## A few words about the symbols used in the fruit section

To help you get a quick sense of the salient features of the hundreds of varieties in the guide, we have used a series of symbols. The following notes are designed to help you understand the symbols more fully. For example we show Almond Ingrid (below) as being fresh eating, picking in September and self fertile.

These varieties are rated as having good dessert quality. All can also be cooked, although results are variable.

Primarily for cooking due to their higher acidic qualities. Some varieties if stored for long periods and allowed to ripen well can be eaten fresh, especially if you prefer a more tart and firm quality.

The month is indicated for picking time for apples and pears. To determine the best time within the month, keep an eye open for the first few fruits falling from the tree; also when the pips have turned from white to dark brown. As plums, cherries and other stone fruit are best eaten fresh, then the 'part' month for picking is shown.

The storage month is only an approximate guide. Depending on picking time and storage conditions provided this period can vary.

Best eaten straight from the tree. Storing in a refrigerator will extend shelf life for a few days.

All fruits are divided into 5 flowering periods from early 1 to late 5. As an example: a variety in group 3 will cross pollinate with any variety in groups 2, 3 or 4. For a more detailed explanation see our guide to pollination page 287.

These varieties will pollinate themselves without the need of a partner.

Heavy flowering varieties that also produce good viable pollen followed by good crops. Excellent pollinators for other varieties.

Triploid varieties are generally very strong, vigorous growers producing extra large fruit. They will not pollinate other varieties. See further explanation in the pollination section page 287.

These varieties are those that in general have high yields, abundant flower and rated reasonably disease resistant to mildew and scab.

Varieties that perform well throughout the UK. This will include a good resistance to frost at blossom time.

This specifically refers to a high degree of Scab resistance in apples and pears. For further information on Pest and Disease control in the garden see pages 302.

These varieties are particularly suitable for growing in pots, if they are grown on dwarf rootstocks such as M27 for apples and Tabel for cherries.

Tip bearing varieties are very few. Most of the fruit bud forms on the terminal buds of each shoot. Pruning needs to be in sympathy. See pruning guide for fruit trees page 294.

Where practical, and in particular on wall trained fruit, it would be worthwhile covering the blossom with fleece or other suitable material on frosty nights. Early flowering fruit such as apricots, nectarines, and peaches would benefit.

 Suitable for making Perry.

Suitable for making Cider.

Good for juicing.

The Royal Horticultural Society's Award of Garden Merit (AGM) indicates that the plant is recommended by the RHS.

Please see www.rhs.org.uk for further information.

## ALMOND

Also described in our ornamental section. Although not a reliable fruiting tree the fresh March flower is cheerful.

### Ingrid

This is the most reliable cropper of the selected varieties, with reasonable leaf curl resistance (in most areas) and good fruit quality. Plant in a sheltered position.

# APPLE

The Apple is part of our cultural heritage, with thousands of known varieties. Chapters have been written on single varieties, combining mythology, religion, art and language connections and, most important, local history. The varieties illustrated here are a small selection, but combine a geographical spread of some of the most interesting old favourites and the very latest introductions. The way they perform in gardens has been the main criterion for their inclusion and description.

## Adam's Pearmain

A distinctive late apple with attractive lenticel spots, red-brown skin and a rich, aromatic, nutty flavour. An excellent keeper. (Norfolk/Hereford 19th Century)

## Allington Pippin

King of the Pippins x Cox's Orange Pippin. Pale yellow, flushed red. Juicy and sharp with a pineapple flavour. Can be cooked. (Lincoln 19th Century)

## Annie Elizabeth

Orange with red flush. Large fruit with cream-white flesh and a sweet light flavour. Good keeper. Ideal for stewing, needing little sugar. Upright tree. (Leicester 19th Century)

## Arthur Turner

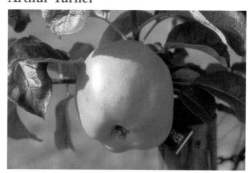

Large yellow-green fruit. Cooks to a delicious yellow purée, needing hardly any sugar. Very attractive flower. (Slough, Bucks. 1912)

---

**The story of the Apple**

The apple originated in the Dzhungariskiy Alatu region on the border between western China and Russia. Only recently plant scientists from Oxford University found apple trees, pears, plums and cherries all still growing wild.

This is beautifully documented in *The Story of the Apple* by Barrie Juniper and David J Mabberley. See Further Reading page 318.

## Apple Crump Recipe

One of the easiest dishes to produce for any fruit, particularly plums and rhubarb; but cooking apples too are perfect.

*Ingredients*

- 100g butter, at room temperature
- 100g granulated sugar
- 4 heaped tablespoons plain flour
- 450g Bramley or another cooking apple.

Pre-heat the oven to 170°C.

*Method*

1 For the crump topping, place the flour, sugar and butter into an oven proof bowl.

2 Pop the bowl into the oven for 10-15 minutes until the butter has melted.

3 For the filling, peel, core and slice apples, place in another ovenproof dish and put in oven for 5 minutes.

4 Remove the crump mixture from the oven and stir the ingredients together and spread over the part cooked apples.

5 Place in oven at 170°C for 40 minutes.

## Ashmead's Kernel

Pale green aromatic fruit with strong, sweet-sharp, intense, acid drop flavour. Firm white flesh. Beautiful flowers. (Gloucester circa 1700)

## Baker's Delicious

Handsome, flushed bright orange. Deep cream flesh, rich and juicy with lots of sugar. Strongly acidic. A good early cooker. (Wales 1932)

## Ballerina Obelisk Syn: *Flamenco*

Cox's Orange Pippin x Court Pendu Plat. This is the best quality apple of the Ballerina range with a very columnar habit and dark red crisp fruit. (Kent 1992)

## Bardsey

The 'sainted' apple found on Bardsey Island. This pink over cream skinned, lemon scented apple has a fine refreshing flavour and cooks well without sugar. (Ynys Enlli 1998)

## Beauty of Bath

Bright red flush on yellow. Flesh, often stained pink under the skin, is sweet and juicy when fully ripe. Can drop from the tree quite suddenly and needs to be eaten in haste to be at its best. An old remedy for reducing bruising was to scatter straw beneath the tree for a softened landing. (Somerset 19th Century)

## Blenheim Orange

Yellow-gold fruit has orange flush and a few red stripes. Nutty taste, sweet crumbly texture. An old favourite – cooks, eats and keeps well. When baked it keeps its shape and will produce a thick purée. (Oxford 1740)

## Bloody Ploughman

An old variety from Carse of Gowrie. The story goes that this apple arose from a pip on the grave of a ploughman shot by a gamekeeper for stealing. Very red and ribbed in appearance. Classified as an eater, but likely to do better as a cooker.

## Bountiful

Cox's Orange Pippin x Lane's Prince Albert. Soft juicy fruit which is light and sweet when cooked. Slices retain their shape. A good garden tree. (Kent 1964)

### Why do we need so many kinds of apples?

"Because there are so many folks. A person has a right to gratify his legitimate tastes. If he wants twenty or forty kinds for his present use, he should be accorded the privilege. Some place should be provided where he may obtain trees and scions. There is merit in variety itself. It provides more point of contact with life and leads away from uniformity and monotony."

From *The Apple Tree* by Liberty Hyde Bailey, a noted American plantsman.

## Braeburn

Crisp, firm, aromatic fruit. Excellent all round quality, but needs a good climate. Many highly coloured forms have been selected for commercial growers such as 'Hillwell', 'Loch Buie' and 'Helena' – they all taste the same! Plant in a sheltered, sunny spot.
(New Zealand 1950)

## Bramley 20

A compact version of Bramley's Seedling – 20% less vigorous with heavier crops. Highly recommended for the garden especially if grown on M27 dwarf rootstock to create the perfect mini Bramley. (Bristol 1970)

> **Bramley's Seedling**
> Unique and loved passionately, this variety is one of the most famous apples in the world and over 200 years old. As probably the best Bramley reference it is worth reading Roger Merryweather's *The Bramley – a world famous cooking apple* ISBN 0 947810 06 4 and published by Newark & Nottingham District Council. It encapsulates all one would want to know about this unique apple!

## Bramley 'Original'

*© Archie Miles*

Propagated from the original tree in Southwell, Nottinghamshire by kind permission of the owner Mrs Nancy Harrison. There is a belief by many enthusiasts, that over time, the 'modern' Bramley has lost flavour and quality. Propagation from the original tree provides an opportunity to experience this variety in its original and pure form.

## Bramley's Seedling

The finest cooker in the world! Green to greenish-yellow with a strong acid flavour.
(Nottingham 19th Century)

## Broadholme Beauty

From the village of the same name in Lincolnshire, this excellent disease resistant, long keeping cooking apple was raised by Cecil Lovely, blind for almost his entire life (1914-2007) and each tree sold contributes a donation to the Blind Dogs Association, in his memory. It is ideal for diabetics as there is little need for adding sugar. It also retains its shape well. With a shiny, smooth green skin, almost translucent in appearance, this apple produces heavy, regular crops. Its branches often appear to have a mild case of canker, a physiological condition. Thought to be a cross between James Grieve and Lane's Prince Albert. (Lincs. 2002)

## Brownlees Russet

A juicy flavour like acid drops, keeps well into February. Very attractive pink blossom. (Herts. 1848)

## Captain Kidd

A better coloured form of Kidd's Orange Red. Yellow with red stripes. Sweet, crisp and aromatic. A good alternative to Cox. (New Zealand)

### Apples and health – fact and folklore

There are numerous ancient rhymes and sayings about the benefits of eating apples. It appears our forebears knew what they were talking about, since recent science tells us that  apples are indeed very good for us. Here is a selection...

*An apple a day keeps the doctor away*
(Welsh folk proverb, 1866)

*Apple in the morning – Doctor's warning*
*Roast apple at night – starves the doctor outright*

*Eat an apple going to bed – knock the doctor on the head*
(United States in 1913)

*Three each day, seven days a week – ruddy apple, ruddy cheek*

*In Scandinavian mythology Iduna was guardian of the golden apples which the gods tasted whenever they wished to renew their youth.*

Here are six reasons for eating apples:

- High flavonoid content reduces the risk of heart disease.
- High concentrations of fibre regulate cholesterol levels and lower blood pressure.
- The risk of diabetes and cardiovascular diseases is lowered.
- Pectin and apple juice protect against colon cancer.
- Improves memory and cognition and helps prevent Alzheimer's disease.
- Reduced incidences of Asthma are known particularly in children whose mothers have eaten apples during pregnancy.

(US Apple Association nutrition-health research)

## Captain Tom

A distinctive large dual purpose angular shaped fruit. It also has unusually beautiful large pink blossom. (Colwall, Malvern)

## Carlisle Codlin

Cooks to a white juicy purée with a tart, fruity flavour. (Carlisle 1830)

## Catshead

Large angular fruit, green-pale yellow. Cooks to a sharp firm purée. A suitable shape for parcelling up as dumplings for farmers packed lunches. (West Midlands 17th Century)

## Charles Ross

Peasgood's Nonsuch x Cox's Orange Pippin. An easy to grow apple with orange-red flush. Sweet flavoured eater which also bakes well. Valued garden apple. Good for northern areas. (Newbury 19th Century)

## 'Sporting' Apple

Nature offers unpredictable but interesting oddities on occasions, no more so than when apples show skin colour variations. Caused by the sun's natural radiation, apples often 'sport' and fruit growers will use this opportunity to introduce improvements. Many commercial apples are improved colour versions of the original variety and some of these are identified in our descriptions. Occasionally a variety will 'revert' to its original colour and the apple shown here is particularly rare and has decided to take on a split personality.

The pale half is the original variety and the red half the high coloured 'sport'.

## Chivers Delight

Golden crisp and juicy with a sweet, honey flavour. Keeps well. A good garden apple for all areas. (Cambridge 20th Century)

## Claygate Pearmain

Rich and aromatic with a nutty taste. Combines the qualities of Blenheim Orange and Ribston Pippin. Flushed orange-red over greenish-yellow background. Produces good crops. (Surrey 1921)

## Cobra

Cox's Orange Pippin x Bramley's Seedling. The perfect dual purpose apple with a fine dessert flavour developing by mid winter. It is a fine cooking apple from mid September onwards having a refreshing acidic, tangy quality for a multitude of culinary uses from firm baked apples to pie fillings. In all cases requiring little added sugar. (Bred by Hugh Ermen, Kent 2007)

## Applefests

Apple Day is an annual celebration of apple, orchards and local distinctiveness, initiated by Common Ground in 1990, it has since been celebrated each year by people organising hundreds of local events. The official apple day is the 21st October and most 'applefests' are generally held on Saturdays on or around this time.

It is on these occasions that the passion of local fruit enthusiasts is on show for all to behold. Part of this scene is the local 'expert' who is on hand for variety identification. Their opinions are valuable and should be nurtured and appreciated, as they come with years of acquired knowledge and instinct. For more on this subject turn to Fruit Identification on page 298.

## Cornish Aromatic

Handsome bright red flush with russet patches. Sweet, sharp pear drop and spice flavour. (Cornwall 1813)

## Cornish Gilliflower

*'Gillyflower'* is the old English name for the carnation which, with this apple, shares the scent of cloves. Dark red flush with red stripes over gold. Knobbly exterior conceals yellow perfumed flesh. In late October it is intensely flavoured, rich and aromatic. (Cornwall 1800)

## Court of Wick

Red flushed russet freckled over gold with intense fruity flavour. Sweet yellow flesh. (Somerset 18th Century)

## Court Pendu Plat

Greenish yellow flushed orange-red. Rich, fruity, strong pineapple-like acidity mellows to become sweet – holds flavour well until February. One of the oldest recorded varieties and very disease resistant. (France 1613)

## Cox's Orange Pippin

The original Cox with all the qualities expected from the finest flavoured apple in the world. Orange flush over greenish-yellow. Deep cream flesh has sweet aromatic flavour. Too difficult to grow successfully in gardens. Prone to disease. (Bucks. 19th Century)

## Cox's Orange Pippin Self Fertile
Syn: *Cox S.F.*

A self fertile form of Cox's Orange Pippin highly recommended for less than ideal Cox areas. Heavy crops of the best eating apple in the world. (Bristol 1975)

## Crawley Beauty

Medium to large flat shape. Bright yellow, orange-red flush, with red stripes. Crisp, firm with slightly sweet flavour. Early in season will cook to lightly flavoured purée. Loses acidity with storing. (Sussex 1870)

## Crispin Syn: *Mutsu*

Golden Delicious x Ludo. Greenish-yellow, sometimes with brown flush. Crisp, sweet, juicy flesh, similar to Golden Delicious but with a coarser texture. One of the latest keepers improving in flavour after long storage. Originally came to the UK as 'Mutsu' meaning 'elephants ears' due to the extra large leaves. Re-named 'Crispin' in a W.I. naming competition. (Japan 1930).

## D'Arcy Spice

Bright green becoming gold with red flush. Hot, spicy nutmeg flavour. Enjoys the sea air! (Essex 18th Century)

### Apples Dessert, Culinary or Cider?

The grouping of varieties into these categories began as far back as Theophastrus in ancient Greece and still there are conflicting opinions. It is very much an arbitrary matter decided by the individual palate. One thing for certain is that there is an abundant choice for all preferences including those who enjoy unripe cooking apples for fresh eating or the sweetest of apples to make their preferred cider. We are indeed all experts.

We apologise if any of the descriptions in the fruit section of this book concerning flavour, aroma or texture are in any way misleading.

## Dabinett (Cider)

The most reliable cider variety producing a high quality juice. (Martock, Somerset 19th Century)

## Devonshire Quarrenden

A strong flavour of berried fruit, sweet but with good acidity. Dark crimson flush with yellow background. (Devon or France 1676)

## Discovery

Worcester Pearmain x Beauty of Bath. Bright red flush. Crisp and juicy with a hint of strawberry. An excellent early dessert apple with good disease resistance. (Langham, Essex 1949)

## Doctor Hogg

Large with yellow skin flushed pale red with slight stripes. Flesh tender, white, sweet flavoured and sub-acid. Cooks to a good purée. (Sussex 1880)

## Downton Pippin

Orange Pippin x Golden Pippin. Medium size. Yellow skin, slightly tinged red, dotted with russet. Flesh firm, crisp yellowish white with a sweet flavour. Also cooks and will keep its shape. (Shropshire 1806)

### Apples and alcohol

The connection between apples and alcohol is ancient. It is thought that the Celts and their predecessors in central Europe made cider. Today it is still the practice for families to make their own cider, cider wines, vinegars and calvados in apple growing districts, whilst the juice industry is a multi-million pound business in many parts of the world.

## Dumelow's Seedling

Medium, pale yellow fruit. Firm, crisp, white flesh which cooks to a sharp flavoured pale cream purée. Good for baking. (Leicester 1800)

## Edward VII

Blenheim Orange x Golden Noble. Green-yellow with russet dots. Good round shape ideal for easy peeling. Cooks to a good cream purée. Pale pink flowers. Resistant to scab and frost. An excellent all round cooker. (Worcester 1906)

## Egremont Russet

The flesh is cream, tinged yellow, sweet and firm with a rich nutty flavour. The usual russet to be found in shops. (Sussex 19th Century)

## Ellison's Orange

Cox's Orange Pippin x Caville Blanc (probably D'Été). Medium striped, red, juicy apple. Aniseed flavour develops after picking retaining its melting juicy flesh. Scab resistant. (Lincoln 1904)

### Frost resistant varieties

Apples are probably the toughest of the tree fruits, with a degree of frost tolerance in their flowers. Those known to have good resistance are: Edward VII, Ellisons Orange, Fiesta, Lord Derby, Red Devil, Red Falstaff, and moderate resistance are: James Grieve, Lanes Prince Albert, Lord Lambourne and Scrumptious. Cox's Orange Pippin and Bramley's Seedling are sensitive.

## Elstar

Ingrid Marie x Golden Delicious. Very heavy crops of good quality fruit, eating well at picking time and with reasonable storage. The sweet, crisp, juicy flesh has an intense honeyed flavour. (Holland 1972)

## Epicure

Wealthy x Cox's Orange Pippin. Red stripes over greenish-yellow. Sweet and juicy fruit. Early and small but heavy cropping and high quality. Popular garden variety. Bred by Laxton. (Bedford 1909)

### Parents in breeding

Most fruit varieties have known parents that have been selected by the breeder. The first name (in the case of Epicure being 'Wealthy' above) is always the female or the flower from whence the apple will be produced and the second name (in this case 'Cox's Orange Pippin') always the male or pollen donor. Many parents of apples are not known and are 'Chance Seedlings' such as Bramley's Seedling. Where only the flower is known but not the pollen donor this is often referred to as 'OP' or **open pollinated**. For more on fruit breeding see 'Hugh and Laura Ermen' page 233.

## Falstaff

James Grieve x Golden Delicious. Green-red striped fruit with superb crisp, juicy flavour. One of the heaviest croppers year on year. Frost resistant. Excellent pollinator. Available as 'Red Falstaff' which has an improved colour. (HRI, East Malling, Kent 1965)

### Fiesta Syn: *Red Pippin*

Cox's Orange Pippin x Idared. Rich, aromatic and sweet with a crisp texture. Excellent garden tree with Cox-like characteristics. Very heavy crops. Ideal for northern areas. (Kent 1972)

## Fortune Syn: *Laxton's Fortune*

Cox's Orange Pippin x Wealthy. Similar to and an early Cox's Orange Pippin type but slightly sweeter flavour and easier to grow. Best left on tree for as long as possible to allow flavour to develop. Bred by Laxton. (Bedford 1904)

## Fuji

Ralls Janet x Delicious. Orange-red flush. Crisp, firm, sweet, juicy flesh. Crops well despite being a very late season picker in early November. Best eaten after Christmas. Various 'sports' have been introduced of late with better colour, such as 'Aztec'. (Japan 1939)

### The Fuji Bag

In Japan the apple is considered a luxury fruit of high value. The 'Fuji' bag was one of the first ways to protect individual fruits from attack from pest and disease. Each apple in mid summer would be enclosed in a paper bag that was removed a few weeks before picking to allow the apple to develop colour. This painstaking operation can be performed on fruit clusters or individual fruits with any easy to use breathable material such as nylon stockings and old muslin bags that are particularly good at repelling wasps.

## Gala

Kidd's Orange Red x Golden Delicious. A reliable cropper of good, small, crisp and well flavoured fruit with a thin skin. One of the most popular eating apples in the world. Improved colour forms are grown commercially such as 'Mondial' and 'Royal' Gala which appear in the shops. (New Zealand 1934)

## Galloway Pippin

Large and yellow with a russet freckle finish. Keeps its shape well when cooked, best eaten before Christmas. (Wigtown, Galloway 1871)

## Gennet Moyle

Orange-red flush with a slight russety cheek. With little sugar this variety cooks to a sharp, flavoursome lemon purée. Makes a mild cider 'fit to be drunk by ladies in summer' and even good for jam.
(Possibly Hereford 19th Century)

## George Cave

Carmine stripes over green background and white flesh. Strong, sweet, sharp taste. A good follow on from Beauty of Bath. Fruit liable to cracking. (Essex 1923)

## Golden Delicious

Well known crisp eater. Greenish-yellow turning gold. Sweet, honey flavour. Flavour is superior to imported fruit when grown in the UK. (USA 19th Century)

## Golden Noble

The apple we know as Golden Noble was discovered in an old orchard on a country estate in Norfolk in 1820. It is thought that the original tree might have been in Pontefract, Yorkshire where it is mentioned in 1769. Handsome golden cooker, one of the very best. Sharp and well flavoured, making it ideal for pies. When baked has a creamy texture and needs very little sugar. (Norfolk 18th Century)

### Family apple tree

Family apple trees can be very successful for small gardens. They generally come in suitable combinations for differing seasons of eating and/or cooking and for good pollination. This picture shows the grafting technique used in the nursery to produce this type of tree. Eventually one variety will possibly weaken or another becomes more dominant but this is easily overcome by simple pruning. For pruning and other information on tree management please see pages 294.

## Golden Pippin

Gold with russet dots. Sweet rich taste with a lemon tang. Cooks well despite being a small apple. Good for pippin jelly. (UK 1629)

## Golden Spire

Golden with deep cream flesh. Sharp, almost cider flavour. Cooks to a well flavoured purée. Named for its shapely spired nose. Slightly weeping in habit. (Lancs. 1850)

## Granny Smith

Bright green and juicy but with no strong taste. This good keeper needs a long hot summer to perform well. Ideal for those who like firm, crisp apples. (Australia 19th Century)

## Greensleeves

James Grieve x Golden Delicious. A reliable mid-season variety. Pale, greenish-yellow. Crisp, tangy, easy to grow, and a good pollinator for other varieties. (Kent 1966)

### Fruit thinning

The need for thinning of all tree fruit is often ignored in the hope that the tree will produce a miracle crop of quality fruit well beyond its capacity. Remember to follow these golden rules.

- The main benefit of thinning is larger and better flavoured fruit.
- The tree will have the capacity to produce quality fruit bud for the following year's crop.
- Thinning is a good opportunity to remove damaged fruits caused by pest and disease.
- At any time fruits are touching there are too many.
- June drop often occurs in July so some of the work could be done for you.
- Weak trees should have only one fruit per cluster.
- Over heavy crops can lead to biennial bearing, see page 222.
- If fruit thinning is considered too time consuming then summer prune the tree lightly instead.

## Grenadier

Easy to grow, large early fruit which cooks to a sharp purée. The tree is compact making it ideal for the garden. A very good pollinator for Bramley. (Bucks. 19th Century)

   DNK **3** ✓ UK 🏆

## Harry Masters Jersey (Cider)

Often known as 'Port Wine' this dark red fruit produces a full bitter-sweet taste with a soft astringency. (Yarlington, Somerset 19th Century)

 **5** Ci

## Herefordshire Beefing

Deep red flush with stripes. Sharp, firm but not very juicy flesh. Rich flavour, keeps shape when cooked so very good in open tarts. Best early in season. (Herefordshire late 1700)

   **4**

## Herefordshire Redstreak (Cider)

A cider apple that at one time was unsurpassed. In its day it was often preferred to imported wines and poetry and song were often enlisted in its praises. It arose from a pip collected and grown by Charles I's Ambassador to France, Lord Scudamore. It is quite special, firstly for a high specific gravity and therefore high alcoholic content (11%) and secondly for its pretty pink coloured juice, making a fine 'Cyder' in all respects.

 **5** Ci

---

**Cyder**
by John Philips (1676 – 1709)

"Let every tree in every garden own
The Red Streak as supreme, whose pulpose fruit,
With golden irradiate, and vermilion, shines
Tempting, not fatal, as the birth of that
Primeval, interdicted plant, that won
Fond Eve, in hapless hour of taste, and die

This of more bounteous influence, inspires
Poetic raptures, and the lowly muse
Kindles to loftier strains; even I, perceive
Her sacred virtues.
See! the numbers flow
Easy, whilst, cheer'd with her nectareous juice,
Hers, and my country's praises, I exalt"

# Apple Herefordshire Russet

## Herefordshire Russet

Cox's Orange Pippin x Idared. The russet with a Cox flavour.
Exceptional eating quality with a rich aromatic flavour. A winner
in 'taste testings' around the country. Picking in early October
with storage until late January. The tree is well spurred, well
shaped and moderately vigorous. The fruit set is heavy with
small to medium sized fruit. Bred by Hugh Ermen. (Kent 2002)

## Honeycrisp Syn: *Honeycrunch*

A very large, attractive, crisp apple with a fine sweet flavour and texture. Although not aromatic it would please most palates. Little experience in the UK to date. (USA 1990)

## Howgate Wonder

Blenheim Orange x Newton Wonder. Large, yellow striped red cooker. Keeps shape well when cooked but has a very light taste. Can also be used as an eater as it is quite sweet and juicy. Often holder of the "biggest apple in the world" prize. (Isle of Wight 1915)

## Irish Peach

Small yellow fruit, red flush. Slightly perfumed and juicy. Like a peach it should be eaten straight from the tree. Popular during Victorian and Edwardian times. (Sligo, Ireland 1819)

## James Grieve

Red flush stripes over pale green. Crisp and juicy. Excellent flavour and reliable cropper – deservedly popular. (Edinburgh 1893)

### James Grieve

James Grieve is just one of many famous Scottish apple varieties, some of which are mentioned in this section such as 'Bloody Ploughman' and 'Scotch Dumpling'.

For an excellent account of choosing and growing varieties in Scotland one should read, John Butterworth's *'Apples in Scotland'* ISBN 1-904078-00-1. Landford Press.

## Jumbo

Red Charles Ross x Tetraploid Jonathan. Flushed and striped red on pale green background with a deep red blush and attractive red flecks. Golden cream flesh. Very large and dual purpose, particularly good for baking as it retains its colour. For eating fresh it has a good acidic, aromatic flavour. Tree vigour is moderately strong. Bred By Hugh Ermen (Kent 2000)

## Jupiter

Cox's Orange Pippin x Starking Delicious. Large Cox-flavoured apples, but a more robust variety. Sweet, juicy, aromatic flesh. A strong growing tree performing well on all semi dwarf and dwarf rootstocks. (Kent 1966)

## Katy Syn: *Katja*

James Grieve x Worcester Pearmain. Heavy crops of bright red early fruit, with sweet, juicy, acid, firm flesh. Makes excellent fresh juice and even a palatable cider. Good pollinator. (Sweden 1947)

## Kent Syn: *Malling Kent*

Cox's Orange Pippin x Jonathan. A very rich flavour combining sugar and acidity. Coarse-fleshed with a tough skin. A good cropper for any area, disease resistant and an excellent eater after Christmas. (Kent 1949)

## Keswick Codlin

Found on a Cumbrian rubbish tip in 1790. Pale green-yellow with darker yellow flush. Cooks to a juicy cream froth and purée which hardly needs sugar. Good for jelly. Very profuse in flower and very heavy crops – dual purpose. (Lancashire 18th Century)

### Codlins and Cream

Codlin is a generic name for a certain type of cooking apple usually yellow/green, conical in shape, used between August and October and originally an ingredient in the national dish 'codlins and cream'. The name is derived from to 'coddle' or parboil, a process used to retain the apple's shape. There are many 'Codlins': English (includes Old English, Quodlin and Common), Carlisle, Kentish and more.

## Kidd's Orange Red

Cox's Orange Pippin and Delicious (direction uncertain). Sweet, crisp and aromatic, with a good balance of sugar and acidity. A good Cox alternative. (New Zealand 1924)

## King of the Pippins
Syn: *Princess Pippin/Reine des Reinettes*

© Claire Higgins

Medium size, orange-red flush on greenish yellow-gold background. Firm, crisp, juicy apple. When cooked keeps its shape and colour, so perfect for open tarts. Also used for cider. (UK or France 19th Century)

## King's Acre Pippin

Sturmer Pippin and Ribston Pippin (direction uncertain). A large fruit, green with brownish red flush and russet patches. Very rich flavour with a crisp, juicy texture. A good late keeping garden apple. (Hereford 1899)

## Lane's Prince Albert

Russet Nonpareil x Dumelow's Seedling. Shining green flushed orange-red with red stripes. Useful, late keeping cooker, greenish-white soft flesh. Cooks to a lemon purée. So named when Prince Albert and Queen Victoria called at the Kings Arms for a change of horses. (Berkhamstead, Herts. 19th Century)

## Laxton's Superb

Wyken Pippin x Cox's Orange Pippin. Sweet and aromatic possessing certain similarities to Cox. Can become biennial bearing. A good substitute for Cox's Orange Pippin in colder exposed areas. Purple flush and red stripes give this an old fashioned attractive appearance. (Bedford, 1897)

### Biennial Bearing

This condition often afflicts old apple trees and particular varieties such as Laxton's Superb. In the 'on' year the tree fruits so heavily that it uses all its energy to sustain and mature its current crop and has no reserves to form flower bud for the following spring. The best solution is to prune the tree heavily in the early summer in the 'on' year, thereby reducing the overloaded crop and giving the tree a chance to produce flower bud as well. For more on pruning see page 294.

## Lemon Pippin

Lemon coloured and shaped, large with a strong lemon aroma. Quite sweet, rather dry, firm, coarse yellow flesh, good in tarts and jelly. (Normandy or Kent 1700)

## Limelight

Discovery x Greensleeves. This improved Greensleeves type is abundant in cropping. The apple has a clean, smooth finish and seems to glow when ripe with the occasional attractive pink blush. It is crisp, refreshing, and very disease resistant. Makes a neat, compact tree. Bred by Hugh Ermen. (Kent 2000)

## Lord Derby

An excellent quality cooker. Large, firm, attractive, green fruit with a distinctive ribbed angular shape. Cook early when green for a sharp taste. Good for pies. Similar ribbed angular shape to Catshead. (Cheshire 19th Century)

## Lord Hindlip

A very handsome apple with a crimson flush and rich aromatic flavour. Cream coloured flesh with a coarse texture. A native West Midland variety. (Worcs. 1896)

## Lord Lambourne

James Grieve x Worcester Pearmain. An old favourite and a reliable cropper. Bright striped fruit, moderately sweet, aromatic with some flavour of strawberry. (Bedford 1907)

## Melrose

Large fruit blushed pink/crimson over milky yellow background. Sweet, sharp flavour. A popular apple of the 19th century Tweedside orchards. (Melrose Abbey, Roxburgh 1831)

## Meridian

Cox's Orange Pippin x Falstaff. Striped orange-red on pale green background. Juicy with aromatic flavour. Heavy cropper, disease resistant. Good keeping qualities.
(HRI, East Malling, Kent 1972. Introduced 2000)

## Michaelmas Red

McIntosh x Worcester Pearmain. Dark red flush becoming deeper red with keeping. Juicy, quite soft flesh and firm skin. Very heavy crops of small, sweet apples. (HRI, East Malling, Kent 1929)

## Michelin (Cider)

Medium size firm fruit. Reliable and heavy cropping – juice low acidity. Stiff upright habit, spurs fairly well. (Normandy, France 1782)

## Monarch

Peasgood's Nonsuch x Dumelow's Seedling. Large quality cooker and a fair eater. Green with pink flush. Cooks to a juicy purée with a creamy texture, a highly prized cooker for mincemeat. Can be slightly biennial. (Essex 19th Century)

## Newton Wonder

Very late keeping, large yellow and scarlet. Cooks to a juicy, mild purée. Later in season makes fruity eating apple. Good in salads, stuffing and mincemeat. (Melbourne, Derbyshire 19th Century)

## Norfolk Royal Russet

A lovely looking and quality dessert apple. The russet finish also has a bright red cheek giving it an old fashioned look. A sport of Norfolk Royal but with a richer and superb intense aromatic flavour. (Burnham Overy Staithe, Norfolk 1983)

## Northern Greening

Very old variety recorded by Forsyth and Hogg. Valued as a superb sharp, juicy sauce apple. Keeps well throughout winter. Small but abundant fruit. (England 1802)

## Orleans Reinette

Golden-yellow fruit flushed red, nutty and aromatic, firm, sweet flesh. Early fruit can be cooked – slices keep shape – makes a sweet baked apple. (European, 18th Century)

## Peasgood's Nonsuch

The largest dessert apple. Pale green with broken red stripes and orange flush. When cooked makes a sweet, deliciously flavoured purée. Juicy when eaten fresh – good in salads. (Grantham, Lincs. 1850's)

### Apple harvesting & storage

"Fruit does not quit the tree until it be filled with its full compliment of nourishment" Marshall 1796.

- Do not pick too early. Home grown can fulfil its potential for flavour unlike commercially grown fruit that often lacks flavour because it is picked too early to reduce bruising during robust handling and the many food miles it travels to market.
- Fruit rarely ripens evenly through the tree. The south side or fruit in the sunniest position should be picked first.
- Do not store early varieties – although the fridge can be very useful to extend the eating period.
- A cool moist atmosphere is best.
- Only keep fruit in a single layer.
- Eat the blemished fruit first.
- Watch out for mice.

See further information on page 300.

## Pink Lady Syn: *Cripps Pink*

Golden Delicious x Lady Williams. A firm, solid apple with cream flesh and a sweet and honey flavour. This variety would need an unusually long hot summer to mature and develop flavour well in the UK. (Australia 1989)

## Pinova

Clivia x Golden Delicious. A high quality eater, scab resistant and a good late keeper. Conical, yellow skin with a late developing pinkish-red flush. Precocious cropper with a degree of frost resistance. There is a red sport called 'Evelina' or 'Red Pinova' (Germany 1986)

## Pitmaston Pine Apple

Small, conical and golden with rich distinctive flavour of pineapple, blended with honey and musk. Can be biennial bearing. (Hereford 1785)

## Pixie

Good crops of small apples ideal for children, yellow with attractive red stripes and orange-red flush. Finely flavoured, rich with plenty of sugar. Keeps well. The picture above shows 'Red Pixie', a sport with more attractive colour. (RHS Wisley, 1947)

## Princesse

Heavy cropping russet of average quality. Less nutty flavour than Egremont, but easier to grow. Very disease resistant. (France)

### Mistletoe

The festive season would not be the same without mistletoe; and yet as a parasitic plant it needs to be controlled otherwise it can become a burden on fruit trees in particular, competing for nourishment with the crop and often breaking limbs due to its considerable weight. There are male and female plants. Females only bear fruit if pollinated by a male plant. A single male plant would be enough for a small orchard. The fruiting females can also be pruned at the same time as the tree to a more sustainable volume.

## Queen Cox Self Fertile 18

A self fertile selection of Queen Cox. The best commercial form of Cox with attractive colour and occasional russet spots. Good yields due to its precocious self fertility. (Bristol 1975)

## Rajka

Sampion x Katja. Rated as a very disease resistant apple, pleasing to the eye, with an even shape. A small apple but regular and heavy crops. Pleasant eating quality. Pronounced 'Raika'. (Czech Republic 1983)

## Red Devil

Discovery x Kent. Excellent garden variety with deep scarlet skin and red stained flesh when fully ripe. Superb fruity strawberry flavour. Makes an excellent pink juice. Disease resistant. Named after the 'Red Devil' parachute display team. Ideal for all areas. Bred by Hugh Ermen. (Kent 1979)

## Red Falstaff

The select red sport of 'Falstaff'. Fruity, well balanced flavour, crisp and juicy. Frost resistant and self fertile. One of the heaviest yielding varieties. Can be stored easily and eaten throughout the winter. Highly recommended for every garden. (Norfolk 1983)

## Red Miller's Seedling

Red sport of Miller's Seedling. Medium, pale yellow with bright red flush. Crisp, soft, white, sweet flesh with refreshing acidity. Ideal for children. Can be biennial bearing. (Sport found Canterbury, Kent 1960)

### Apple tree vigour

Why are apple varieties noticeably more weak or vigorous than average? It is probably due to the type of rootstock they are grown on and for a full explanation see page 286. OR there may be other reasons:

**Stronger growth:**
- A minority of varieties are 'triploids' ✖ (see explanation in the pollination section page 287). They are naturally more vigorous than the majority of varieties and are identified with 'Triploid' symbol in this section.
- The trees are growing in excellent deep, well drained and fertile soil.

**Weaker growth:**
- The variety is naturally less vigorous. Such varieties as Bardsey, Charles Ross, D'Arcy Spice, King of the Pippins, Pitmaston Pine Apple, Red Devil, Red Windsor, St Edmund's Russet and Worcester Pearmain.
- The variety is self fertile and therefore flowers more profusely and sets heavy crops of fruit. Examples would be Limelight, Red Falstaff and Red Windsor.
- The tree is growing on thin/poor soil.

**Natural Tree Shape:**
- Have been bred for compact or restricted growth such as Ballerina trees or are naturally extreme in their growth habit either naturally upright or spreading.

For tips on managing the above extremes refer to the Pruning section on page 294.

## Red Windsor

Superb Cox type flavour and very heavy crops. Frost hardy and very compact growth. An ideal garden variety, easy to grow with good disease resistance and some frost resistance at blossom time. A sport of Alkmene which has Cox's Orange Pippin parentage. (Hereford 1985) *See next page for image.*

## Redprince Syn: *Red Jonaprince*

An exceptional form of Jonagold coloured fully red by late September. Excellent flavour, keeps well. There are over 70 different clones of Jonagold and this is one of the best. (Holland 1990. Introduced 2000)

## Redsleeves

Exeter Cross x scab resistant seedling. A sister seedling to Greensleeves introduced at the same time. Crisp and juicy red fruits ideal for children, disease tolerant and frost resistant. (HRI, East Malling, Kent 1986)

## Reverend W. Wilks

Peasgood's Nonsuch and Ribston Pippin (direction uncertain). Compact trees producing enormous fruit which bake superbly. Cooks to a light, sweet, pale, lemon purée, hardly needing any sugar. The best early cooker. A delicate fruit, handle with care. (Slough, Bucks. 1904)

Apple Red Windsor

## Ribston Pippin

Sweet, aromatic, crisp fruit with yellow-red flush. Firm, deep cream flesh, more acid than Cox. Resistant to scab. Described as being 'like a good dessert wine'. (Little Ribston, near Knaresborough, North Yorkshire 18th Century)

## Rosemary Russet

Orange-reddish brown flush over greenish-yellow, russet patches. Flesh firm, fine white, tinged yellowish-green. Sweet and aromatic, with a taste of acid drops. (UK, described Brentford, Middlesex 1831)

## Rubinette Rosso

©Richard Barrie

An attractive Swiss apple with a delicious aromatic flavour as good as a Cox but with better crops. Although on the small side and slightly prone to scab this is probably one of the finest tasting apples in the world. A newly introduced form of the original Rubinette. (Switzerland circa 1978)

## Sam's Crab

Medium size, slightly greenish-yellow flushed and streaked red. Firm flesh, sweet flavour, slightly sub-acid. (Herefordshire 1831)

## Sandlin Duchess

An 'Improved Newton Wonder' when it was introduced by William Crump. Sweet, crisp and juicy with an open texture. (Sandlin, Malvern 1880)

## Saturn

Falstaff x Cox's Orange Pippin. Very resistant to scab. Heavy crops of attractive, red blushed, conical fruit. Juicy, crisp and refreshing. Not particularly aromatic. (HRI, East Malling, Kent 1980)

## Scotch Bridget

Ribbed, quite rich with cream, crisp flesh. A favourite in the Hereford and Worcester area, particularly the Teme Valley. (Scotland 1851)

## Scotch Dumpling

Large apple, cooks to a well flavoured frothy purée. Very attractive pink flowers. (Scotland 1949)

### Beautiful Apple flowers

Rubinette (previous page) and Scotch Dumpling are two examples of stunning apple flowers that provide that ornamental bonus to having them as trees. Others worthy of note are: Arthur Turner (large white and red), Captain Tom (shell pink and white), Discovery (just pure white), Golden Spire (predominantly shell pink), Lord Derby (pink and white), Red Falstaff (white with pink and maroon shades).

## Spartan

McIntosh x Yellow Newton Pippin. A very popular eating variety. Fruit dark red, sweet, juicy, crisp with a white flesh. (Canada 1926)

## St. Edmund's Russet
Syn: *St Edmund's Pippin*

The best mid-season russet. Sweet, juicy, rich, densely textured, pale cream flesh. Very attractive with a golden-red russet and silvery sheen. (Suffolk 1875)

## Stoke Edith Pippin
Russet freckled over gold. Sweet, slightly perfumed when eaten at its best from November onwards. Quite soft, juicy, pale yellow flesh. A small 'pearmain' shaped fruit. (Herefordshire 1872)

# Hugh and Laura Ermen – Fruit Breeders Naturel

Many of the apples grown commercially today were, in the past, either chance seedlings found by accident or latterly raised by professional and enthusiastic amateur breeders. Successful breeders are rare and have instinctive natural abilities and none come more acclaimed than Hugh and Laura Ermen.

Hugh and Laura combined Hugh's professional experience of a life's work in Horticulture with his rare and natural instincts in parent selection, with Laura's invaluable help in all aspects, such as pollen testing, pruning and keeping accurate records. Cobra, Herefordshire Russet, Limelight, Red Devil, Scrumptious and Winter Gem are all from their stable and Hugh had this to say about their achievements.

"Of course it is always helpful to have Lady Luck smile on a few of our seedlings but we need to provide luck with opportunity. This is made possible by careful parent selection and we have found that there are many unpredictable results. Many good apples in their own right do not necessarily produce similarly good offspring and some unusually odd parents can often produce winners, such is nature's way.

We aim to raise new varieties for people to enjoy a wider spectrum of flavours and textures, as variety is the spice of life. We keep things simple, work with nature and not try to manipulate it too much. An example is that we prefer to cross varieties that flower at the same time rather than different flower times. This we hope will give improved compatibility by imitating what happens in the wild.

Disease resistance is all important for the modern garden and whilst we are aware that this breaks down because disease also adapts itself to survive, we utilise a broad range of characteristics within the parents we use to strengthen this resistance.

Our scope for fruit breeding in a small town garden is limited. No DNA or GM technology are used though these can stimulate innovation. It can take up to 15 years from pollination to introduction and in this time 98% of seedlings may be discarded. There are many good varieties already and to produce new ones is a great challenge. The culture and breeding of fruit is to us a fascinating way of life which hopefully contributes in a small way to our fruit industry and country."

Hugh died in 2009 and is greatly missed.

# Apple Scrumptious

## Scrumptious

Starkspur Goldon Delicious x Discovery. This apple is something very special. Named for its wonderful complexity of flavours it has been carefully bred and selected specifically for our garden conditions. It is a mid season variety suitable for planting in all areas of the UK. It is self fertile, frost hardy when in flower, thin skinned for children and can be eaten straight from the tree at any time during September. The fruit will naturally stay on the tree without falling. When tasted by apple lovers, descriptions include: fragrant and honeyed, liquorice and wine, a bunch of cherries, fresh, aromatic, soft and delicate, crisp and sweet.

## Sturmer Pippin

This greeny-brown apple picks late and keeps well. Crisp, juicy and sweet but needs plenty of autumn sunshine to build up the flavour. Southern areas only. (Haverhill, Suffolk 19th Century)

## Sunburn

An aromatic, sweet flavoured variety of Cox parentage. Good regular crops although small in size and a long eating season from November to March. (Hornchurch, Essex 1925)

## Sunrise

An excellent early eater. Bright red, well sized apples with soft, white juicy flesh. Its best attribute is that for an early apple it retains its crispness and flavour on the tree for several weeks. Prone to scab in some seasons. (Canada 1990)

## Sunset

Similar to Cox but more disease resistant and slightly earlier. Red stripes and orange flush over gold. Sharp intense flavour. Heavy cropper. Excellent garden apple. (Ightham, Kent 1918)

## Sweet Society

Ingrid Marie x Elstar. Part of a range of plants and trees selected by the RHS to celebrate their Bicentennial in 2004. Sweet Society is an attractive classic Cox type apple, slightly small but with a superb aromatic eating quality. Appearance is similar to a good coloured Cox with attractive russet streaks and a good red flush on a yellow green background. The flavour is sweet and rich. The tree is quite bushy in habit, produces spurs well. Shy cropping. Bred by Hugh Ermen. (Kent 2004)

## Tom Putt

A very handsome large cooking apple with bright red crimson streaks. Firm, crisp and sharp, sweet when cooked. Very disease resistant. (Devon 18th Century)

## Topaz

Rubin x Vanda. A deep orange-red striped attractive colour. Juicy, sweet and firm initially, softening in storage. (This is a very disease resistant variety, good crops and a compact tree). (Germany 1984)

## Tydeman's Late Orange

Laxton's Superb x Cox's Orange Pippin. Orange-red colour with some russet. Firm and sweet. Trouble-free. As rich and aromatic as Cox when eaten before Christmas. (HRI, East Malling, Kent 1930)

## Warner's King

Very large, pale green fruit turning pale yellow with slight brown-pink flush. Juicy and acidic – cooks well to a sharp purée. (Kent 18th Century)

## William Crump

© Claire Higgins

Cox's Orange Pippin x Worcester Pearmain. Green-yellow with red stripes and orange-red flush. Rich, intense and aromatic mellowing to Cox flavour. (Worcester 1910)

## Winston

Cox's Orange Pippin x Worcester Pearmain. Green-yellow with dull purplish-red flush and attractive lenticels as russet dots. Flavour like Cox but sharper and will keep much longer. Will only ripen well in southern districts. (Berks. early 20th Century)

## Winter Banana

Known to develop an aromatic flavour and scent of banana and very juicy when ripe. Large, smooth skinned with a bright red flush on yellow background. (USA 1876)

## Winter Gem

Grimes Golden x Cox's Orange Pippin. Wins flavour contests consistently. Exceptional quality. Attractive pink flush. Rich and aromatic. A strong grower and needs good pollination as a shy cropper in some years. Best on a dwarf rootstock such as M27 or M9. Bred by Hugh Ermen. (Kent circa 1985)

## Worcester Pearmain

Reliable crop of delicious orange-red fruit. Firm, juicy flesh is very sweet with strong strawberry flavour. A seedling of Devonshire Quarrenden. At its best when ripened on the tree and just before it falls off. (Worcester 19th Century)

## Yellow Ingestrie

Orange Pippin x Golden Pippin. Greenish-yellow fruit turning yellow. Sharp, fruity and firm. A charming lawn tree due to its drooping habit. Highly decorative in table displays and kissing bows.
(Shropshire circa 1800)

## Yorkshire Greening

Cooks to a sharp pale green pureé. Good Flavour.
(York 1803)

# APRICOT

Apricots are often mistakenly considered tender. They are actually a very hardy plant that can be grown as a free standing tree and all varieties are self fertile. Their early flowering habit requires some caution and good air drainage is important to their fruiting potential in an open situation. If this is not possible, then growing on walls will enable easy protection from spring frosts.

## Alfred

This is a hardy and successful variety for our climate. Less prone to die-back than other varieties. (USA)

## Early Moorpark

An earlier form of this famous variety which was supposedly introduced from the continent to Moorpark, Herts. in the mid 18th Century. Skin pale yellow with an orange blush on the sunny side. Deep reddish-orange flesh, very juicy. Ideal for planting on walls or in a sheltered spot to protect from spring frost.

### Islam and horticulture

Islam's historic contribution to horticulture is perhaps no less than that it made to mathematics. In Spain especially a centre of horticultural expertise was established. Our word Apricot comes from the Spanish albaricoque, and this in turn comes from the Arab words al burquq. Places in Spain and Mexico named Alburquerque mean 'place of the apricot tree'.

## Goldcot

A good reliable modern variety. Quite vigorous and healthy with regular crops of good sized fruit. Selected for its suitability for cold wet climates such as the UK. The tree is very hardy, vigorous and resistant to leaf spot. The fruit are medium to large, golden yellow with quite a thick skin, making them ideal for storage in the fridge for some weeks. Also good for freezing and bottling. Freestone. (USA)

## Golden Glow

Found on the side of the Malvern Hills, this variety is very hardy. Crops and performs well as a free standing tree or trained on walls where spring frosts can be avoided. (Worcs. 1985)

## New Large Early

A very large fruit with an almost white skin and pale flesh. Slightly earlier than Early Moorpark. (circa 1873)

## Tomcot

This variety is far more reliable than other Apricots producing masses of flower and very large fruit with a strong red blush on an orange background. An intense apricot flavour. (USA)

   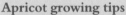

### Apricot growing tips
- Apricots do not suffer from peach leaf curl disease but they do get bacterial canker quite badly during prolonged wet weather (random dead branches and 'gumming' symptoms).
- Only prune in early summer (mid May) as part of the fruit thinning operation in heavy cropping years or after picking in light cropping years. If no crop then do not prune...never prune between and including October and April.
- Good drainage is essential.
- Pot growing is acceptable provided there is even moisture supply otherwise fruit can split when watered heavily after a dry period.
- As flowering is early when few pollinating insects are present, a touch with a camel hair brush or rabbit's tail is recommended to help with self pollination.
- For the very best success a southerly wall is perfect...they deserve a prime position.

# ASIAN PEAR

See Pears

# BULLACE

See Damsons

# CHERRY

For sweet cherries we recommend the planting of new, self fertile varieties on dwarf rootstocks, especially Gisela 5 which is ideal for orchard, garden and patio trees. These will fruit far better in the garden situation, as well as being easier to protect from birds. Fruit growers are planting orchards as far north as Perthshire, which gives an idea of their potential. Picking from late June to early September, the range of varieties now covers a lengthy season to suit all needs. The very reliable cooking 'Morello' cherries should be considered for north facing walls. Pollination: Due to various flower incompatibilities, the flowering times are not relevant and therefore not mentioned by symbol. Each variety, if not self fertile, states the best pollinator by variety.

## Bigarreau Gaucher Syn: *Gaucher*

Large, round, black. Flesh dark red, fairly firm, juicy, very good quality. Pollinated by Bradbourne Black and Stella. See also illustration on page 244. (Kent 1907)

## Black Oliver

Medium-large round black fruit. Flesh dark red, soft, juicy. Vigorous, upright spreading tree. Pollinated by Stella, Sunburst and Sweetheart. See illustration of tree on page 244. (West Midlands)

## Bradbourne Black

Very dark red with similar flesh. A vigorous tree with sweeping branches. Pollinated by Stella, Sunburst and Sweetheart. See illustration on page 244. (Kent)

## Celeste Syn: *Sumpaca*

Van x Newstar. Dark red, large, and of excellent eating quality. Ideal for patio growing due to its naturally dwarf compact habit. (Canada 1990)

## Colney

A true, large, black cherry of the finest eating quality. Less prone to splitting. Pollinated by Stella or Sunburst. (Norwich)

## Early Rivers

Large, heart-shaped, red to black. One of the earliest to ripen. Pollinated by Merton Glory, Noir de Guben or Stella. See also illustration on page 245. (Sawbridgeworth 1869)

## Kordia

A quality mid to late season, large, dark carmine-red to black heart shaped fruit of a good acidic/sweet balance. Penny and Van and any self-fertile variety will pollinate. (Czech Republic 1963)

## Lapins Cherokee

Van x Stella. Large, black fruit, a garden favourite. One of the first self fertile varieties to appear. Will shed its fruit readily when green but there is always plenty left to ripen later. Upright and strong growth habit. (Canada 1984)

## Merchant

One of the best early to ripen varieties. Highly productive, large black with good flavour. Pollinated by Merton Glory, Lapins and Noir de Guben. (Norwich circa 1970)

## Merton Bigarreau

Knights Early Black x Napoleon Bigarreau. A traditional high quality firm black cherry with outstanding flavour. Pollinated by Napoleon Bigarreau, Roundel and Stella.

## Merton Glory

Very large, sweet, heart-shaped fruit. An outstanding early white cherry. Shapely compact trees. Can bruise easily if roughly handled. Pollinated by Stella or Sunburst. (John Innes Institute, Surrey 1931)

# Cherries

*Loveliest of trees, the cherry now*
*Is hung with bloom along the bough*
*And stands about the woodland ride*
*Wearing white for Eastertide.*

A.E. Houseman,
'*A Shropshire Lad*' (1896)

## Modern varieties and rootstocks

New varieties and rootstocks are at the forefront of tree fruit improvements – and no more so than in very recent times with cherries. First came the self fertile forms like 'Stella', 'Sunburst' and 'Sweetheart', then genuinely dwarf rootstocks of which 'Gisela 5' is the current winner, and finally improved fruit size and quality with such varieties as 'Penny'.

The combination of these improvements also increases the tree's ability to hold its fruit through to ripening. In the past, on the more vigorous rootstocks, the tree would often shed its crop in May during cold weather.

See rootstock information for all fruit trees on page 286.

*Picture left shows a modern commercial tree on Gisela 5, compact and full of flower, all influenced by the rootstock. On the right the variety 'Celeste' in its second season, self fertile and very compact in habit.*

## Sour cherries

- Morello and all other sour cherries are self fertile.
- They will tolerate heavy shade and perform well on north facing walls.
- The birds will only take them when they are very ripe.
- Cherry pie and ice cream is a must.

## Fruit splitting

Logic suggests that fruit splitting is due to the impact of heavy rain on the tender ripening fruit. It is actually caused by a combination of circumstances. During and after rain, the tree takes up water through the roots too fast, the fruit swells too quickly and the high humidity in the air does not allow the pores of the skin to breathe – hence the splitting occurs. The best solution, in pots at least where watering is more controllable, is to keep the compost barely moist, using an old umbrella – and then place a net over this to deter the birds!

## Patio cherries

It is possible to grow any fruit tree in a pot especially on a dwarf rootstock. This is particularly so in the case of the modern cherry variety and rootstock combination as explained on page 286. Not only does this control growth and promote flower production, the resulting fruit have a very good chance of developing and ripening when net covered.

# Cherries
## by Norman H. Grubb

This wonderfully old-fashioned book is still considered by many as the definitive work on Cherry trees – more than half a century after its publication. The author, Norman H. Grubb, worked at the East Malling Research Institute in Kent which, from its foundation in 1913, made a unique contribution to the breeding of fruit-tree rootstocks. Until 1913, seedlings were used to provide rootstocks for propagation, but the fruit trees which resulted were of varying size and disease resistance. In 1917, East Malling Research Station introduced a range of clonally propagated dwarfing rootstocks that revolutionised the fruit industry. These produced smaller trees which did not compromise the size of fruit and were particularly suitable for domestic gardens. It is estimated that up to 80% of the world's orchard trees today grow on rootstocks originating from East Malling. And as well as rootstocks, the centre has been the source of a wide range of fruit, ornamental plants and trees.

CHERRIES

BY
NORMAN H. GRUBB
EAST MALLING RESEARCH STATION

FOREWORD BY
H. V. TAYLOR
C.B.E., D.SC., B.SC.(CHEM.), A.R.C.S., V.M.H.

PLATE XIV.

FIG. 3.—BLACK OLIVER.

FIG. 4.—VICTORIA BLACK A.

**Black Oliver**
See description on page 240.

PLATE I

BIGARREAU GAUCHER

**Bigarreau Gaucher** Syn: *Gaucher*
See description on page 240.

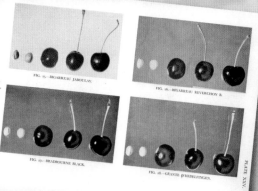

FIG. 45—BIGARREAU JABOULAY.

FIG. 46—BIGARREAU REVERCHON B.

FIG. 47—BRADBOURNE BLACK.

FIG. 48—GEANTE D'HEDELFINGEN.

PLATE XXV.

**Bradbourne Black**
See description on page 240.

**Early Rivers**
See description on page 241.

**Napoleon Bigarreau**
See description on page 246.

**Noir de Guben**
See description on page 246.

**Roundel Heart**
See description on page 246.

## Morello

The popular cooking cherry. Acid flavour. Very hardy and very reliable cropping. Ideal for north walls and makes the most delicious cherry pie, just add ice cream! 'Nabella' is often available which is another good sour cherry with slightly larger fruit.

## Napoleon Bigarreau

An old fashioned variety with large, long, heart-shaped fruit. An excellent white cherry with a shiny finish. Pollinated by Bigarreau Gaucher, Merton Bigarreau, Stella and Sunburst. See illustration on page 245. (Germany)

## Noir de Guben

A large, dark red to black cherry with a distinctive heart-shape. The fruit resists cracking well and has a good shelf life. Pollinated by Colney, Early Rivers or Merton Glory. See illustration on page 245. (Germany)

## Penny

An outstanding quality black cherry that is firm, large and very late in the season. A recent UK introduced variety and one of the best commercial cherries for fruit growers. Not self fertile but is pollinated by any other self fertile variety. (East Malling, Kent 1998)

## Roundel Heart

Large, heart-shaped, red to dark red. One of the old varieties of excellent quality. Pollinated by Stella and Sunburst. See illustration on page 245. (Kent)

## Stella

Lambert x J.I.2420. This was the first self fertile sweet cherry to appear that set a standard for modern high yielding varieties for garden and orchard. A large, dark red, reliable, sweet, juicy cherry with good flavour. (Canada 1968)

## Summer Sun

This variety is very hardy and produces crops even in unfavourable areas. A good bushy shape makes the tree easy to manage. Fruits are red to dark red, firm and crunchy and have an exquisite flavour. Sets fair crops on its own, but more prolific if pollinated by any other self fertile variety. (Norwich 1970)

## Sunburst

Van x Stella. Large fruit, sweet with great flavour and texture. Self fertile and easy to pick. (Canada 1975)

## Sweetheart

Van x Newstar. Very precocious, firm, with good flavour. One of the later picking varieties but well worth the wait as fewer cherries are available in the shops at this time. Ripens unevenly to spread the season. A good pollinator. (Canada 1990)

## Van

An old variety from Canada used in breeding of the self fertile modern varieties. A very firm and large, true black. Eating quality is superb. Pollinated by Lapins, Stella or Vega. (Canada 1944)

## Vega

A very large, white exhibition cherry often over 12 gms in weight. Exquisite flavour. Pollinated by Lapins or Stella. (Canada)

# CHESTNUT

There are several named varieties of sweet chestnut, selected for the large size and superior quality of their nuts, among which we consider those listed below to be suitable for the UK, certainly in southern areas. They are generally early to harvest and should have some disease tolerance for our changeable climate. Fruiting should begin within two – four years of planting.

## Maraval

A mid-season hybrid variety, upright with moderate vigour, producing shiny, dark mahogany-red nuts.

## Marlhac

Laquepie x C. crenata. An early mid-season hybrid. Vigorous tree with large, mahogany-red nuts that will store well.

### Chestnut Facts

- The Botanical name of the sweet Chestnut tree is Castanea sativa. Spanish castanets are often made from the hard wood of the chestnut tree.
- Chestnuts are happier on light soils, acid to neutral is best, avoid chalk if possible and they will fruit better in southern England.
- They dislike water logged soils, which encourage 'ink disease' (phytophoracinnamomi and P. cambivora) symptoms being a black liquid oozing from the trunks.
- They are also a traditional wood used for fencing and coppicing, see ornamental section page 73.
- They need to be cooked before eating and will explode unless scored first – nature's big popcorn!
- For heavy crops another variety needs to be planted within 50 metres as a 'wind blown' pollinator.
- Harvest the nuts daily to avoid the attention of hungry vermin.
- Inflatable plastic snakes have been used to scare away squirrels!
- They are prone to frost, so are best planted on the upper levels of sloping ground.

For interesting and thorough information on many native, fruiting and forestry trees contact the Agroforestry Research Trust. www.agroforestry.co.uk

## Marigoule

This is an early variety with large, dark brown marron nuts. The best variety to plant on its own if only space for a single tree.

## Marsol

An early mid season. Very large with good storage and best for wet areas due to its resistance to anthracnose and ink disease.

## CORNELIAN CHERRY

There are several 'fruiting' forms of the ornamental tree Cornus mas and these are known as the Cornelian Cherry. These specially bred forms, primarily from eastern Europe, have large fruit for making into highly nutritious jellies and compotes. They also have attractive, small but abundant yellow flowers in February to cheer the winter landscape. These specialist 'fruit' trees should become more available in the near future. Cornus mas is described in the Ornamental Section.

# FIG

These wonderful deciduous trees can be very successful in the UK if grown in sheltered sites and allowed some space. They will be surprisingly large and spread up to 3m. 'Bayernfeige Violetta', 'Brown Turkey' and 'Ice Crystal' are the best for outdoor growing and the others would benefit from reasonable shelter.

## Bayernfeige Violetta

This is a unique fig. Not only does it have luscious, sweet, dark red flesh with a superb flavour it is also extremely hardy to -20°C. It can mature early in late July and is very heavy cropping. (Germany)

## Brown Turkey

Large, brown, pear-shaped fruit with a sugary, rich, red flesh and a good compact habit.

## Brunswick

Large pear-shaped fruit with green-yellow skin. Yellow flesh with a red centre. Leaves are 'hand' shaped.

## Dalmatie

Very large, green fuit of high quality and attractive foliage.

## Ice Crystal

Very unusual, deeply divided leaves that appear in the shape of ice crystals making this a very ornamental plant. It is very hardy and also produces small, sweet, edible fruits.

## Noir de Carron

As suggested in the name this is a black fig of very high quality eating.

## White Marseilles

Large, round, pale green fruit with translucent white flesh.

## Fig facts

- Only the small embryonic fruit that appear in the spring on the tips of the previous year's growth will develop into ripe fruit in the UK in August and September. A second crop appears later in the summer but these fruit will not mature and should be removed in the autumn as they can attract mould and then wood infection.
- All varieties grown from cuttings are female and will produce fruit.
- Figs in pots are ideal as they can be given a sunny spot, moved inside if necessary and have their roots restricted to reduce vegetative growth and encourage fruiting.
- Figs are full of natural sugars and minerals including calcium and iron and are good for treating warts.
- 'Syrup of figs' is a laxative and good for diabetics.

## Growing tips

- Hard pruning is recommended to encourage young replacement shoots on old 'woody' plants.
- Figs ooze a white sap when pruned in spring or summer. This is not harmful but can cause irritation to the skin.
- Even centuries old neglected barren figs can be rejuvenated by heavy pruning.
- Pinching out of strong growing tips in mid summer encourages the development and ripening of the current crop.

# DAMSON

Damsons, with their richly astringent flavour, are peculiar to England, and are easily grown in most situations. They originate from the native plum, Prunus insititia from which Bullaces, Mirabelles and the Delmas Fruit also arise. The 'Westmorland' damson is famous in the Kendal area and has an enthusiastic local following. Damsons were grown primarily in the past as a dye for clothes and uniforms. The 'Sloe' or 'Blackthorn' also present in our hedgerows is Prunus spinosa widely dispersed in Europe, Asia and north Africa.

The word Damson comes from the Medieval English damascene and the Latin damascenum. It means, literally, the Plum of Damascus. This city in what is now Syria has long been a centre of trade. It was whilst on his way to this city that Paul the tax gatherer is said to have converted to Christianity.

Damsons are so versatile, being used for gin, beer, wine, vinegar, jam, cheese, jelly and even chocolate. Some, such as 'Blue Violet', 'Delma' and 'Merryweather' are even eaten fresh.

## Blue Violet

A famous 'early' damson from Westmorland first brought to notice between the Wars. A true sweet 'dessert' fruit more of plum quality. Dropping from the tree very early in mid August. Slightly oval-shaped tapering to the apex. Dark blue-black with an attractive bloom. (Kendal 1932)

## Delma

This is an early picking variety that is sweet and able to be eaten fresh or made into delicious jam, cheese or compote. It will often harvest at the end of August. Found by chance in her garden in Hampshire, Delma Grant brought this interesting variety to notice in 1997. It is unique and recognised as a distinctive form in its own right.

### Damson Cheese
*Keith Atkey's Grandmother's recipe*

Damson Cheese, there is nothing remotely cheesy about it! Even nicer than damson jam and more flavoursome than damson jelly.

*Ingredients*
- 6lb damsons • 1 pint water
- 1lb sugar to each lb of fruit pulp
  (or 1¼lb to each pint of pulp)

Wash damsons and stew them in water until tender. Rub through a sieve, using a wooden spoon. Weigh pulp obtained, place in a pan and add an equal weight of sugar; stir until it comes to the boil and simmer for 15-20 minutes. Test on a cold plate for jelling; as soon as it sets pour into hot jars and cover immediately.

## Farleigh

PLATE VIII.

DAMSON FARLEIGH

*This colour plate is from 'The Plums of England' by H.V. Taylor published in 1949, see the plum section on page 274 for further information.*

Very small with a blue-black bloom. Good quality. Known to be very hardy and most likely to crop regularly in northern districts. (Farleigh, Kent 1820)

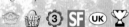

## King of the Damsons Syn: *Bradleys King*

Blue-black bloom and large fruit. Reliable cropper in mid September. (Notts. 1880)

## Langley Bullace

Farleigh x Early Orleans. Small round to round-oblong, blue-black with a good bloom. Picking mid October. Self fertile. (Raised by Veitch 1902)

## Merryweather

© *Claire Higgins*

An unusually large plum sized damson both for dessert and culinary use. Reliable heavy crops. Self fertile. (Nottingham 1907)

## Shropshire Prune

© *Claire Higgins*

The 'Greengage of Damsons'. Native of the West Midlands. Small hedgerow damson – very reliable cropper with intense flavour. Similar to the 'Westmorland' damson. (Shropshire 17th Century)

# FILBERT

Closely related to the Hazels and Cobs, the Filbert is considered superior to both for size and flavour, although the crops are less heavy. When eaten 'green' in September they are succulent and their flavour delicate. They can also be collected for winter storage – if we can beat the squirrels! Pollination: Any two varieties, including Hazels, will cross pollinate. However, specific pollinators are mentioned where known. If planting near a hedge containing the wild nut (Corylus avellana), a pollinator is less essential.

## Cosford

Slightly larger than the Cobnut with a long husk (full beard). Good pollinator for other varieties. Pollinated by Gunslebert Hazel.

## Red Filbert

Also listed in our Ornamental Section. This worthy selection has striking long, claret red catkins, rich purple foliage and very edible purple skinned fruits.

Filberts are named as such because they were known to ripen (in France at least) around St. Philberts day – 22nd August. There are other connections between Christian saints and fruit. St. Malachy has an apple as his symbol, St. Uban has a vine, whilst St. Nicholas has three golden apples. St. Nicholas is, among other things, the patron saint of pawnbrokers, the three balls of the pawnbrokers shop representing the saint's apples.

# GAGE

Gages are small plums that have a more delicate constitution but with superior flavour and sugar content. They are often shy to crop but will have the occasional good year where patience will be rewarded. Green, yellow and red fruiting forms are available. Generally the yellow gages are better cropping and with comparable flavour to the green types.

## Cambridge

Small, yellowish-green, juicy fruit, reliable. Good cropper and self fertile. Prefers a sheltered warm site. Will cross pollinate with plums. (Cambridgeshire)

## Coe's Golden Drop

Green Gage x Dame Aubert. Large, yellow gage, oval-shaped with a long neck. Good quality for fresh eating or preserving. It is supposed to be stored in good condition for many months by hanging in a dry place or wrapping in tissue paper, according to Lindley's 'Guide to the Orchard'. (Suffolk 18th Century)

## Denniston's Superb Syn: *Imperial Gage*

The most reliable cropping gage. Transparent sweet flesh with red flushed skin. High yields. Recommended for Midlands and Northern regions. Average quality. (USA 19th Century)

## Early Transparent

A most unusual gage with very sweet golden melting flesh. Large with an attractive red cheek. Regular cropper. (Herts. 19th Century)

## Jefferson

A medium, round, yellow gage, very sweet. A hardy selection suitable for open areas and northern districts. Pollinated by Denniston's Superb.
(USA 19th Century)

## Old Green Gage

This form was selected by the RHS for its excellent old fashioned flavour and more reliable crops. Partially self fertile. (UK)

## Oullins Golden

Large, golden yellow fruit of good gage-like flavour. Can be picked early for cooking. Excellent for bottling and freezing. (France 1860)

## Reine Claude de Bavay

This variety is the same as the imported gages we see in the shops. A very reliable cropper and if allowed to ripen on the tree is well flavoured. (Belgium 1832)

## Stella's Star Syn: *Hector's Greengage*

A variety introduced by the late plant breeder Hector Harrison. This self fertile greengage is very productive from an early age. Turns slightly yellow when ripening. The flavour is not intense, but is compensated for by such a productive tree.

## Willingham

As with the Old Green Gage form this was selected by the RHS for its good cropping and excellent quality. Found in the native hedgerows around Willingham in Cambridgeshire this is one of the finest eating qualities. (Cambridge)

# HAZELNUT

The varieties listed here have been selected for their heavy, regular crops. The catkins are also prolific and provide some late winter cheer to the garden. As with Filberts, picking can begin in September for fresh eating or left until fallen to the ground for collection for winter storage. See also 'Trazels'. Pollination: Any two varieties, including Filberts, will cross pollinate. However, specific pollinators are mentioned where known. If planting near a hedge containing the wild nut (Corylus avellana), a pollinator is less essential.

## Butler

Large nut, very good texture, strong flavour. Moderately vigorous tree, heavy cropper. Pollinated by Gunslebert or Filbert Cosford. (USA)

## Gunslebert

Medium-large nut with good texture and a strong nutty flavour. Moderate vigour, very heavy and reliable cropper. Clusters of six or more nuts. Exceptional catkin display in winter. Pollinated by Butler. Good pollinator for Filbert Cosford. (Germany)

## Gustav's Zeller

One of several more recent commercial selections producing two or three times the crop of the old Kentish Cob and with much larger fruit. Pollinated by Butler and Gunslebert.

## Hall's Giant Syn: *Merveille de Bolwiller*
Very large attractive nut with glossy rust-brown shell. Resistant to nut gall mite. Excellent quality. Best in a sheltered well drained site. Pollinated by Filbert Cosford and Gunslebert. (France)

## Kentish Cob

The traditional cob is planted extensively in Kent to this day and is unique for its history and cultural heritage within Kent. There is an enthusiastic following amongst its growers who are members of the Kentish Cobnut Association. www.kentishcobnutsassociation.co.uk. It is a species of its own and is not technically a hazel. Medium large nuts in clusters of two to five fruits of excellent texture and flavour. Compact tree habit. Can be slightly biennial.

## Lange Tidling Zeller

A modern variety with similarly large and heavy crops of quality nuts to Gustav's Zeller, with extra long attractive catkins and a compact tree shape. The most suitable pollinators would be Gustav's Zeller and Gunslebert. (Denmark)

### Hazel facts

- Hazels are the only native British nut.
- Contain healthy mono-saturated fats.
- After coppicing, sturdy vigorous one year shoots are used for basket weaving, hurdles, the top of newly laid hedges or pegs for thatching.
- The name 'filbert' is possibly a corruption of 'full beard' referring to the long husk - or St. Philberts day (August 22nd).
- Best grown on shallow, less than fertile soils.
- Yellow male flowers (catkins) and the female small red stigmas are produced on separate parts of the same tree. Self pollination is however only partially reliable in good weather and pollinating partners are recommended.
- Empty shells (blanks) are a sign of poor pollination.
- 'plats' are a Kentish name for a hazel/cobnut orchard.
- Cobnut is a specific variety of hazel only grown commercially in Kent.
- Common pests include weevils, winter moths, aphids and gall mites, none of which reach epidemic proportions and require no spraying in a domestic situation.
- Summer pruning is recommended in the form of 'brutting' see pruning section page 294.
- Hazels and even walnuts can be stored 'wet' in winter in moist sand and will remain edible and in good condition until they germinate.

## Tonda di Giffoni

A moderately vigorous and precocious variety. A large nut with easy 'husk' removal. One of the first to leaf out and yet retains its foliage long into the autumn. Pollinated by Gunslebert and Butler. (Italy)

## KIWI

Luscious health giving fruit for sheltered sites. Also hardy, vigorous, twining climbers, with highly ornamental leaves and flowers, excellent for covering walls or stumps.

## Solo

A reliable, self fertile, very free flowering and fruiting form. Fruit almost round, slightly smaller than other cultivated varieties, maturing in January, can serve as a pollinator for other cultivars.

# LOQUAT

The Loquat (Japanese medlar or plum) *Eriobtrya japonica* is a native of eastern Asia and often found in our gardens as a semi-hardy evergreen large shrub or small tree planted for its attractive foliage. Any fruiting ability of this species is generally confined to the southern counties and the fruit will only mature in the late autumn in the best of summers. It is however possible that with new selected cultivars these trees will eventually give regular fruit production in the UK. Loquats prefer a well-drained loam although they seem to cope with sandy or clay soils. Yellowish, white fragrant flowers are produced on the ends of new growth and these are self fertile.

# MEDLAR

Medlars require reverential consideration for their unusual fruit and the ornamental features of the tree.

### Nottingham

An attractive small tree, flat topped, with a spreading semi-weeping habit. The small russet fruits can be eaten when fully ripe from October onwards. Even when quite young the tree takes on a picturesque and architectural appearance. The flowers are large and pure white and the large leathery leaves turn a lovely russet-copper colour in autumn.

### Royal

Although smaller in size to Nottingham the fruit of this variety has better flavour and is one of the few to be taken slightly seriously for fresh eating.

### Palatable or otherwise

When picked, the fruit should be stored in sawdust in stone jars until soft (bletting) and eaten with wine, port and cheese, or made into excellent jelly. Not everyone's cup of tea; Bunyard in his 'Anatomy of Dessert' likened Medlars and Dickens as equally distasteful.

'Quiets the heated stomach'. This old saying has been scientifically supported by findings that show pectins, sugars, tannins and gums in medlars to be in ideal combination for easing indigestion.

# MIRABELLE

These interesting fruits, usually small and sweet, often crop in abundance. Golden Sphere, Gypsy and Ruby have been bred in the Ukraine, are dessert quality and can be used for a host of bottling and other culinary uses. All mirabelles are partially self fertile and will benefit from a companion variety or will cross pollinate with the early flowering plums in groups one and two.

## de Nancy

Yellow-orange with green tinges and red spots. Very small, roundish-ovate, freestone. Partially self fertile. Resistant to frost. Eat fresh from the tree or use for bottling and preserves. (France 16th Century)

## Golden Sphere

Large, yellow almost translucent fruit with golden flesh and a sweet plummy flavour. Partially self fertile.

## Gypsy

Large, bright red fruit with a sweet orange flesh. The flavour is sugary and rich. Partially self fertile.

## Ruby

This is the largest fruit of the mirabelles recorded with exceptionally sweet peach flavoured dark red flesh. The tree is unusually upright in habit in comparison to the wide spreading bushy habit of most varieties. Partially self fertile.

# MULBERRY

Trees of great character that become gnarled and picturesque with age. Eventually they fall over but continue to survive. They have large, broad, heart shaped leaves turning butter yellow in the autumn. The delicious fruit have a sharp and intense flavour.

## Chelsea Syn: *King James I*

There is a fascinating history to this black mulberry. It is derived from a tree that existed in the 17th century, in a garden in Swan Walk, which became the Chelsea Physic Garden, during the time of King James I. During the 1939/45 war the last remaining tree was about to be grubbed to make way for an air shelter when cuttings were taken and this variety has survived ever since in the trees of this name.

Unusually large and succulent fruit cropping early in life. Harvesting is best done each day. If hand picked the fruit will be bruised causing staining to fingers and clothes – children enjoy the experience of course! For a clean operation take a large sheet and lay it under the tree and shake the boughs vigorously. Any perfectly ripe fruit will fall and are subsequently gathered with ease. An intensely rich flavour. Add sugar, microwave, seive and pour over ice cream!

*Mulberry bark*

# NECTARINE

The smooth skinned peach is often considered to have a superior flavour to its well loved cousin. Varieties such as Lord Napier and Pineapple were bred by Rivers at Sawbridgeworth in the late 19th and early 20th century, and have a superb flavour.

## Humboldt

Raised from a seedling of Pineapple. Orange fleshed and richly flavoured. The tree produces flowers freely. (Rivers of Sawbridgeworth)

## Lord Napier

One of the earliest and largest of all the nectarines. The skin has a very dark crimson cheek in full sun. Flesh very white, melting and juicy. The flesh separates well from the stone (freestone). (Sawbridgeworth 1860)

## Nectarella

A dwarf nectarine of very good quality. Sweet orange-red flesh and a freestone. Like Garden Lady Peach, this genetic dwarf is very slow growing and would be ideal for pot growing, making it very easy to protect this tree under cover in the spring from 'leaf curl' disease. See page 261.

## Pineapple

A clean pale skinned variety with yellow flesh and rich aromatic flavour slightly reminiscent of a sprightly pineapple. (Rivers of Sawbridgeworth)

# PEACH

This luscious fruit comes from Persia (Prunus persica). Included here are the classic traditional English varieties bred by the Rivers Nursery in Hertfordshire in the latter part of the 19th century, all of exceptional quality.

Growing tips: Both white and yellow fleshed varieties are available. Fan training on a sheltered wall (except north facing) is recommended to avoid leaf curl. Picking times relate to growing under glass, therefore if planting outside at least two weeks need to be added. All varieties are self fertile. Early flowering outside make these trees prone to frost damage. Fruit is best picked when still firm for final ripening indoors.

## Amsden June

The earliest ripening peach. White skin with a bright red blush. White flesh, freestone. Very tender and juicy. (Missouri, USA circa 1865)

## Bellegarde

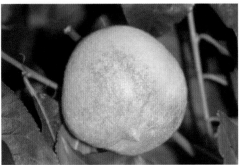

Deep red skin striped with dark purple. Flesh pale yellow, slightly red at the stone. Rich, vinous and juicy. (France 18th Century, known UK since 1732)

## Duke of York

One of the finest early white fleshed peaches. The flavour is intense and aromatic and the flesh very soft and juicy. (Rivers of Sawbridgeworth 1902)

## Garden Lady

A genetic dwarf peach with beautiful pink flowers. The fruit has yellowish flesh which is sweet and juicy. It is best used as a patio tree. As with Nectarine Nectarella, if grown in a pot, this tree can be moved inside during the early spring. See 'Leaf curl disease' opposite. Freestone. (New Zealand)

## Hale's Early

This is a hardy early variety for our climate. Skin is crimson streaked, flesh pale yellow, tender, melting and delicious. Freestone. Produces heavy crops. (USA)

## Kestrel

A beautiful white fleshed peach, full of flavour. (Rivers of Sawbridgeworth)

## Peregrine

Still the most revered of all white fleshed peaches. The flavour is intense and rich. Heavy cropping and suitable for sheltered situations. Freestone. (Rivers of Sawbridgeworth 1906)

## Red Haven

A firm, yellow flesh of good quality. The flowers are small and dark pink. Freestone. (USA)

## Rochester

The largest and most suitable of yellow fleshed types for outdoor cultivation. The flavour is very good with soft and juicy texture. Reliable cropper. Flowers late, missing early frosts.

## Royal George

Later to ripen than most, this delicate variety needs careful choice of situations and is best for southern walls only. Crops heavily, round, juicy flesh with a very rich flavour. Also good under glass.
(Known UK 18th Century)

## Saturn Syn: *Java Peach*

An unusual, small, flat-shaped fruit, very sweet and succulent orange flesh, ideal for children especially with its nick-name Sat-on!

**Leaf curl disease**
Picture above shows an innovative shelter (courtesy RHS Wisley) to keep a trained peach tree dry during the spring but allowing ventilation and access by pollinating insects. Keeping rain off the tree at this time of year will prevent leaf curl disease and frost damage. Several varieties have been released in recent times with claims of leaf curl resistance. It is hoped that they prove to be reliable in this respect.

**No pruning**
The picture below shows a peach 'Garden Lady'. This and the nectarine 'Nectarella' are ideal for low maintenance trees for very small spaces, requiring no pruning.

# ASIAN PEAR

These distinctive pears, often seen in shops, resemble russet apples in appearance. They have very crisp white flesh, with a mild strawberry flavour, and are excellent as a dessert of salad fruit. They can be stored in the fridge for some time. The trees are strong growing, with attractively tinted foliage. Due to their early flowering, they are most productive when grown with the protection of a wall. Several Asian pears x European pears have now been bred and these are closer to the Asian pear than the ordinary pear in appearance and flavour.

## Kumoi

A beautiful, rich golden russet finish makes this 'Nashi/Chinese' pear also an ornamental tree. Flavour is better than other varieties and the fruit can be kept for many weeks in the fridge. (Asia)

## Shinseiki

One of the first varieties to appear in the UK and has been a consistent cropper. Has very attractive leaves with bronze tinted young growth. (Asia)

## Tree names in our settlements

The names of fruit and other trees feature prominently in the way the landscape is described the world over. There are towns called *Almond* in both New York and Wisconsin, USA, and a *Mount Almond* in British Columbia, Canada, which stands at 2318m above sea level.

Other allusions stretch from *Applewood* in Colorado to Antarctica, on which no tree has grown for thousands of years, which has an *Apple Glacier* and a *Cherry Island*. As you'd expect from the ubiquitous Birch, places named after that tree stretch from British Columbia to the Cayman Islands, from New Zealand to the wonderfully descriptive *Birchy Bay* in Newfoundland.

Closer to home it is in the naming of villages and towns that the connection is most striking. We find *Almondbury* in the West Riding of Yorkshire, and *Almondsbury* near Bristol. *Appleby* in Westmoreland is echoed by settlements called *Appledore* in Devon and in Kent with *Appleton Wiske* and *Appletreewick* in North Yorkshire. Near Blackburn you'll find a village called *Cherry Tree* and near Cambridge, *Cherry Hinton*. There are plenty of hazels: *Hazel Grove, Hazel End* and *Hazel Bank*; there are *Pear Tree Greens* and *Perry Greens* in both Essex and Hertfordshire and there is a place called *Plumtree* south east of Nottingham.

There are *Ashfords* in Ireland and Kent, and *Eight Ash Green* near Colchester. We find *Alderford* in the fen country near Norwich, and *Aldershot* in Surrey. We have *Beech Hill* and *Beech Wood* and not to be outdone by the rest of the world we have places called *Birch* in Essex and Manchester plus Birch Greens, Heaths, Woods, and Vales! We can find *Crabtrees* in South Yorkshire and West Sussex, *Elm Park, Elm Bridge* and indeed *Elm* itself near Wisbech. As you might expect the oak features prominently with *Oak Cross, Oakington, Oaklands, Oak Green* (to name but a few) together with *Fair Oak, Five Oaks* in the Channel Islands, and *Five Oaks* in Wessex (not to be confused with *Five Ashes* in East Sussex) and *Five Oak Green* in Kent. *Willow Green* near Northwich in Cheshire and *Yew Green* near Warwick round off our tour, but this small taste of the ways in which trees of one kind or another inform the naming of our settlements can be greatly enhanced by a study of the Ordnance Survey map of your own area, which will reveal many, many more. One final thought: try walking round the streets in your own neighbourhood and see how many are named after trees of one kind or another. You might be surprised!

PEARTREE · YARD

# PEAR

To many fruit lovers the pear is the queen of fruits especially when eaten at that perfect moment. It is that 'moment' that is often hard to predict. This combines picking not too early and ripening not too fast. When in balance the experience is sensational. Pears sold in shops are so often unable to reach this peak, so the home gardener has an opportunity to fulfill a worthy challenge.

As with apples, pears have a rich history but many have their origins in other countries. Those that are derived from the UK are generally the best for our gardens. They respond well to spur pruning so cordons and other trained forms are highly recommended. Due to their distinctive historical relevance there is a separate section for perry pears on page 271.

© Sue Griffith

## Beth

Beurré Superfin x Williams' Bon Chrétien. An excellent garden variety. Pale green, turning to pale yellow with smooth skin. Small, sweet, juicy flesh. Good cropper. (Kent 1938)

## Beurré Hardy

Medium-large, light green almost covered with bronze russet. Rough skin. Tender and juicy with rose water flavour. Good cropper. Vigorous tree and good for poor soils. (France 1820)

### Fruit Ripening

The secret to eating pears at their best is to pick (unhook the fruit) just before they are ripe to reduce bruising but with enough sugars to develop the flavour during the final ripening process.

## Beurré Superfin

Medium size, mid-green turning yellow with many light brown russet patches. Rough skin. Pale yellow melting flesh has delicious scented flavour. A high quality pear which does not crop well in all areas, but well worth growing in warm sheltered sites. (Angers, France 1837)

## Black Worcester
Syn: *Parkins's Warden: Pound Pear*

Large, dull green almost wholly covered with brown russet. Many fruits have purplish flush. Crisp, coarse, fairly juicy flesh. An excellent stewing pear. This is a type of 'Warden' pear, see below. When Queen Elizabeth visited Worcester in 1575, on noticing the tree and its beautiful fruit she directed that it should be added to the Arms of the City. (16th Century)

### Cooking Pears

These were originally known as 'Warden' pears after Warden Abbey in Bedfordshire where they were first cultivated in the UK. Most varieties, such as Catillac ripen very late and if prepared in the autumn will take hours of cooking. Store for as long as possible, even if this is well after Christmas, and they will cook in half the time. Besides, this is still nature's way to provide nourishment during the long harsh winters.

## Catillac

Large, dull green fruit changing to greenish-yellow. Some fruits develop an attractive red flush and slight russet. Only suitable for cooking, and turns pink in the process, but also a good exhibition pear for its even round shape and general good looks. Vigorous spreading growth. Heavy cropping. (France 1665)

### Celebration Syn: *Nuvar Celebration*

Conference x Packham's Triumph. A large 'pyriform' fruit of excellent dessert quality. Light green on a yellow background. The tree is strong growing and healthy. (Kent 1972)

## Concorde

Conference x Doyenné du Comice. Medium to large fruit. Pale green turning yellow, some with large patches of gold or brown russet. Pale yellow flesh is sweet and juicy with a pleasant mild flavour. Very heavy cropping and compact grower. Recognised as one of the best varieties for organic growing. (Kent 1977)

## Conference

One of the most reliable varieties with good self fertility. Medium size yellowish-green with brown russet over areas of the fruit, occasionally pink flushed on chalk soil. Sweet and juicy. Good cropper. (Herts. 19th Century)

## Doyenné d'Été

Bright green changing to pale yellow. Sweet and moderately juicy. One of the earliest of pears to ripen. (Raised by Capucin Monks. France circa 1700)

## Doyenné du Comice

A superb quality pear. Medium-large, pale green changing to yellow. Some fruits have a red flush. Pale yellow flesh has rich juicy flavour. Recognised for superb eating quality but needs good pollination – Conference or Williams' Bon Chrétien would be ideal. (France 19th Century)

## Durondeau

Medium to large with attractive lenticels and red to brown russet skin. The white moderately juicy flesh has a sweet pleasant flavour. (Belgium 1811)

## Émile d'Heyst

Light green, medium size fruit, turning to yellowish-green. Some solid and some mottled areas of russet. The flesh is green under the skin turning yellow in the centre and has a moderately juicy, sweet subacid flavour. Can be grown successfully in the North of England and Scotland. (Belgium 1847)

## Fondante d'Automne

High quality and quite reliable, a good garden variety. A green turning yellow fruit with a pinkish flush with mottled brown russet. A fine melting juicy texture. (France 1825)

## Glou Morceau

Medium to large size fruit is pea green turning to pale yellowish-green, with very little russet. An excellent pear with fine, melting and juicy texture and a classic pear flavour. Reliable cropper. Good pollinator for other varieties. (Mons, Belgium 1750)

## Gorham

Pale green turning yellow. Some fruits are heavily russeted. Cream, fine and juicy flesh with a sweet musky flavour. A reliable pear. (New York, USA 1910)

## Humbug Syn: *Pysanka*

This highly unusual green, yellow and pink striped pear offers something very special for the garden. In its native country it is known as the 'Easter Pear' as it is traditionally stored through winter and paraded as a table decoration before eating at Easter time to celebrate the onset of spring. It has a sweet and juicy texture despite its rather thick skin. The tree is healthy and even the young shoots appear stripey in winter. (Ukraine)

## Invincible Delwilnor
### Syn: *Delwilnor Fertilia*

Invincible is well named because it is tough and hardy, setting heavy crops each year and will often produce a second flowering after a heavy frost. The fruit quality is fair with a host of dessert and cooking options. The strength is in its yield and precocity. Would make an ideal pollinator for other varieties in a similar flowering period. Ideal for exposed areas where a pear tree is a must.

## Jargonelle

Pale yellow with brownish-red flush on some fruits. The pale yellow flesh is tender and juicy with a musky flavour. One of the hardiest and longest lived pears, making a majestic tree. Performs well in the north if on a sheltered wall. Like many earlies it can drop from the tree unexpectedly. (1629)

## Josephine de Malines

A small, conical, greenish-yellow variety of delicious flavour with a dark red flush. Sweet and moderately juicy. Shows good resistance to pear scab. Keeps very well. (Belgium 1830)

## Louise Bonne of Jersey

Small-medium, pale green turning yellowish-green fruit, with a dark red flush. White flesh is melting and sweet. Good quality and reliable cropper. Moderately vigorous. (France 1780)

Despite its name, the pear Louise Bonne of Jersey was raised around 1780 at Avranches in Normandy. Perhaps it came to the United Kingdom via the Channel Islands. Even before this there are strong historic links between fruit tree varieties in France and England, links that were greatly strengthened by contact between members of monastic orders on either side of the Channel.

## Merton Pride

Glou Morceau x Double Williams. Large, green fruit turning yellow, most with some russet. Creamy white flesh is soft, sweet and juicy, with excellent pear flavour. Good cropper. Excellent garden variety. (John Innes Institute. Surrey 1941)

## Moonglow

Bright lemon skin when ripe. Mid season, similar to Williams' Bon Chrétien, but with a finer flavour and texture. (USA 1960)

## Onward

Laxton's Superb x Doyenné du Comice. This is an excellent quality pear, quite resistant to spring frosts. Medium size. Light green fruit changes to yellow-green, some with a pinkish flush and others a heavy russet. Creamy white flesh has a sweet rich and juicy flavour. Good cropper. Will not pollinate Doyenné du Comice. (Wisley, Surrey 1947)

## Packham's Triumph

Medium fruit prone to being small, when it can frequently crop very heavily. Bright green changing to pale yellow with occasional russet. Has an unusual bumpy appearance. Pale yellow flesh is juicy, with a musky flavour. Crops and keeps well. Compact growth. (Australia 19th Century)

## Pitmaston Duchess

Duchess d'Angoulême x Glou Morceau. Very large, long, golden-yellow russeted fruit. The yellowish white flesh is juicy with a rich flavour. One of the finest eating quality. Shy cropper but partially self-fertile despite being a triploid. Vigorous habit. (Pitmaston, Worcestershire 1841)

## Precoce de Trevoux

One of the finest flavoured pears but early flowering so would benefit from a sheltered site. An attractive fruit flushed carmine red, with some russet streaks. A buttery rich flavour with a musk perfume. (France 1862)

## Robine Syn: *Royale d'Été*

Rather similar to the 'Bergamot'. Small, green turning yellow with small brown dots and an open 'eye'. White, crisp flesh with a dry but sugary, musky flavour.

## Sensation

A sport of Williams' Bon Chrétien, with red skin and striking red foliage in the spring. Creamy-white, fine texture, melting and juicy. Best pollinators are Conference, Doyenné du Comice and Winter Nelis. (Australia 1940)

## Shipova

The 'Bollwyller Pear'. The best of the Sorbus x Pyrus (Sorbopyrus) rare intergeneric hybrids between the pear and the whitebeam. A small to medium sized tree with very attractive white flowers and large leaves felted beneath. The fruit are typical 'pear', small and quite delicious. A good ornamental fruiting tree.

## Williams' Bon Chrétien

A good early eating variety, medium-large, pale green turning to golden yellow. Very juicy and sweet. Regular good cropper. (Aldermaston, Berkshire 18th Century)

## Winter Nelis

Small but a good late variety with frost resistance. Pale green turning to yellowish-green, almost covered by russet. The greenish-white flesh is juicy and sweet. (Belgium 19th Century)

### Whitty Pear

Similar to the 'Bollwyller Pear' described on this page is the Whitty Pear (Sorbus domestica) also described on page 167 in the ornamentals section.

The first known 'Whitty Pear' tree was observed by Edmund Pitt, an alderman of Worcester, in 1678 in the Wyre Forest, with little knowledge of how it arrived. Descendents (raised from seed) of this tree were planted in the Precentory in Worcester and near the Chapter House and one in the Oxford Botanical Garden in 1790. The fruit appear as small bunches of green pears tinged with yellow on one side when ripe, and are comparable with medlars when eaten. In central and southern Europe from where the tree originated the fruit was made into a wine or perry and the wood of its tree, being very hard, was sought after by cabinet and musical instrument makers for its ability to take on a high polish.

© Claire Higgins

# PERRY PEAR

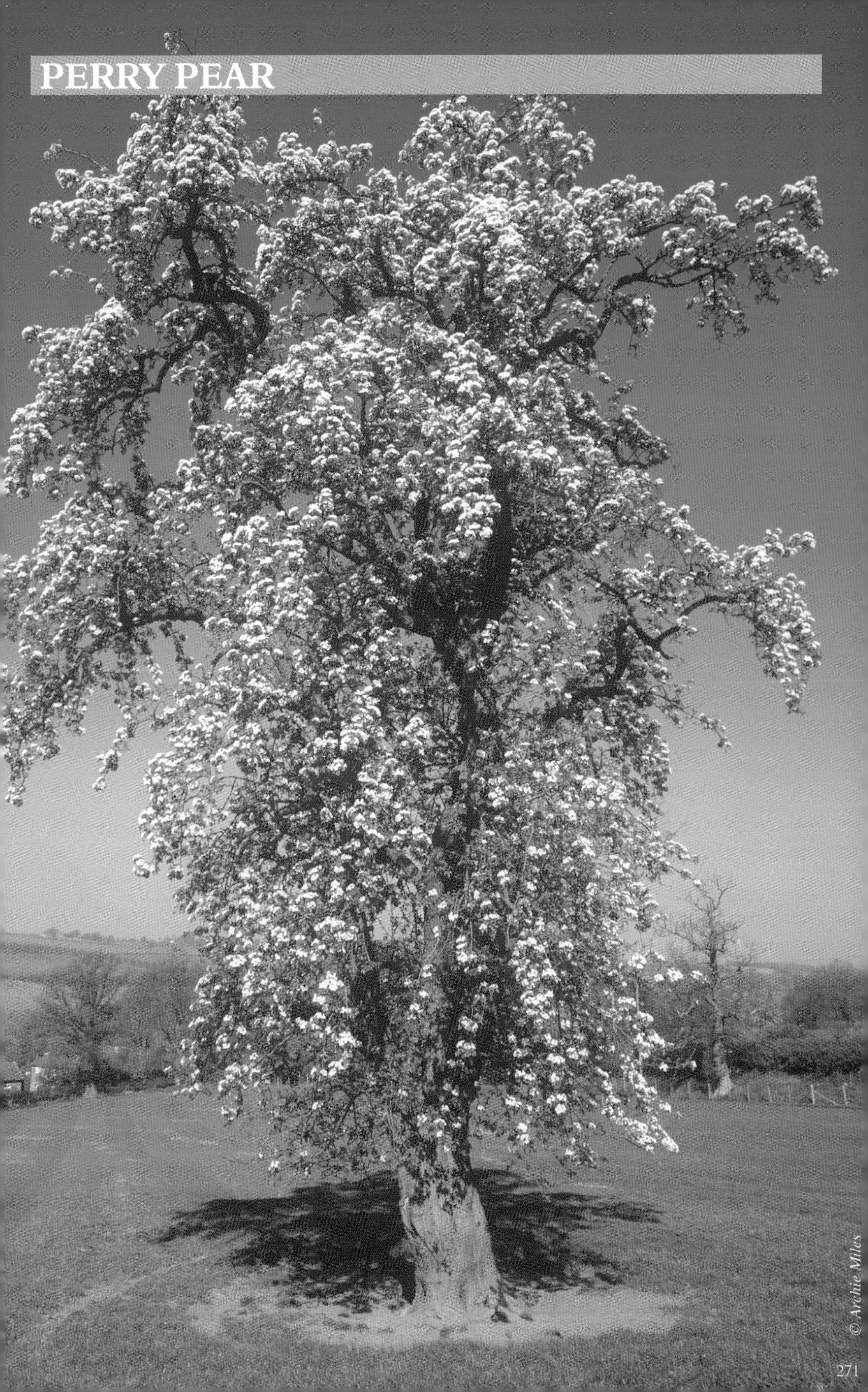

© Archie Miles

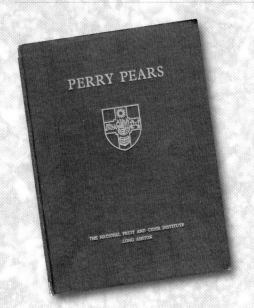

## Pioneers of Perry

This classic work was first published in 1963 by J. W. Arrowsmith Ltd, Bristol, printers to the University of Bristol. Long Ashton Research Station (closed in 2003) had been for exactly 100 years a government agricultural and horticultural research centre set up to improve the west country cider and perry industry. 'Perry Pears' was one of its most significant publications and is used today as the bible for a resurgent perry industry. With kind permission we are able to provide just a small glimpse of this unique reference now available as a ring bound copy.

## Taste and Explore

For those interested to learn more about cider and perry making and view over 100 different perry varieties in a unique orchard collection, visit *The Orchard Centre & Hartpury Perry Park* just west of the A417 at Hartpury, Gloucestershire.

*Professor B.T.P. Barker – a leading expert on cider and perry – to whom the book 'Perry Pears' was dedicated*

## Brandy (Perry)

The fruit is small and pale greenish-yellow with a bright red flush. Crops heavily with a tendency to bear biennially. The tree is small to medium and makes an average quality perry. (Gloucester 19th Century)

   Pe

## Cannock

A small general purpose pear for perry, bottling and stewing. Best to store until the spring to reduce what can be considerable cooking time, the result is still satisfying. (Staffs.)

     Pe

## Hellens Early (Perry) Syn: *Sweet Huffcap*

One of the best early Perry pears.
A strong growing tree with wide angled branches that become pendulous at the ends. Heavy crops of small, round, green-yellow fruit. Has low to medium tannin making an average to good quality perry.
(Gloucester/Hereford 18th Century)

   Pe

## Hendre Huffcap (Perry)

A large tree with upright branches. Crops are generally large and regular often causing broken branches. Fruit is elliptical and irregular, yellowish-green or yellow with a russet around the stem end. A clean grower suffering little disease. Good vintage quality perry. (Bromsberrow, Gloucester)

   Pe

## Thorn (Perry)

A small tree with upright habit and multi spur systems. Produces abundant crops of small yellow fruits with some russet. The perry vintage is average to good with low tannin. (Gloucester circa 1670)

  Pe

## Tettenhall Dick

"Tettenhall Dicks are as hard as bricks" so the saying goes! Part of Black Country life for more than 500 years when they were sold on street corners for two pence or six pence per flat capful. A very small multi-purpose pear for fresh eating, bottling or stewing, can also be used for perry. This self fertile pear fruits in abundance.

     SF Pe

*Old traditional perry pear trees are one of man and nature's combined triumphs. It is undoubtably the most majestic of fruit trees. Tall with a rugged elegance, these beautiful trees reach for the sky with showy flowers and attractive autumnal fruits, with a twist in the trunk that shows off its fissured bark.*

*The Perry pear revival has begun, but we have missed a whole generation of planting and the old trees are diminishing in number at an alarming rate. Despite supreme efforts by a few enthusiasts much more needs to be done. The increasing interest in this fine traditional drink may yet provide the extra impetus to save the Perry pear for posterity.*

# PLUM

These hardy fruits can be picked from early July to late September. They include varieties mostly derived from Prunus domestica, the European plum and the occasional Prunus salicina, the Japanese plum. For fresh eating and various culinary uses, they come in all shades of red, blue, purple and yellow.

## The Plums of England

The pages below and the colour plates reproduced in this section are from The Plums of England by H.V. Taylor, published in 1949.

The colour plates which show not only whole fruit but leaf, stone and fruit section, convey much more information than simply a photograph of the fruit on the branch.

H.V. Taylor was a noted fruit expert but credit should also be given to Mr. A.G. Symmons of the Sun Engraving Company of Watford for undertaking the origination of the colour plates using skills and equipment which are now part of a lost art.

## Avalon

© Claire Higgins

Large, round-oval, red colour. One of the finest quality desserts. A strong growing tree with a tendency to be shy cropping in its early years and therefore recommended on Pixy rootstock. Partially self fertile. (Bristol circa 1980)

## Belle de Louvain

Very large purple fruit, firm texture and sweet. Good for culinary and dessert use. (Belgium 1845)

274

## Blaisdon Red

This variety is probably the best jam maker of all, with a vibrant purple-red coloured skin that turns the golden yellow flesh bright red when cooked. The tree yields heavily with large crops of medium sized fruit and is fairly disease resistant. (Blaisdon, Gloucester)

## Blue Tit

Czar x Green Gage. An old Laxtons variety with a blue-black bloom and yellow flesh. Good quality. (Bedford 1938)

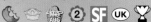

## Czar

Prince Englebert x Early Rivers. So named, as the first year it fruited was 1874, the year Tsar Alexander II visited Britain, the last Russian head of state to visit before President Putin in 2003. A medium, dark purple plum with a sweet yellow flesh. Can produce very heavy crops and always reliable. Self fertile. Good for eating, cooking and bottling. (Herts. 19th Century)

  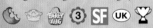 

## Edda

Czar x Pêche. An excellent dessert plum. Blue skin and yellow flesh with a fine rich flavour. Opal and Victoria are good pollinators. (Norway circa 1950)

## Excalibur

A vigorous tree, shy cropping but sacrificing quantity for quality is worthwhile in this case. Pollinated by Victoria. (Bristol circa 1980)

## Giant Prune

d'Agen x Pond's Seedling. A very large, red, oval, and freestone fruit which crops very heavily indeed. Not the best dessert eating quality but tough and reliable for exposed areas. (USA 1893)

## Gordon Castle

A native hardy plum for northern districts. Greenish-yellow but sweet with an excellent flavour. (Scotland)

## Guinevere

This is a large, heavy cropping plum around Marjorie's Seedling time with probably better eating quality and has extended shelf life when fridge stored. Self fertile. A healthy, well shaped and manageable tree. Formally WJ96. (Kent 2000)

## Herman

Czar x Ruth Gerstetter. Medium, blue-black, very early, freestone, golden flesh and excellent eating quality. Two to three weeks earlier than Czar and with improved flavour. Self fertile. (Sweden 1970)

## Heron

Medium-large, blue mottled purple. Very good quality dessert. Traditional to the Vale of Evesham. (Raised by Rivers. 1875)

## Jubileum Syn: *Jubilee*

Victoria x Czar. A plum of superb eating quality. Similar in appearance and flavour to Victoria, but much larger fruit, and picks one week earlier. A strong growing tree, recommended on Pixy rootstock. Self fertile. (Sweden 1985)

## Kirke's Syn: *Kirke's Blue*

Large, dark purple with a bright blue bloom, firm, juicy and sweet but rich flavour. A favourite of the past. (London 19th Century)

## Laxton's Cropper

Victoria x Aylesbury Prune. Average quality but an excellent cropper especially for hardy areas. Red turning blue-black, oval, medium. (Bedford 1906)

## Mallard

Red with bloom. Medium oval, oblong, mid to late August. Good quality dessert. Needs a pollinator. (Rivers of Sawbridgeworth 1885)

## Marjorie's Seedling

One of the latest picking plums for mid to late September. Large and good quality purple fruit. Dual purpose. Good cropper. (Berks. 1912)

## Methley

One of the best of the Japanese plums (Prunus salicina) with blood red flesh and juice. A refreshing little plum, extremely juicy and sweet with mild flavour.

## Opal

Oullins Green Gage x Early Favourite. One of the most reliable garden plums. Known as the early Victoria. A medium, reddish-purple fruit with superb flavour. Self fertile. (Sweden 1925)

   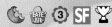

## Purple Pershore

## Monarch

A large, round, blue-black fruit producing heavy yields for eating and cooking. Green-yellow flesh. A strong growing tree. (Rivers, Sawbridgeworth 1883)

Diamond and Early Rivers (direction uncertain). A very useful robust plum with good regular crops. Purple to almost black and very large. A good dual purpose. (Worcester)

## Queens Crown
Syn: *Denbigh or Cox's Emperor*

A large, round oval pink-red fruit with yellow flesh similar to Ponds Seedling but of better flavour. Good crops, flesh clings to stone, partially self fertile.

## Reeves

One of the best flavoured red plums, similar if not superior to Victoria quality. Can be shy cropping. Pollination by Victoria as first choice. (Canada 1940)

### Another saintly connection
Sanctus Hubertus was Saint Hubert, a Bishop of Liege in the 9th Century. St Hubert is the patron saint of huntsmen since, according to legend, whilst out hunting one day when he should have been seeing to his religious duties, he was visited by a stag bearing a crucifix to warn him of the consequences of neglecting his work.

## Rivers's Early Prolific Syn: *Early Rivers*

© Claire Higgins

As the name suggests a good, heavy cropping early season plum. Small, bluish-purple. A good dessert variety when fully ripe. (Herts. circa 1820)

## Sanctus Hubertus

© Claire Higgins

Mater Dolorosa x Early Rues. Large, purple-blue, oval fruit for early August. One of the best croppers of the early varieties although the fruits do need to ripen well before eating. (Belgium 1966)

## Seneca

Italian Prune x Prinlew. Reddish-purple, large, oval fruit. Flesh yellow and very sweet, when picked in the first week of September. Very good quality. Freestone. (New York State 1937)

## Apriums, Pluots and Plumcots

These are 'hybrids' or 'interspecifics' that are essentially crosses between plums and apricots. Pluots and plumcots are smooth skinned expressing the dominant plum and Apriums are slightly fuzzy showing the apricot dominance. They can now be purchased in the shops and are certainly well flavoured.

Trees are beginning to be available from certain sources, but it is worth noting that they are very early flowering, and that the fruit is generally produced in superior climates such as southern Europe and California. They are best treated as apricots, by training on walls.

*Plumcot*

© Claire Higgins

## Swan

Red-purple with a bloom. Good sweet flavour, a good dessert and a favourite of the Evesham plum growing area. (Sawbridgeworth, Herts. 1875)

## Thames Cross

Coe's Golden Drop x Giant Prune. A very large oval-shaped yellow plum, juicy and sweet with good flavour. Suitable also for jam making. Partially self fertile. (Bristol 1938)

## Valor

Imperial Epineuse x Grand Duke. Large, dark purple fruit with greenish-yellow flesh, useful as a dual purpose fruit very late in the season. (Vineland, Canada 1968)

## Verity

Imperial Epineuse x Grand Duke. A large, oval fruit with a blue-purple bloom. Another good dual purpose plum, for the late season. Clingstone.
(Ontario, Canada 1938)

## Victoria

Oval, bright red fruit in late August-early September for dessert, bottling or canning. A clean freestone. Unfortunately disease prone but tolerable considering the quality and quantity that this variety produces. The most popular plum even to this day.
(Sussex 19th Century)

## Violetta

Blue skin with yellow, sweetly flavoured flesh. A compact grower and heavy cropping. (Sweden 1990)

## Warwickshire Drooper

An old favourite. Always crops well and regularly. Large yellow fruit, very juicy and good for eating and cooking. The tree has a spreading, drooping habit from which it was named. In its county of origin this variety was fermented into an alcoholic drink called Plum Jerkum reputed to 'leave the head clear while paralyzing the legs'. (Worcester/Gloucester pre 1920's)

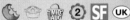

## Yellow Pershore Syn: *Yellow Egg*

The fondly named 'yellow egg' plum traditional to the West Midlands. A large, reliable cropper for dessert as well as the ideal bottling plum. Self fertile.
(Worcestershire 19th Century)

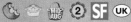

281

# QUINCE

The quince (Cydonia oblonga) is an ancient fruit known to the Greeks and Romans who dedicated it to Venus and Aphrodite. To them it was a symbol of love, happiness and fertility often used in marriage ceremonies. After the Romans left, quinces were found to be growing wild in Sussex. The flavour of quince is rather austere in its raw state but is very tasty as a stewed fruit (often added to that of apple), or as a jelly or marmalade – in fact it was the first fruit that was made into a marmalade, well before the use of citrus. 'Marmelo' is Portuguese for Quince. Quince are high in nutritional benefits for fatigue and debility and as a laxative. In addition to the showy fruit are lovely soft pink flowers and large leaves, making this tree worth its place in the garden.

## Champion

A regular cropper, round pear-shape and greenish-yellow fruit.

---

### Quince Vodka

Incredibly easy to make and can be served at room temperature or chilled.

*Ingredients:*

- 1lb Quince
- 1/2 lb Granulated or Caster Sugar
- 1/2 litre Vodka

1. Grate the quince (the easiest way to do this is in a food processor).
2. Put the grated quince in a 1 litre Kilner Jar.
3. Add the sugar.
4. Fill the jar to the top with vodka.
5. Shake well and store in a cool place (e.g. garage).
5. Shake the jar twice a week for 4 weeks.
6. Continue to shake (when you remember) for the next 5 months (once a week will be fine).
7. Strain through a sieve.
8. Pour the reserved liquid back into the jar, and let it settle for 48 hours, so the sediment sinks to the bottom.
9. Using a length of pipe syphon the liquid into a bottle.

It is now ready to drink.

Thanks to the Higgins family for the above recipe.

---

## Meech's Prolific

Like all quinces, has fruiting and ornamental qualities producing large, subtle pink flowers and very large, pear-shaped fruit. Yellow when ripe. Self fertile. (USA 1880)

## Portugal

An early ripening variety of high quality for cooking and preserving, particularly good for marmalade. Turns pink when cooked.

## Serbian Gold Syn: *Leschovach*

Highly productive variety from Serbia locally known as 'Leschovach', used for all culinary purposes including Quince Liqueur. A very healthy tree worthy of planting in larger numbers. Self fertile. (Serbia)

## Vranja

Large, pale green-yellow fruit similar in shape and size to Meech's Prolific and also similar to Bereczki. (Serbia 1800)

### Quince Cheese

As a change from quince jelly try making this delicious quince cheese. Again it is not at all cheesy, more like the nicest possible kind of Turkish Delight, less sweet, intensely fruity, with a slightly grainy texture. It will keep perfectly in the fridge for at least 12 months. It is popular in Spain where it is known *Membrillo*.

**Ingredients**

- 1kg preserving sugar
- 750ml water
- 1.2kg Quinces, peeled, cored and grated or cut into small pieces.

Dissolve the sugar in the water and bring to the boil. Continue to boil for about 5 minutes to make a light syrup. Stir the quince into the syrup, bring back to the boil and simmer very gently, stirring every so often for anything from 45 minutes to 1½ hours, until the mixture turns into a thick grainy paste. This is a slow process; giving it an occasional whisk helps speed things up a bit. It is ready when the spoon, dragged across the bottom of the pan, separates the paste, showing the clean bottom of the pan. Spread the paste into lightly greased shallow dishes or trays and place in the oven at its lowest possible temperature for 3-4 hours to harden further. Remove from the oven and leave to cool.

Once cool, wrap in greaseproof paper in useable slabs. Store in the fridge in sealed containers. It will keep for at least 12 months, retaining its wonderful freshness. To serve, cut into Turkish delight size cubes.

Thanks to the Atkey family for this recipe.

## TRAZEL

Trazels are so called from a corruption of **tr**ee h**azels** and are a hybrid cross between the common hazel C. avellana and the Turkish hazel C. colurna. They have both fruiting and ornamental features with good edible nuts along with the highly ornamental envelopes, frilled in appearance. The trees are vigorous and upright. They will cross pollinate each other or be pollinated by other hazel varieties.

### Chinoka

### Freeoka

# WALNUT

The good fruiting forms of walnut have been selected over considerable time and include many from other countries. The common walnut (Juglans regia) is included in the ornamentals section of this book as it is well regarded as a valuable tree for large gardens and the landscape. Unfortunately they are very inferior in fruiting to the selected varieties, shown here, that are generally large, thin shelled and of excellent eating quality.

## Broadview

Currently the best form for the UK. Precocious from an early age and slightly resistant to frost at flowering time. It is also a compact tree compared with other varieties. (British Columbia, Canada)

## Buccaneer

*Wet walnuts*

A healthy robust form. The nut is round and carried in abundance, particularly suited for pickled walnuts. (Holland)

## Fernette

Franquette x Lara. Large, good quality globular nut similar to Fernor and a good pollinator for the same variety. (France)

## Walnut facts

- The male and female flowers on an individual tree are produced at slightly different times so self fertility of a variety is rare.
- Trees can still pollinate each other up to 250 metres away as long as the wind is blowing in the right direction!
- 'apoximis' is a process in which a female flower is able to set fruit without pollination.
- Walnuts are difficult to establish in the first year of planting and some die-back in the shoot tips is to be expected. Plenty of water and no competition from grass and weeds is important.
- Walnuts for pickling are best picked in late June/early July before the shells are formed. Test with a pin or skewer.
- Pruning should only be done if absolutely necessary and in the autumn before the leaves have fallen.
- 'Wet' walnuts are sold in nets as 'dongers'. They should be dried quickly before they go mouldy. In an airing cupboard, in single layers is ideal. Turn regularly.
- The green husks can be boiled to produce a yellow dye and is a good source of tannin.
- Romans used to throw walnuts at the bride and groom, representing fertility.
- Rich in antioxidants and omega-3 fatty acids.
- For information on the chemical *Juglone* go to page 89 in the ornamental tree section.

Walnuts can take some years before cropping begins. Applying a large cable tie to the tree trunk in May will restrict growth and promote the onset of fruit bud for the following year. The cable will need to be released in the autumn. This process can be repeated each year if desirable. For information on the pruning of fruiting trees see page 294.

## Fernor

Similar to Fernette. A late leafing (avoiding spring frost damage), precocious flowering and late ripening form. Thin shelled for kernel extraction.
Pollinated by Fernette and Broadview.

## Franquette

Superb late season quality nut which is large with a thin shell. Suitable for all purposes. Broadview is the best pollinator. The tree is a strong grower. (France)

## Lara

A potentially good cropper and compact grower. The nut is large, thin shelled and excellent quality. Franquette would be the best pollinator.

## Plovdivski

A Bulgarian variety for both fruit and timber. Large fruit and blight resistant.

## Proslavski

Also a Bulgarian variety, vigorous tree and blight resistant. Large nut of good quality.

## Rita

A Carpathian variety, hardy, slow growing and very productive. Appears to have partial self fertility.

## Nutshell Guide Books by Clive Simms

For interesting and practical information the Nutshell Guide Books from Clive Simms are delightful reading and a must for the enthusiastic amateur.

5 Topics are covered to date:

Figs.............................ISBN 0-9544607-1-5

Hazelnuts ...................ISBN 0-9544607-5-8

Walnuts ......................ISBN 0-9544607-0-7

Grapes.........................ISBN 0-9544607-2-3

Blueberries, Cranberries
and Lingonberries .....................ISBN 0-9544607-3-1

# Fruit rootstocks

**Fruit trees are grown on a range of rootstocks in order to control the rate of growth. These tables show approximate size of mature trees and various suggested uses.**

A full explanation of rootstocks, background and history can be found at:
www.frankpmatthews.com/rootstock-information.htm

| Very Dwarf | | Dwarf | | Semi Dwarf | | Semi Vigorous | | Vigorous | | Very Vigorous | |
|---|---|---|---|---|---|---|---|---|---|---|---|
| Fruit | Rootstock | Fruit | Rootstock | Fruit | Rootstock | Fruit | Rootstock | Fruit | Rootstock | Fruit | Rootstock |
| Apple | M27 | Apple | M9 | Apple | M26 | Apple | MM106 | Apple | MM111 | Apple | M25 |
| | | Pear | Quince C | Apricot | Torinel | Pear | Quince A | Pear | Pyrodwarf | Pear | Pyrus communis |
| | | Cherry | Gisela 5 | Plum | Pixy | Plum | St Julien A | | | Cherry | F.12.1 |
| | | | | Gage | Pixy | Gage | St Julien A | | | Plum | Brompton |
| | | | | Damson | Pixy | Damson | St Julien A | | | | |
| | | | | | | Cherry | Colt | | | | |

## Apple tree vigour

Why are apple varieties noticeably more weak or vigorous than average?

It is probably due to the type of rootstock they are grown on as shown above **OR** there may be other reasons:

### Stronger growth:

- A minority of apple varieties and the occasional pear are 'triploids' (see explanation opposite). They are naturally more vigorous than the majority of varieties and are identified with a 'Triploid' symbol ✪ within the description pages.
- The trees are growing in excellent, deep, well drained and fertile soil.

### Weaker growth:

- The variety is naturally less vigorous. Such varieties would be Bardsey, Charles Ross, D'Arcy Spice, King of the Pippins, Pitmaston Pine Apple, Red Devil, Red Windsor, St Edmund's Russet and Worcester Pearmain.
- The variety is self fertile, flowers more profusely and therefore sets heavy crops of fruit. Examples would be Limelight, Red Falstaff and Red Windsor.
- The tree is growing on thin/poor soil.

### Natural Tree Shape:

- Have been bred for compact or restricted growth such as Ballerina trees or are extreme in their growth habit either naturally upright or spreading.

For tips on managing the above extremes refer to the Pruning section on page 294.

*Apple rootstock stoolbeds on a commercial nursery*

*The fruit rootstock influence on tree size control is often manifested by unnatural swellings at the union between variety and rootstock. This is quite normal.*

# Pollination made simple

**The subject of pollination is often made unnecessarily complicated. This brief outline will hopefully be of some assistance.**

## All fruit trees

Most suburban situations provide naturally good cross pollination due to the proximity of other gardens and the activity of bees and other insects that is helped by such a diversity of plant material. Gardens are generally well sheltered, so all fruit trees have an excellent chance to be visited at the optimum time.

## Pollination periods mentioned in this book

Each of the fruit trees (apples, pears etc) are divided into 5 flowering periods. This covers approximately a month from the beginning of period 1 to the end of period 5.

Each period overlaps with the one before and the one after. For example: a variety in group 3 will cross pollinate with varieties in group 2, 3 and 4, and a variety in group 2 with those in 1, 2 and 3.

## Self fertile varieties

Each of the fruit groups have varieties that are self fertile, a few in apples, pears and cherries and all apricots, nectarines and peaches. All these are shown with the SF symbol.

## Triploid varieties

Fortunately there are few triploid varieties to have to consider.

Triploid varieties are marked ✪ in the fruit section. They are mostly apples with the occasional pear. The rules are:

- Triploids are poor pollinators for any other variety.

- They should be accompanied by two other non-triploid varieties that will also pollinate each other or one variety that is self fertile. An example would be Red Falstaff which is self fertile and is a very good pollinator for Bramley Seedling, which is a triploid.

## Malus Crab apples

These are a very useful range of trees where many varieties will pollinate apples. See Malus in the ornamental section of this book for this information. Also remember that mostly all Malus are self fertile themselves indicating how useful their pollen is for cross pollination.

## Blossom

Even though we have been quite precise about blossom timings of varieties, the picture below shows how blossom on older two year wood on the right opens before the young one year wood on the left, on the same branch. It is therefore more receptive and available as a pollen donor for a longer period of time.

Like all subjects, pollination can be taken to a higher level and a very readable account by Hugh Ermen is available to view in the pollination section at www.frankpmatthews.com

# Bees

**We are hugely reliant on the pollination work of bees for our food production. This enthusiast's account provides an insight into a fascinating life cycle.**

It is very unusual to have to wait for more than a very short while on a warm, sunny day, before a honey bee is seen visiting some flower; as early as mid February on crocus through to the late autumn on michaelmas daisies and the early mahonia flowers and of course on the very many others in between, from the lowly ubiquitous dandelion to a thirty foot native cherry.

They do this to gather food – pollen and nectar, their proteins and carbohydrates. Nectar is a watery solution of sugars, mainly sucrose and it is after the action of enzymes, added both by the foragers on their way back to the hive and then by those 'house bees' who receive the nectar there, that a transformation takes place; so that by the time it is stored away in the comb, water content is down to 18%, the sucrose broken down to roughly equal parts of glucose and fructose – making up 50% with a percentage point or two of trace elements and vitamins. It has now become honey.

It is this food gathering activity that affects pollination: honey bees are 'master' pollinators. The hairiness of their bodies picks up pollen grains from the dehisced anthers and, crucially, they tend to move to a flower of the same kind i.e. apple to apple, thus carrying that pollen to and depositing it on a receptive stigma of the same or another flower, this leading eventually to seed and fruit development.

There is no substitute for strong colonies, headed by young queens to pollinate cultivated crops. Such colonies can be moved and, as long as the move is more than about 3 miles, they quickly reorient and can be seen in as short a time up to thirty minutes after release from the hive, bringing in pollen. The practice of moving colonies to work top fruit, oil seed rape, field beans, borage, phacelia and raspberries for example is known as migratory bee-keeping and when the flowering of such crops is over, the colonies are moved to other flora.

Honey bees visit many wild flowers, with ling potentially the most productive – especially when burning is practiced as on the grouse moors and fells. The regeneration results in young high pollen and nectar yielding plants. Many of our woodland trees are wind pollinated – oak, beech and hazel as examples but some others such as sycamore, sweet chestnut, lime and acacia are visited by honey bees for pollen and nectar. Hedgerow plants include sloe, blackberry and hawthorn – the latter not always a reliable yielder despite the myriads of flowers. Later in the year willowherb and the streamside balsam are visited.

Many garden plants are visited by honey bees thus adding to the interest. Ornamental malus, prunus, and chaenomeles along with numerous perennials and annuals are valuable sources. Though not plentiful enough in an individual garden to have a bearing on honey yield, it is surprising what can be gathered from those residential areas with good gardens.

Many aspects of honey bee biology are fascinating – the structure within the hive for example – the comb. Built with wax secreted from glands in the lower abdomen of worker bees a few days old, then moulded into those perfectly shaped hexagonal cells – all carried out in the  dark and very crowded hive. It is in these cells that the queen lays eggs, where larval and pupal development takes place and from which adults emerge. It is in this same comb structure that pollen and honey is stored to meet the needs of the colony through times of dearth – in England, end of October to March and, those inevitable inclement spells during the English summer.

Unique too is their ability to maintain a constant temperature – in the lower 90°F, in the brood area. They do this from as early in the year as the end of January/early February when the queen commences laying, it is almost incubator-precise – and all in a wooden box (the hive) with walls about ⅞" thick.

The majority of bee keepers are hobbyists, their apiary generally in the garden, the bees visiting suitable flora within up to a two mile radius. The results and returns of their endeavours: enhanced seed and fruit crops, and not least, honey and beeswax.

**Jack Cox**

# We have ways of making you fruit

**Commercial fruit growers in England and other parts of the UK are extremely dedicated to their profession and continually look for innovative ways to improve their skills and subsequently their orchards' cropping potential. This approach is key to their survival.**

They openly compete with imported fruit from superior growing climates and lower labour costs, but still manage to produce high quality and in many instances better flavour in their fruit despite these disadvantages.

Most consumers never see the attention to detail and innovation that happens on fruit farms and the illustrations here provide a glimpse of some of the clever methods employed to make trees produce earlier and better fruit. Most of these techniques come from the 'stress factor'. By limiting vegetative growth from day one, trees will respond by producing fruit blossom. This is a natural reaction. These ideas can be easily exploited at home in our gardens.

For other more traditional forms of trained trees see pages 290 and 297.

*Wide angles will support heavy crops. Start them young with toothpicks*

*Electricity tie cables encourage fruiting in walnut trees. Apply in May and remove in October. See Walnuts page 284*

*Alternate angled trees will expose fruit to maximum light*

*Apple wigwams also solve pollination problems*

*Planting S shape encourages earlier and lower fruit*

*Covers to reduce cherry splitting and a white carpet to reflect light for earlier ripening*

*Bending and even cracking branches encourages heavier blossom*

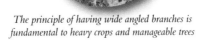

*The principle of having wide angled branches is fundamental to heavy crops and manageable trees*

289

# Fruit tree forms... the choice is yours

Fruit trees are particularly suitable for growing into all sorts of shapes and forms. Some of the pure trained forms are photograghed on page 297 Here we illustrate a full range of options for different situations all of which began life as a one year (maiden) tree in the nursery.

Where a particular shape of tree is unobtainable 'off the shelf' it is quite possible to grow your own starting with a one year (maiden) fruit tree. By cutting the maiden tree to a measured point above ground level all the shapes shown are possible.

All you need is courage and a very sharp pair of secateurs. On the left is shown a dormant maiden tree with various pruning heights that can be matched by code to each illustration.

The other rule to obey is that only some of these forms are suitable for 'stone' fruit i.e cherries, plums, apricots, peaches etc. Apples and pears however are entirely suitable for all forms. We therefore indicate 'apples and pears' only for those tree forms unsuitable for other fruits.

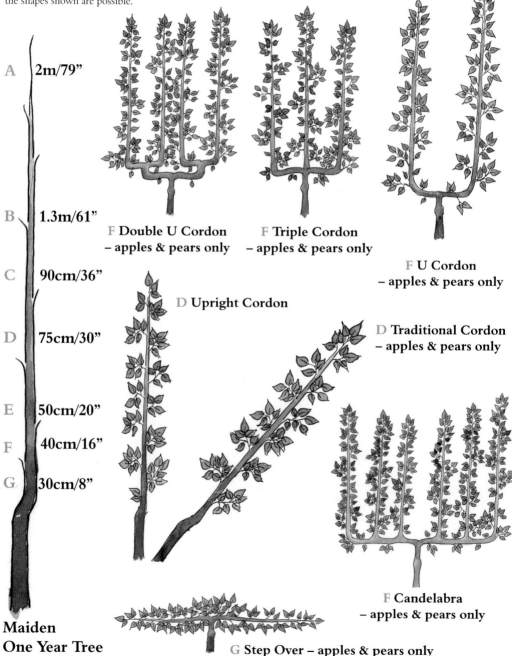

A   2m/79"

B   1.3m/61"

C   90cm/36"

D   75cm/30"

E   50cm/20"

F   40cm/16"

G   30cm/8"

**Maiden
One Year Tree**

F **Double U Cordon
– apples & pears only**

F **Triple Cordon
– apples & pears only**

F **U Cordon
– apples & pears only**

D **Upright Cordon**

D **Traditional Cordon
– apples & pears only**

F **Candelabra
– apples & pears only**

G **Step Over – apples & pears only**

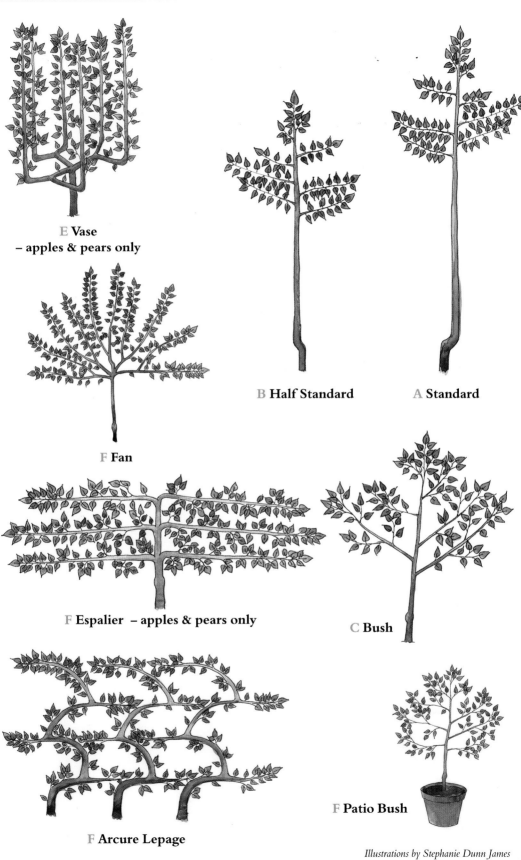

E **Vase**
– apples & pears only

B **Half Standard**

A **Standard**

F **Fan**

F **Espalier** – apples & pears only

C **Bush**

F **Arcure Lepage**

F **Patio Bush**

*Illustrations by Stephanie Dunn James*

# Traditional standard orchards

The old traditional standard fruit tree orchard has declined in recent times as they are uneconomical as commercial plantations. Their positive environmental and ecological impact has only been appreciated latterly, however, the gap between the old declining trees and the more recent replacement plantings are too far apart and the latter too few. Various initiatives, including private plantings and local support grants are helping, but more effort is needed to reverse the decline of a very important part of our landscape.

This information gives some important practical advice to achieve successful traditional orchard establishment, including rootstocks, tree guarding, pruning and aftercare. At the time of writing further help and advice can be obtained from the Farming and Wildlife Advisory Group (FWAG), www.fwag.org.uk

## Rootstocks
Rootstock selection is important for vigour, good anchorage and longevity and only vigorous rootstocks should be used as follows:

**Apples:** M25, Malus sylvestris (wild apple) or Malus 'Bittenfelder'

**Pears:** Pyrus communis (wild pear)

**Cherries:** Prunus avium (wild cherry) or Prunus Mazzard F.12.1

**Plums, Damsons, Gages etc:** Brompton, Myrobolan.

(see page 286 for further rootstock information).

## Trees from the nursery
One year (maidens) or two year (straight lead) or three year (finished standards) are the choices generally available. Planting older and larger trees is expensive and they will be slow to establish. The transplanting of older trees is not recommended either as this could lead to poor anchorage, stress and the likelihood of disease.

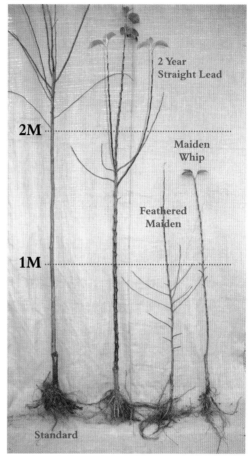

*Typical 'standard', 'straight lead' and 'maiden' trees from the nursery*

*The proud owners of a fine young traditional orchard*

The '2 year straight lead' is the ideal choice for economy and substantial enough to be staked and guarded permanently at planting time. 'Standards' (not always obtainable and more expensive) provide the most instant tree and 'maidens' (one year) are generally more available but do require careful attention in the first few years. Quite often a compromise has to be made combining tree age and the varieties available.

Good quality trees can take two-three years to grow in the nursery, so it is worthwhile planning the orchard and ordering the trees well in advance. This will cater for more choice and certainty when it comes to seeking out rare and historically important varieties.

## Ground Preparation & Planting

Orchard renovation often requires planting into the same position as the original tree and although not ideal this has to be done to maintain the symmetry of the plantation. In these circumstances additional fertilizer, such as bone meal and extra mulching will give the tree a good start. Here are some useful suggestions:

1  If possible spray off a metre square with weed killer at least a month before planting. Where an old tree has been removed the soil should be cultivated well in advance, removing old roots and incorporating well rotted compost or manure.

2  For new plantings do not dig holes in advance as unexpected rain will 'puddle' the hole and the backfill. Well rotted manure or bone meal should only be mixed with the backfill and not directly in contact with the roots.

3  Plant the tree with the rootstock/variety union at least 6-8cm above ground level.

4  Always mulch the tree after planting with any organic matter, bark or old carpet.

5  If a pot grown tree is used make sure a good proportion of the compost is knocked off the root ball (only when dormant) and spread the roots as much as possible.

6  Prevent further competition from weeds and grass for at least three years.

(For a more detailed look at planting trees please see page 14).

## Tree staking and protection from animals, rabbits & hares

Young trees up to 10 years old can be severely damaged by animals unless protected with good staking and guarding until well established. Good quality stakes also provide a purchase for proper rabbit guarding. It is very important to protect from rabbit and hare damage from the day the tree is planted.

Wire mesh guards are preferable and more reliable than spirals or plastic shelters. For cattle it is better to erect a 3 or even 4 post guard with 1.5m posts, wire stock fencing and barbed wire to be certain of full protection.

*3 or 4 post supports are recommended for cattle or sheep*

*Single stake support with wire mesh and barbed wire is barely adequate protection from farm animals*

Single stake support or a post either side with rabbit or stock fencing for sheep will reduce the cost but will not protect trees from the most mischievous animals. Whatever the method of tying it is imperative that this is slackened each spring. It should be possible to be able to place your index finger between tie and tree at all times.

*Any spacer between tree and post will prevent damage from rubbing*

## Pruning

The initial pruning of a young tree at planting time and then for its formative years is important. Establishing a good clean straight stem and a balanced shape should be the aim. It is not complicated and there are a few specific suggestions for standard trees as follows:

### Maiden Trees

If planting maiden trees prune off all lower branches (feathers) and leave the main leader of the tree undisturbed to 'run on'. Thereafter when the tree has reached approx 2m a further cleaning up of the stem to 1.5m can take place. The tree will form a natural head over a period of time. If a maiden tree is well over 2m the tree can be immediately pruned to this height at planting time. This will encourage the development of side branches at the right height in the first year.

### Straight Lead Trees

After planting, any tree over 2m can be topped off at this height and all side branches can be removed up to 1.5m in year one and 2m at the end of year two.

### Standard Trees

After planting, reduce all branches in the head of the tree by one third. This will reduce planting shock and encourage the formation of fruiting laterals.

## Pruning In Later Years

It is best to take a simple approach to pruning as the trees age. More general fruit tree pruning information can be found overleaf.

# The pruning of fruit trees

## General principles

**It is not the intention to give extensive details of the general pruning of fruit trees in this section, as there are several excellent books devoted to this subject alone. These are listed in the recommended reading section on page 314.**

The intention here is to cover some of the basic principles, hopefully encouraging the reader to 'have a go' in the knowledge that more good than harm can be achieved, whatever the saw cut, or secateur snip.

### Perfect trees do not exist

Many beautiful photographs of perfectly manicured fruit trees (and some of these decorate our pages) suggest that only the truly dedicated and experienced are capable of creating such perfect trees. This is not the case and there are no mysteries.

**It is important to realise that even a manic chainsaw user will rarely kill a fruit tree.**

### Why do we need to prune?

- to remove unwanted parts i.e. shoots, branches, roots, fruit buds.

- to let in sunlight and air – by removing congested and crossing branches to enable the tree to produce better quality fruit in appearance, flavour and size.

- to reduce pest and disease – by removing damaged or diseased wood.

- to limit the size and shape to the space allotted to each tree.

### What method should I use?

The pruning of fruit trees can be approached in a very detailed, precise way, or in a more relaxed manner. Your own personality as a gardener will determine the choice of tree form you wish to grow.

## Tools

A good pair of secateurs (left) is essential. Beware the cheap offers, you get what you pay for!

A Grecian pruning saw (below) is very useful and surprisingly easy to use. They cut on the return stroke which makes for light work.

## Informal pruning

The more informal free standing forms such as bushes, half standards and standards, will need less attention to detail and will therefore be favoured by those who can take life as it comes.

### Unproductive trees

If trees are non productive, be careful not to prune too hard in the belief that this will encourage fruiting. It is better to prune lightly and tie down strong, upright branches (see **Festooning**). This will encourage the formation of good fruit bud for the following spring.

*The two pictures above show before and after informal pruning of a typical neglected pear tree. Five minutes work and only five main cuts within the centre of the canopy have been enough to open up this tree after several years of neglect.*

### When and how hard?

The general rule should be: little and often. It is better to prune a little each year than to take drastic action every 10 years. A continual renewal of young replacement branches is possible and better for regular fruiting potential each year. Air and light are important; the former to reduce disease and the latter to ripen fruit for the best flavour and keeping quality.

- Apple and Pear – anytime and hard.

- Apricot, Bullace, Cherry, Damson, Gage, Nectarine, Peach, Plum – summer only and lightly.

- Medlar and Quince – anytime and lightly. (See **Tip bearing varieties**).

- Walnuts – avoid pruning if possible.

- Dwarf rootstocks control growth. For further information see page 286. Dwarf rootstocks reduce the amount of pruning required. The combination of dwarf rootstocks and patio planting (see symbols explanation page 200) virtually negates any need for pruning, in fact pruning would only be required to reduce crop load and maintain a reasonable fruit size.

## Tip bearing varieties

A small percentage of apple varieties, all medlars and quinces are 'tip bearers' (see symbol for 'tip bearing' varieties in the fruit pages.) These varieties should have the occasional whole branches removed to stimulate fresh growth, but at the same time whole fruiting bows of the tree should remain untouched. The very tip of each extension shoot will bear fruit.

*© Stephanie Dunn James*

## Summer is a good time for pruning

Tradition has it that pruning is a winter job, however here are a few reasons why summer pruning has many advantages:

- The weather conditions make it more enjoyable!
- If trees have a visibly heavy crop, heavier pruning can be used to lighten the crop load and encourage some replacement growth.
- This also helps to cure trees that have the tendency to 'biennial bear' (every other year).
- Stone fruit (Cherries, Plums etc.) will also suffer fewer disease problems if pruned when in leaf.
- It is the most effective way to contain tree size.
- It is essential to use summer pruning when maintaining "trained" fruit trees. See **Formal pruning**.

### Painting wounds

Do not paint wounds – it is purely cosmetic. Nature has a wonderful capacity to heal wounds, even if made by heavy pruning cuts. Natural healing callus can be inhibited by excluding wounds from air and light.

## Festooning

Upright shoots are generally vegetative and are less fruitful than horizontal branches that are more naturally inclined to produce fruit bud. Tie down vigorous upright shoots or branches in the late spring or early summer when they are more flexible, due to sap movement. This is called 'festooning'. This will also make picking easier in the years to follow. The two pictures below show an apple tree having had its branches tied down during blossom time and similarly (bottom) a plum on the right having the same treatment in early summer.

# Formal pruning

Symmetrically trained and elaborate forms of fruit tree such as fan, espalier, step overs and cordons are enjoyable to create and maintain. If pruned correctly following some simple principles they will remain very productive year after year and within their original allotted space. Perfect for walls, wire or wooden trellises or pergolas, they are also a great opportunity to grow successfully the more tender earlier flowering fruits such as apricots that benefit from a more sheltered spot.

The basic principles are as follows:

## Summer spur pruning and tying-in

The best time of year to prune formally trained trees is in late June, July and early August when the new growth is flexible and can be manipulated easily. The diagrams below and opposite should help to illustrate the simple principles of spur pruning and fruit bud development.

The picture opposite shows a typical spur system on a young pear cordon. 'A' are summer pruning points where young shoots have been removed and 'B' where plump fruit buds have formed for blossom the following spring. These fruit buds form naturally as terminal buds on the less vigorous shoots or are encouraged by the action of summer pruning on the more vigorous shoots.

The drawing below shows a single horizontal spur pruned branch in various stages of development (1-3 years old). Again 'A' is a summer pruning point where young vigorous shoots are reduced to only one or two buds. 'B' shows 'fruit' buds formed as a result of the pruning action. 'C' is the tied down leading shoot used as an extension of the branch system. This can be stopped and spur pruned itself when it has reached its desired length.

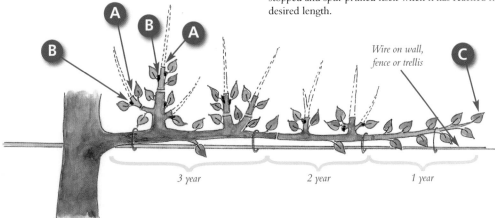

*Wire on wall, fence or trellis*

*3 year*     *2 year*     *1 year*

## Important:

- Espalier is often used as a generic term for all forms of trained trees on walls, pergolas and fences. It should only refer to horizontal/parallel systems of training.

- Productive espaliers should ideally have a spacing of 15"-18"(30-40cm) between tiers.

- Only one additional tier should be trained in each year otherwise the lower tiers do not develop

sufficiently strong enough to sustain good fruit production in the forthcoming years.

- All trained forms are able to be contained to a given area of wall, fence or pergola by spur pruning on at least two occasions during the summer. If it is ever considered a chore then it is well worth remembering that with each snip one encourages more fruit the following year. 'If in doubt, cut it out'!

*Step over*

*Fan*

*Fruiting arch*

*Arcure*

*Espalier*

*Cordon*

*Lattice*

*Oblique espalier*

- **The advantages of summer pruning**

  1. Increases fruit bud for the following year.

  2. Allows sunlight to colour and ripen the fruit.

  3. Reduces excessive vegetative growth.

- **Winter pruning**

  Winter pruning should be used to generally re-shape a tree by removing large undesirable branches and to tidy up the summer spur pruning.

- **Apples and Pears**

  These respond well to heavy spur pruning.

- **Plums, Cherries, Peaches & other stone fruit**

  Spur pruning is less well suited to stone fruit. A lighter approach to pruning should be adopted and the use of more tying in of the current season's new shoots is advised. Fan, Informal Fan and Arcure are the most suitable forms.

# Fruit identification (apple & pears)

**Fruit identification is not an exact science, as much influenced by local folklore, semantics, an experienced eye and nose, a touch of mystery and as many variety synonyms as there are villages in the country.**

Science will eventually provide a more exacting system of identification through a national DNA fingerprinting database. We will have more accurate answers but fewer puzzles, interesting opinions and wonderful characters to entertain us.

Apples can be sent to: Fruit Identification, Brogdale Horticultural Trust, Brogdale Road, Faversham, Kent. ME13 8XZ. A fee is charged.

One of the keys to identification is shape as this is unaffected by maturity, colour, flavour and texture considerations which can be so variable and so dependent on picking and eating at the right time. The terminology mentioned here will hopefully be helpful to decipher the apple identification language.

## Apple shapes
The illustrations shown here are the main distinctive shapes for apples and pears. This is not to say that some varieties will fall somewhere in between just to make the job of identification just that little bit more challenging. Most varieties given as examples are illustrated fully in this book.

*Flat*

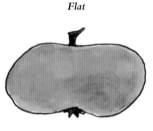

Beauty of Bath
Court Pendu Plat
Discovery

*Flat-Round*

Ashmeads Kernel    Dumelows Seedling
Blenheim Orange    Egremont Russet
Bramley's Seedling    Pixie

*Short-Round-Conical*

Brownlees Russet    Irish Peach
Epicure    Lanes Prince Albert
Fortune

*Round*

Chivers Delight    Golden Noble
Crawley Beauty    Grenadier
Edward V11

*Round-Conical*

Bakers Delicious    Cox's Orange
Carlisle Codlin    Pippin
Charles Ross    Ellisons Orange

*Conical*

Howgate Wonder    Tom Putt
Lord Derby    Worcester Pearmain

### Long-Conical

Cornish Gilliflower
Lord Hindlip
Norfolk Royal Russet

### Oblong-Conical

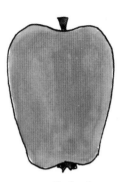

Catshead
Claygate Pearmain
Cornish Aromatic
Golden Delicious
Pitmaston Pine Apple

### Oblong

Crispin
D'Arcy Spice
Gala
Greensleeves
King of the Pippins

## Pear shapes

There are four main shapes for pears that are quite distinctive and some varieties are offered as examples.

As with apples, pear shapes will vary from one season to the next.

### Bergamotte

Catillac
Doyenné d'Été
Fondante d'Automne

### Oval

Émile d'Heyst
Glou Morceau
Gorham

### Pyriform

Black Worcester
Doyenné du Comice
Jargonelle

### Callabasse

Concorde
Conference
Durondeau

The terminology used for describing fruit is a language of its own. In addition to the main features such as stalk, eye and cheek other logical descriptive terms are used to describe other features such as flattened apex, flat sided, five-crowned, ribbed, broad at base, wasted at apex, lop-sided, scarf skin, lenticels, areolor, hair line, bumpy and beading!

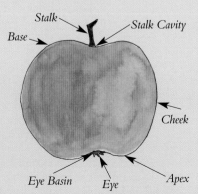

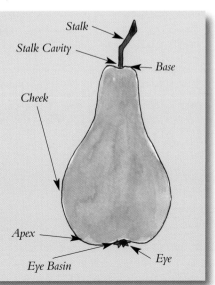

# Harvesting and storing fruit

**Our desire to store fruit defies Nature's own intentions to ripen fruit as soon as possible to enable seed dispersal and germination.**

Commercial fruit production today involves the use of controlled atmosphere cold storage where temperatures are lowered and oxygen is taken from the atmosphere to slow down the natural ripening process. This is not possible for home grown fruit that will need more natural methods to extend its shelf life. This is often referred to as 'barn storage', taken from the literal meaning when farms and small holdings had no better place to store their crops for the winter.

The key objective is to gather fruit in peak condition and store in as cool a place as possible. Domestic refrigerators are ideal, however the capacity of the modern 'fridge is very limited so other ideas are worth considering. Here we share some worthwhile tips to help you extend the eating period of your hard earned bounty. All fruit varieties described in this book have picking and storage times for guidance.

## General Tips

### Harvesting

- Fruit should be harvested just before full maturity. Fruit ripening is the process of starch converting to sugars and if you pick too early, fruit does not have the capacity to convert all the starch to sugar. Flavour and sweetness will suffer as a result.

- Always pick fruit when dry, this includes avoiding dewy mornings. Wet fruit attracts mildews and rots.

- Fruit ripens unevenly with those most exposed to the sun and on the outside of the tree ripening before fruit on the north or shaded fruit further inside the tree canopy.

- Fruit from trees on clay or heavy soils will store longer than from trees growing on light sandy soils.

- Retain stalks on fruit if possible. When picking be careful to 'unhook' fruit rather than pull in haste.

- Handle with extreme care, bruising will take time to appear, often after the fruit has been stored away with obvious consequences.

### Storing

- The small fruit will store longer than the large fruit, which should be eaten first.

- Blemished fruit should not be stored but eaten or processed without delay.

- Wrapping individual fruit will extend its storage and many materials can be used. Newspaper is probably the most handy and economical but aluminium foil and grease proof paper in particular work well at extending shelf life.

- Store in a cool airy place and in single layers if space allows.

- Cellars and out-buildings with earth floors are ideal for keeping day/night temperatures low and even. Those with cellars are fortunate but those without can still help by opening windows and doors at night and closing them during the day.

- Rats and mice will run riot given the opportunity.

- Remove stones from fruit before freezing while fruit is still firm.

## Now a few specific tips

### Apples
Avoid storing early varieties other than in the 'fridge and mid season only for a short period. Eat from the tree daily and give surplus fruit to friends and schools.

### Apricots
If unable to eat fresh, then dry, bottle, jam or freeze for the winter.

### Cherries
Immerse in cold water as soon as they are picked, they will stay fresher longer. They can also be frozen successfully.

### Hazels, Cobnuts and Filberts
Harvest when the husks are green for fresh eating or as the husks turn yellow for storage. Protect from vermin. Dry in the airing cupboard.

### Damsons, Sloes and Bullaces
Shaking the tree regularly removes only the fruit that has ripened and importantly retains the stalks. All processing including jams, cheeses and bottling can be carried out after freezing if time is short. Certainly freeze before adding to gin – defrosting breaks the skin for better flavour infusion.

### Figs
Store for several weeks in the 'fridge. Pick when the fruit are well coloured and begin to droop or split near the base. Eat fresh or bottle in syrup.

### Medlars
'Bletting' (controlled ripening in sawdust in stone or glass jars) separates the fruit and slows ripening.

### Mulberries
Shake from the tree each day and gather the ripe fruit. Ideal for freezing.

### Peaches and Nectarines
Pick when fruit is still firm but able to be 'unhooked'. Use the palm of the hand rather than gripping with fingers. Place on soft tissue, cotton wool or bubble polythene. Store in a cool, dark place but a 'fridge is ideal. Inspect daily and eat when the stalk end softens.

### Pears
Always 'unhook' fruit leaving stalk intact, pick when firm, store in single layers wrapped individually. Inspect regularly as pears in particular ripen unevenly.

### Plums
Use egg cartons to keep fruit separate. Shriveled fruit can still retain good flavor. Later varieties can be stored in the 'fridge for some weeks. Good for freezing.

### Quince
Pick as the first fruits drop from the tree. Quinces emit high levels of ethylene, like bananas, that will hasten the ripening of other fruits.

### Chestnuts
Collect from the ground, de-husk and dry before storing in a cool dry atmosphere.

### Walnuts
Collect from the ground or pick as the husks split. De-husk and dry quickly in the airing cupboard in single layers. Store in dry sand and salt mix.

# Diseases, pests and disorders of fruit and ornamental trees

**Severe pest and disease problems are very rare since most gardens are a small, well balanced, environment of diverse plant material and living creatures.**

This creates a natural, interdependent, relationship between pest and predator. Diseases, too, are less prevalent where there is a rich tapestry of foliage of many different species. Pest and disease control with chemicals is therefore only necessary in extreme conditions. It is worth accepting minor blemishes and the occasional inconvenience that pests cause in the garden, especially with fruit trees. A 'no spray regime' is a sensible approach – even misshaped fruit need not be wasted.

## The use of natural predators in the garden

Biological control is now becoming a reality in the garden and there are several companies that offer advice to private gardeners. This is generally in the form of predators which can be introduced into gardens to tackle bugs of all types. For example there are:

- Lace wing and ladybird larvae that will eat your aphids;
- Nematodes to control slugs

## A few useful tips

If the comments so far have been helpful it may allow us to take a more relaxed view about pest and disease. There will be instances where pest and disease damage is visible but not necessarily harmful and by closely monitoring problems and using an organic and biological approach combined with predator friendly chemicals, it will be possible to contribute to a safer environment at home.

- Cut out severe foliage distortions caused by pests.
- Cut out mildew and canker.
- Use tree bands and pheromone traps to disrupt pest life cycles.
- Chickens are effective pest control agents.
- Use products such as garlic preparations that, if sprayed on vegetables and fruit trees, will discourage pests.

### Healthy growth means fewer problems
- Healthy trees are less susceptible to damage from pest and disease.

### Turning over a new leaf
- While working in and admiring your own garden, inspect the leaves of trees, especially looking on the undersides as this is where the first pests will appear unseen.

### Learn the art of masterly inaction
- Unless the leaf itself is becoming obviously distorted it is best not to take any action.

### If it moves fast it's friendly
- You can generally tell a pest from a predator because the pest moves slowly and the friendly predator moves fast – logical and true!

### Leaf disorders
- Once a leaf disease strikes a tree it is generally too late to solve the problem that year so make a note to apply some preventative sprays early the following spring. This would apply to scab and mildew in fruit and crab apples and rust diseases. Spray in dry weather and apply when leaves are just emerging well before blossom time. Prevention is better than cure!

### Bark wounds
- Bark wounds and cankers are best treated by removing the infected branch. Do not hesitate to take firm action as most trees will respond by producing strong replacement growth in a very short time. Please see our separate pruning guides for fruit (page 294) and ornamental trees (page 198) and also each ornamental tree listed has specific and simple pruning instructions by the use of easy to follow symbols.

In the following pages we illustrate some of the more common pests and diseases that can be found on fruit and ornamental trees, and their symptoms.

Specific chemicals are not mentioned in the following pages as it has already been established that their use is limited only to the severest of problems in the garden. We do mention 'preventive sprays' as a useful tool to reduce the incidence of some diseases on fruit trees.

## Key to disease, pest and disorder symbols

| No action needed | Prune out infected area | Remove infected leaf by hand | Introduce natural predator | Introduce pheromone traps | Use sprays |
|---|---|---|---|---|---|

| | Problem | Symptoms | Affects | Period | Control |
|---|---|---|---|---|---|
| | **Aphid** <br> **Common Name** <br> Green apple aphid | Considerable leaf curling, shoot tips may be stunted or even killed. | Most fruit trees & Betula | May-July | Only spray if heavy infection. |
| | **Aphid** <br> **Common Name** <br> Rosy apple aphid | Twisted shoots, small leaves followed by shrivelled fruit. | Apple | April - July | Use lacewing or ladybird larvae if unable to prune out. |
| | **Aphid** <br> **Common Name** <br> Damson hop aphid | Considerable leaf and shoot curling. | Plum, damson & gage | April - August | Use lacewing or ladybird larvae if unable to prune out. |
| | **Aphid** <br> **Common Name** <br> Woolly aphid | Sticky white 'wool' produced. Galling may seriously disfigure plants. | Apple | Anytime | Severe infections should be scrubbed with wire brush and painted with methylated spirits. |
| | **Aphid** <br> **Common Name** <br> Blackfly | Severe leaf curl. Shoots may become stunted and tips killed. | Cherry | April - July | Important to detect at early stages. |
| | **Bitter pit** | Multiple black spots throughout flesh. | Apple | August – October | Linked to calcium deficiency but some varieties are particularly prone. Use seaweed products as fertiliser or foliar sprays. |
| | **Brown rot** | Fruit turns brown and concentric rings of yellowish mould appear. | Apple & pear | August – October | Remove bad fruit a.s.a.p. |
| | **Brown rot** | Fruit turns brown and concentric rings of yellowish mould appear. | Cherry & plum | July – September | Remove bad fruit a.s.a.p. |
| | **Canker** <br> **Common Name** <br> Nectria canker | Sunken areas of bark often restricted to one side of stem. Wounds may heal disfiguring cankers at the edge. | Apple & Malus | Anytime | Prune out preferably between June and August. |

## Key to disease, pest and disorder symbols

| No action needed | Prune out infected area | Remove infected leaf by hand | Introduce natural predator | Introduce pheromone traps | Use sprays |
|---|---|---|---|---|---|

| **Problem** Canker **Common Name** Bacterial canker | **Symptoms** Amber gum oozes from affected bark that leaves darkened, sunken stem areas. | **Affects** Plum, cherry & Prunus | **Period** Anytime | **Control** Prune out preferably between June and August. |
|---|---|---|---|---|
| **Problem** Canker **Common Name** Papery bark canker | **Symptoms** Flaking papery brown bark. | **Affects** Apple, pear & Malus | **Period** Anytime | **Control** Acid/wet conditions can be the cause. Trees can recover after pruning and correcting conditions. |
| **Problem** Capsid **Common Name** Green capsid | **Symptoms** Corky patches on fruit. | **Affects** Apple, cherry, peach & pear | **Period** April – September | **Control** |
| **Problem** Capsid **Common Name** Green capsid | **Symptoms** Brownish spots on foliage. | **Affects** Apple leaf | **Period** April – September | **Control** |
| **Problem** Coral Spot | **Symptoms** Dead twigs or patches of dead bark covered in pinkish pimples. | **Affects** Acer & Robinia | **Period** Anytime | **Control** Prune out if on side branches. Tree rarely survives if infection in the trunk. |
| **Problem** Hail damage | **Symptoms** Brown indentations or russetted raised bumps often healed up. | **Affects** All fruit | **Period** April – September | **Control** Damaged fruit will generally heal and become perfectly edible. |
| **Problem** Leaf Curl | **Symptoms** Large reddish blisters on leaves leading to early leaf fall and weakening of tree. | **Affects** Peach | **Period** April – July | **Control** Cover wall grown trees with polythene sheeting during April and May for prevention. |
| **Problem** Leaf Miner | **Symptoms** Shredding of leaves between veins. | **Affects** Aesculus & some fruit trees | **Period** June – September | **Control** This pest is serious but the trees will recover each spring & summer. Long term prognosis is that a predator for this pest will prevail. |
| **Problem** Leaf skeletoniser | **Symptoms** Tissue removed from upper side of foliage, lower surface intact. | **Affects** Apple, cherry, peach & Malus | **Period** April – September | **Control** Not a serious pest. |

| Problem | Symptoms | Affects | Period | Control |
|---|---|---|---|---|
| Problem<br>Magnesium deficiency | Symptoms<br>Brown interveinal centres to the leaves. | Affects<br>Many fruit & ornamentals | Period<br>Growing season | Control<br>Apply Epsom/bitter salts. Foliar spray at 20 grams per 10 litres water mid summer or 40 grams per square metre to soil in spring. |
| Problem<br>Midge<br>Common Name<br>Pear midge | Symptoms<br>Shrivalled fruitlets often turning black before premature drop. | Affects<br>Pear | Period<br>May – September | Control |
| Problem<br>Midge<br>Common Name<br>Leaf curling midge | Symptoms<br>Foliage distorted, leaf margins remain tightly rolled. Affected leaves may turn red and fall. | Affects<br>Apple & Malus | Period<br>May – September | Control<br>Several life cycles each year, catch early. |
| Problem<br>Mildew<br>Common Name<br>Powdery Mildew | Symptoms<br>Young leaves, shoots, and flower trusses may appear grey. Growth stunted, diseased flowers not set, leaf fall. | Affects<br>Apple, pear & Malus | Period<br>April – September | Control<br>If a severe problem spray for prevention from early spring, after winter pruning. |
| Problem<br>Mildew<br>Common Name<br>Powdery Mildew | Symptoms<br>Often affects whole trees late summer and autumn. | Affects<br>Acer platanoides and Campestre and Quercus | Period<br>July – October | Control<br>Impractical to take control measures, varies according to the season. |
| Problem<br>Mite<br>Common Name<br>Blister mite | Symptoms<br>Green pustules on upper side of leaf. | Affects<br>Acer and walnut | Period<br>July – September | Control<br>No harm comes to those trees affected. |
| Problem<br>Moth<br>Common Name<br>Codlin moth | Symptoms<br>Grubs seen in centre core. | Affects<br>Acer, apple, pear, plum, damson, walnut | Period<br>May – August | Control<br>Males are attracted to scent of female and are caught on sticky pads preventing mating. |
| Problem<br>Moth<br>Common Name<br>Codlin moth | Symptoms<br>Red ringed entry hole blocked by dry fruss. | Affects<br>Apple | Period<br>June – August | Control<br>Males are attracted to scent of female and are caught on sticky pads preventing mating. |
| Problem<br>Moth<br>Common Name<br>Fruit tree tortrix moth | Symptoms<br>Leaves spun together or a leaf attached to fruit. | Affects<br>Most fruit trees | Period<br>June – September | Control<br>Males are attracted to scent of female and are caught on sticky pads preventing mating. |
| Problem<br>Moth<br>Common Name<br>Winter moth | Symptoms<br>All flowers and greenery may be eaten. Malformed fruits with corky scars or depressions. | Affects<br>All fruit trees | Period<br>October – May | Control<br>Apply tree bands. Make sure band is above tree tie otherwise tree stake will also need to be treated. |

## Key to disease, pest and disorder symbols

| No action needed | Prune out infected area | Remove infected leaf by hand | Introduce natural predator | Introduce pheromone traps | Use sprays |
|---|---|---|---|---|---|

| | | | | | |
|---|---|---|---|---|---|
| **Problem** Moth **Common Name** Lacky moth | **Symptoms** Severe defoliation. Growth and fruit production affected. | **Affects** Apple, cherry | **Period** July – September | | **Control** Spraying necessary for a complete kill. |
| **Problem** Moth **Common Name** Leopard moth | **Symptoms** Accumulation of frass and wood particles. Later withering and die back of leaves and shoots. | **Affects** Apple, cherry, pear, plum & walnut | **Period** June – July 2/3 yrs | | **Control** Very rare and worth seeing. |
| **Problem** Phytophora (fruit) | **Symptoms** Bark peeling and wet black under bark at ground level. | **Affects** Apple, pear & Malus | **Period** Anytime | | **Control** Avoid poor drainage and excessive grass competition. |
| **Problem** Phytophora (ornamental) | **Symptoms** Black oozing gum on tree bark. | **Affects** Aesculus & Alnus | **Period** Anytime | | **Control** Coppicing will re-invigorate the tree and take away infection in Alnus. Aesculus is serious and known as 'Bleeding Canker'. |
| **Problem** Pigeon damage | **Symptoms** Leaves severely reduced from outside in. | **Affects** Plum & cherry | **Period** May – June | | **Control** Pigeon pie! |
| **Problem** Rabbit and hare damage | **Symptoms** Bark removed leaving rough surface (rabbit) or stripped (hare). | **Affects** Most trees | **Period** October – May | | **Control** Wire guards and encourage predators. Some paints are available but need renewing often. |
| **Problem** Red spider mite (indoor) **Common Name** Fruit tree red spider mite | **Symptoms** Leaves become dull green, brownish, then silvery bronze. | **Affects** Most fruit trees & some ornamentals | **Period** May – September | | **Control** Only a serious problem under glass where predators are very effective. Once they have eaten all the spider they may decline in population. |
| **Problem** Red spider mite (outdoor) **Common Name** Fruit tree red spider mite | **Symptoms** Adults shown in picture. | **Affects** Most fruit trees & some ornamentals | **Period** May – September | | **Control** |
| **Problem** Rust | **Symptoms** Red spots on the leaf topside followed by orange pustules on the underside of the leaf. | **Affects** Plum, quince, Betula & Populus | **Period** July – September | | **Control** Gather up and compost leaves. |

| | Problem | Symptoms | Affects | Period | Control |
|---|---|---|---|---|---|
| | **Problem**<br>Sawfly | **Symptoms**<br>Brown, corky scars radiating out from calyx end. Grubs feed on central core generally causing fruit to stop. | **Affects**<br>Apple & pear | **Period**<br>April – July | **Control**<br>Fruit damage is non-progressive and generally heals. |
| | **Problem**<br>Scab<br>**Common Name**<br>Fruit scab | **Symptoms**<br>Fruits badly disfigured and corky areas develop. | **Affects**<br>Apple and Malus | **Period**<br>May – August | **Control**<br>Worse in high rainfall areas where scab resistant varieties would be recommended. |
| | **Problem**<br>Scab<br>**Common Name**<br>Leaf scab | **Symptoms**<br>Leaves bear dark green or brown spots, twigs are blistered. | **Affects**<br>Apple leaves | **Period**<br>May – August | **Control**<br>Preventative spray advised. |
| | **Problem**<br>Shot hole | **Symptoms**<br>Brown spots on leaves that die and drop out leaving multiple holes. More likely to show up in wet seasons. | **Affects**<br>Cherry, plum & Prunus | **Period**<br>May – September | **Control** |
| | **Problem**<br>Silver leaf | **Symptoms**<br>Silvering of leaves often seen only on part of the tree. | **Affects**<br>Cherry, plum, gage & damson | **Period**<br>Growing season | **Control**<br>Prune out between June & August. If persistent, tree will need to be removed. |
| | **Problem**<br>Sucker | **Symptoms**<br>Petals on partially opened buds turn brown. Flowers may be killed quickly. Often mistaken for frost injury. | **Affects**<br>Apple & pear | **Period**<br>April – October | **Control**<br>Not an invasive pest. |
| | **Problem**<br>Verticillium wilt | **Symptoms**<br>Wilting of whole branches also brown streaks along water conducting tissue under bark. | **Affects**<br>Acer & Tilia | **Period**<br>April – August | **Control**<br>Can be serious, little control measures available. Replant with different species. |
| | **Problem**<br>Water core | **Symptoms**<br>Glassy clear flesh inside. Very seasonal. Often revered in some countries for the 'sweetness' of the affected flesh. | **Affects**<br>Apple | **Period**<br>Growing season | **Control** |
| | **Problem**<br>Weevil<br>**Common Name**<br>Blossom weevil | **Symptoms**<br>Capped blossoms with brown petals. | **Affects**<br>Apple | **Period**<br>April – May | **Control**<br>If persistent, spray before blossom opens. |
| | **Problem**<br>Wilt<br>**Common Name**<br>Blossom wilt /botrytis | **Symptoms**<br>Young shoots and particularly blossoms wilt and remain on tree. | **Affects**<br>Apple, cherry, plum, gage & Malus | **Period**<br>April – May | **Control**<br>Only a problem during wet Springs. |

# The Tree Council

**THE TREE COUNCIL**

**The Tree Council** is the UK's lead charity for trees in all settings, urban and rural, promoting their importance in a changing environment and it works in partnership with communities, organisations and government to make trees matter to everyone. It was launched in 1974 to run the annual **National Tree Week** and act as a forum for lobbying and debate, building on the success of **National Tree Planting Year** with its slogan, **Plant A Tree In '73**. Activities have developed to encompass community action, lobbying, awareness raising and grant giving.

Members of The Tree Council now range from professional, non-governmental, specialist and trade organisations, including other conservation charities, to government departments and local authorities. Although individuals may not be members of The Tree Council, they are encouraged to become Tree Wardens or join one of The Tree Council's constituent organisations.

The annual national programme of community action and awareness-raising around trees has grown over the years to become a major part of the work of this organisation. In addition to **National Tree Week**, The Tree Council also organises and promotes **Seed Gathering Season** and **Walk in the Woods** month, supporting the groups organising local events; all these initiatives are aimed at involving as many people as possible in planting, caring for and enjoying trees and woods and their timing reflects the seasons of the tree year.

**Seed Gathering Season** (SGS) launches annually on 23rd September and continues until 23rd October, encompassing **Apple Day** which is usually held on 21st October, though with regional variations within SGS. The Season provides opportunities and reminders to everyone that they can collect seeds and grow their own trees for eventual planting out, as well as using them for a range of other purposes such as eating, playing games and creative crafts. Events are organised by local volunteers and groups, though informal walks are also encouraged and Tree Council books such as the Good Seed Guide and Trees and How to Grow Them act as guides for both enthusiasts and newcomers alike.

**National Tree Week** runs from the last Saturday in November to the first Sunday in December and marks the traditional launch of the winter tree planting season whilst providing the banner under which trees, woods and everything related can be celebrated. It was launched in the wake of National Tree Planting Year (Plant a Tree in '73) to keep up the momentum and public enthusiasm for tree planting. Upward of a quarter of a million people are now involved in the many tree planting events held during this Week and it is estimated that around a million new trees are put in the ground every year as a result, ensuring the expansion of tree cover and attendant increased biodiversity nationwide. By planning and joining local events with a tree focus, communities are brought together to improve their environment. **Tree Dressing Days** (held at different times across the country) usually take place during the last weekend of National Tree Week when hanging ribbons, shapes, shining lights and anything which draws attention to the trees we take for granted is intended to highlight our responsibility for looking after trees and remind us of their enormous cultural and environmental importance.

**Walk in the Woods** month is in May every year, when trees and woodlands are looking particularly beautiful and the weather is clement enough to tempt even the most stay-at-home environmentalists to don their outdoor clothes and make a foray out to enjoy the spring sights. Trees and woods are great because of their role in health and wellbeing – tree'd areas are good for the nation's condition, places for recreation, exercise and education; they have been proven to have positive effects on mental health and as an antidote to stressful lifestyles, even aiding recuperation from illness. Native trees and woodlands, of course, provide great habitats for wildlife and wild flowers, all of which can be seen on guided walks or events taking place nationwide – or just on an informal stroll out.

In 1990, The Tree Council founded the national volunteer **Tree Warden Scheme**, which it still develops and co-ordinates. There are upward of 8,000 Tree Wardens, community-based volunteers organised in local networks, all enthusiastic environmental activists prepared to devote time – an average of 257 hours a year each – and even use some of their own money to champion the causes affecting their neighbourhood trees. Tree Wardens organise activities, fundraise, research and advise on trees and related topics and are a resource for their communities as well as running events for the community action programme and participating in national campaigns in support of The Tree Council or its member organisations.

After training, Tree Wardens become involved in gathering information, local liaison, practical projects and protecting trees. These four roles are the core of the scheme and obvious environmental benefits are gained from involving the community in these endeavours. The Scheme also offers a large-scale environmental education programme, teaching individuals about the value of trees.

The Tree Council raises money for distribution by means of wide-reaching Grants Programmes, through which funds are made available for a variety of planting programmes. **Tree Futures** is a restricted reserve for schools and youth groups to ensure that children under the age of sixteen are given the opportunity to get some hands on experience of tree planting, creating a new generation of tree enthusiasts with pride in the improvements they have made to their local ground.

Planting funds from commercial organisations are deposited in the **Tree Bank**, from which money is drawn to grant aid replacement of losses, ameliorate damage or balance carbon emissions necessarily sustained in commercial activities. When funds allow, grants may be made from the **Hedge Fund** for hedge planting or drawn from the **Wildflower Bank** to regenerate native bluebells and seed wildflower woodland pasture whilst the **Orchard Windfalls** initiate community orchards, with the emphasis on using fruit trees of local provenance.

Publications, often written in response to feedback from Tree Wardens and member organisations, are an important facet of the work done by The Tree Council. There are specialist books, such as the *Hedge Tree Handbook* or *Trees in Your Ground* and more general interest books such as *Why Are Leaves Green?* and *Great British Trees*. The biannual magazine *Tree News*, however, provides tree enthusiasts with a beautifully presented and well written and researched publication that, with the inclusion of the journal *Sylva*, extends across both professional and amateur spheres.

Working with partners, member organisations and Tree Wardens, The Tree Council is active on particular issues of concern such as the **Green Monument Campaign**, a drive for proper recognition for heritage trees that was launched in 2003 to achieve proper safeguards, resources for custodians to promote their wellbeing and access to information on management best practice; the **Tree Care Campaign** for after-care to increase the survival rates of young trees, refreshed annually between March and September with public information on what to do; and the **Hedge Tree Campaign** in support of the Government Biodiversity Action Plan, taking practical action in collaboration with landowners and farmers to increase the numbers and quality of trees in hedgerows. It also acts as a facilitator, drawing together the interested organisations that want to discuss, lobby or make representations on matters of common significance or interest.

Everything that The Tree Council does is directed towards making trees matter to everyone by encouraging the planting of more trees, of the right kind, in the right places; better care for trees of all ages; and inspiring effective action for trees. We hope that the reader is motivated to play a part by contributing time or resources to this work.

# Where to see trees

**In the British Isles we are blessed with some very fine collections of trees, many of them survivors of the huge expansion of interest in tree collecting which took place between the 17th and 19th centuries. There can be few finer ways of learning about trees than by spending a day among them.**

## England

### Avon & Somerset

**Bath Botanic Garden** Lots of rare species, notable Ginkgo, Golden Catalpa.

**Victoria Park, Bath** Many good trees across a wide variety of species.

**Nettlecombe, near Willaton** Outstanding Himalayan Cypress and many other trees.

**Somerset College of Agriculture & Horticulture, Near Bridgwater** A small but growing collection of Wisteria.

### Bedfordshire

**Woburn Abbey** Pleasure Grounds with Sessile Oaks, Golden Swamp Cypress, big Deodars, mixed collection.

### Berkshire

**Windsor Great Park** A large collection of rare conifers.

**Savill Gardens** A mixed collection with some notable Metasequoia. Also a large collection of Ilex.

**Valley Gardens** A mixed collection of trees including over 200 Magnolia and some Mahonia.

**Titness Park, Sunninghill** A few big conifers, and some broad-leaved trees.

### Buckinghamshire

**Waddesdon House, Aylesbury** A good variety across a broad range of species.

### Cambridgeshire

**Cambridge Botanic Garden** A wide collection, most notably of Catalpa, Metasequoia, Tetracentron, Maples.

**Clare College Garden** Fine examples of Metasequoia and Swamp Cypress.

### Cheshire

**Ness, Wirral The University of Liverpool Botanic Garden** A fine collection of some excellent trees.

### Cornwall

**Glendurgan, Mawnan Smith, Falmouth** Many big and rare trees.

**Heligan, Mevagisey** Part of the famous restoration project.

**Tresco Abbey** An extraordinary collection of trees from the southern hemisphere on the Isles of Scilly.

Some of the collections listed here can be seen free, for others there is a charge. Not all are open all year round or every day. It is a good idea to check before you travel.

For information about trees in national collections visit: **www.nccpg.co.uk**

### Derbyshire

**Chatsworth House** A pinetum with many notable specimens.

### Devon

**Bicton, East Budleigh** A wide selection of outstanding specimen conifers, oaks and many others, many un-equalled elsewhere including Cunninghamia, Leyland Cypress, Deodar, Cypress Oak.

**Knightshayes Court, Tiverton** Many fine and rare trees, Largest Turkey Oak (Quercus cerris), fine Cornish Elms.

**Killerton, Silverton, Exeter** A significant collection of large rare and tender trees.

**Powderham Castle, Kenford, Exeter** Notable for its Cork and Turkey Oaks.

**Dartington Hall, Totnes** Famous for its Davidia and Lucombe Oak.

**Arlington Court, Barnstaple** A fine collection of garden trees.

**Streatham Drive, Streatham Hall, Exeter University** A large conifer collection with notable Santa Lucia Firs.

**Saltram House, Plympton** Some fine trees, notable Monterey Pine, Dutch Elms.

**RHS Garden, Rosemoor, Gt. Torrington, Devon** A large collection of Cornus and Ilex and a superb fruit garden.

### Dorset

**Abbotsbury** Many large and rare trees including Idesia, Pterocarya.

**Minterne, Cerne Abbas** Some fine conifers, Davidia, maples.

**Forde Abbey, Chard** Some large and very rare trees.

### Durham

**Durham College of Agriculture & Horticulture** A small but growing collection of Sorbus.

### Essex

**Hatfield Forest** Some large and uncommon trees including ancient examples of coppicing.

### Gloucestershire

**Westonbirt, near Tetbury** The National Arboretum with 100 acres of landscaped planting of immense variety, including over 200 Salix, plus Silk Wood – a 2km walk lined both sides all the way with rare trees and bays of collections.

**Batsford Park, Moreton-in-Marsh** Large and varied collection, some very big trees, new collection of rare oaks. Superb Magnolias.

**Stanway, near Winchcombe** A good Pinetum with some excellent specimens.

**Hidcote Manor, Chipping Campden** A large and interesting collection of rare broad-leaved trees.

**Speech House, near Coleford** A good collection of groups of less usual and rare trees, mainly conifers.

**Cirencester Park & Abbey** A collection of fine broad-leaved trees.

## Hampshire

**Rhinefield Terrace, public gated road from A35 to Brockenhurst** An 1859 planting of conifers-now huge. Some younger trees have been added.

**Bolderwood Arboretum, below gated road from A35 east to A31** Planted in 1861 and later, notably Noble Fir including specimens in excess of 40 metres in height.

**Exbury, near Beaulieu** Many rare and big trees.

**Jermyn's House, Ampfield** An immense collection of trees, verging on the completely comprehensive with rarities galore.

**Avington House, near Itchen Abbas** A few fine unusual trees, big Ginkgo, Wheatley Elm, Honey-locust.

**Romsey, Sir Harold Hillier's Gardens & Arboretum** A fine collection from one of the nation's oldest nurseries.

**Osborne House, Isle of Wight** Features an avenue of Lucombe and Holm Oaks, big Cork Oaks, varied young trees.

## Herefordshire

**Hergest Croft, Kington** Huge collection, especially of conifers, maples and oaks, many very rare. Also Acer, Betula, and Zelkova.

**Queenswood, Hope under Dinmore** Interesting planting of many unusual trees.

**Whitfield, Wormbridge** A vast collection of mostly huge conifers, some maples, oaks etc. Notable Santa Lucia Firs, Deodars, original Blue Atlas Cedar, Acer lobelii.

## Hertfordshire

**Cassiobury Park, Watford** Including one of our finest Red Oak and many other trees.

## Kent

**The National Pinetum, Bedgebury, near Goudhurst** A virtually comprehensive collection of hardy conifer species and many cultivars, landscaped with over 100 forest plots of different species, mostly conifers. Some rare oaks, maples and other hardwoods. Small collection of Taxus.

**Scotney Castle, Lamberhurst** Some fine, big conifers and traditional parkland trees.

**Sandling Park, near Hythe** Some old and large conifers, and outstanding huge Alder.

**Godinton Park, near Ashford** Fine hardwood trees in a parkland setting.

**Crittenden House, Matfield** A growing collection of rare trees.

**Mote Park, Maidstone** A public park with some big hardwoods, notable Black Walnut, Liquidambar and Field Maple.

**The Grange, Benenden** A famous collection of flowering cherries, with many other rare trees, notably Eucalyptus gunnii, Fagus englerana and Nothofagus spp.

**Dunorlan Park, Tunbridge Wells** A public park with a good show of some big conifers.

**Hernhill, Faversham, Kent Mount Ephraim Gardens** A fine collection of many diverse ornamentals.

**Faversham, Kent** The Brogdale Trust, over 2000 Apples. Also over 200 Cherries and 300 Plums. Over 500 Pears (European, Asian and Perry). A wide range of Cob, Hazel and Filbert nuts.

## London

**Hyde Park and Kensington Gardens** Some remarkable specimens of rare oaks, maples, ash and many other species.

**Regents Park** Fine Elms and other trees.

**Syon House, Brentford** Famous big and rare oaks, maples, Catalpa, Zelkova, Swamp Cypress and many other trees.

**Osterley Park, Hounslow** Very fine and rare oaks.

**Waterlow Park** Excellent hardwoods of many kinds.

**Kenwood, Highgate** Notable Zelkova, Swamp Cypress, Oak.

**Chiswick House** Many large trees, notable Fraxinus angustifolia.

**Marble Hill, Twickenham** A public park with a notable huge Black Walnut and tall Lombardy Poplar and Italian Alder.

**Greenwich Park** With many good trees, notable Euodia hupehensis and Betula papyrifera.

## Norfolk

**Lynford Arboretum, near Mundford** Small plantings of groups of less usual conifers, maples etc. More are always being added.

## Northumberland

**Blagdon, Seaton Burn, Newcastle-upon-Tyne** Owned by Viscount Ridley, 250 or more species and cultivars of Acer.

**Cragside, Near Rothbury** Planting on a huge scale by Lord Armstrong.

## Oxfordshire

**Oxford Botanic Gardens** Some very old trees of rare species.

**University Parks, Oxford** Many fine trees including Zelkova, Poplar spp.

**Blenheim Palace, Woodstock** Notable for Cedar of Lebanon, Sugar Maple, London Plane.

## Somerset

(see Avon & Somerset)

## Staffordshire

**Sandon Park Hall, near Stafford** Many good trees across a wide variety of species.

## Suffolk

**Abbey Gardens, Bury St Edmunds** Some big and unusual trees, notably Trees of Heaven and Buckeye.

## Surrey

**Royal Botanic Gardens, Kew** Still the largest specimens of many of the rarest species, unequalled collections of most genera, notably oaks, Celtises, lime, Zelkova and Catalpa.

**Royal Horticultural Society's Gardens, Wisley, Ripley** A very good pinetum, wide range of other trees.

**Claremont, Esher** Notably splendid Cedar of Lebanon, oldest Cunninghamia, finest Sequoia and Bishop Pine.

**Grayswood Hill, Haslemere** Many fine trees of wide range, notable Montezuma Pine, Nothofagus betuloides, obliqua, etc.

**Winkworth Arboretum, near Godalming** Notable collections of Sorbus and Acer, groups of Nyssa, Oxydendrum, rare oaks.

**Moss's Wood and Leith Hill Place (below Leith Hill)** Public road with some fine conifers at each place.

**Riverside Park, Richmond** Many fine trees in a wonderful setting.

**Ravensbury Park, Morden** A public park with fine London Planes, English Elms and smaller trees.

**Merrist Wood Agricultural College, Worplesdon, Nr. Guildford** A good collection of dwarf and prostrate Cotoneaster. Small collection of Euonymus fortunei.

**Tilgates, Bletchingley, Surrey** Over 300 species and cultivars of Magnolia.

## Sussex

**Royal Botanic Gardens (Kew) Wakehurst Place, Ardingly** Immense collection of conifers and broad-leaved trees, (including Betula), many fine specimens of extremely rare trees.

**Borde Hill, North of Haywards Heath** Huge park and six woods full of rare trees, some unknown elsewhere. Most notable Maple collection, also oak, pine, spruce etc.

**Nymans, Handcross** Two pinetums, three gardens and a large Wilderness filled with rare and some tender trees. Outstanding specimens of rare Nothofagus species, also Austrocedrus.

**Leonardslee, Lower Beeding (Open in May & October)** Many fine conifers, Magnolia, Oak and notable Sassafras, etc.

**Sheffield Park, Uckfield** Wide variety of fine conifers and unique planting of Nyssa, notable Maritime and Montezuma Pines, Pseudolarix, Serbian Spruce, Pond Cypress.

**Highdown, Goring** The famous chalk-garden has many rare trees, notable Acer griseum, and a rare Hornbeam (Carpinus turczaninowii) and a rare Juniper (Juniperus cedrus).

**Cowdray Park, Midhurst** Many very big conifers, notable Wellingtonia (in avenue), Acer buergeranum, Sawara Cypress.

**West Dean Arboretum (Roche's Arboretum)** A wide collection, mainly of conifers, some of great size, to over 46m (Douglas Fir).

**West Dean Gardens, Near Chichester, W. Sussex** Notable for its Liriodendron.

## West Midlands

**Swallow Hayes, Rectory Road, Albrighton** A wonderful collection of Hamamelis.

## Wiltshire

**Broadleas Garden Charity, Devizes** A large collection of Euonymus.

**Stourhead, near Mere** Large collection of very big conifers and hardwoods. Largest Macedonian Pine, Noble Fir, Tiger-tail Spruce, Thuja, Tulip-trees.

**Wilton House, Wilton** Many fine old trees. Look out for the Concord Oak by the bridge.

**Longleat, near Warminster** Many big conifers by roads and in the Paradise.

## Worcestershire

**Spetchley Park, east of Worcester** Notable Metasequoia.

## Yorkshire

**Newby Hall Gardens, Ripon, North Yorkshire** A large collection of Cornus.

**Studley Royal & Fountains Abbey, near Ripon, North Yorkshire** Many big trees, notable Sweet Chestnut and Oaks.

**Thorpe Perrow Arboretum, near Bedale, North Yorkshire** a lovely collection in a beautiful setting.

# Wales

## Cardiff

**Bute Park Arboretum** A wonderful collection in the great tradition.

**Roath Park and other public areas of Cardiff** A wide selection.

## Conwy

**Bodnant, Tal y Cefn, Conway** Huge collection of Conifers, Magnolia, Maple. Notable Nothofagus obliqua, Low's Fir, Lodgepole Pines, Grecian Fir, etc.

## Denbighshire

**Vivod Forest Garden above Vivod House, near**

**Llangollen** An arboretum of many rare species, forest plots of wide range.

## Monmouthshire
**Gliffaes Country House Hotel** Open daily in summer to see a wide variety of classic trees.

## Powys
**Dingle Gardens, Welshpool.** Four acre sloping garden with lakes. Rare and unusual trees and shrubs, year round interest.

**Powis Castle Gardens, Welshpool.** The park has big trees, including tallest Douglas Fir and Pinus ponderosa. Gardens have Ginkgo, big Silver Firs and Sequoia, Davidia and Populus lasiocarpa.

# Scotland
## Argyll & Bute
**Brodick Castle, Arran** Many trees including rare Maples.

**Strone, Cairndow** The tallest tree in Scotland in group of very big conifers. (Grand Fir, 54m.)

**Inveraray Castle Gardens** Many fine conifers, notable Leyland Cypress, Grand Fir and Sitka Spruce by bridge and across river visible from terrace.

**Benmore, Younger Botanic Garden (Part of the Royal Botanic Garden, Edinburgh)** Large areas of huge conifers and garden with comprehensive collection. Notable Western Hemlock (48m), Wellingtonia avenue, Abies amabilis, Picea jezoensis. Very tall trees (to 50m) in Glen Masson nearby.

**Crarae Gardens & Forest Garden, Furnace** A wide collection of rare trees, plots of rare conifers.

**Kilmun Forest Garden, near Benmore** Plots of rare Conifers and Eucalyptus. (Forestry Commission).

## Ayrshire
**Culzean Castle, Girvan** Many fine conifers and other trees, especially in Happy Valley.

**Glenapp, Ballantrae** Small group of big conifers in valley off main valley.

**Kilkerran, Maybole** Small pinetum above house, notable Scots Pine, Noble Fir. Big Araucaria, and Wellingtonia. Big Larch and Silver Firs in Lady's Glen.

## Borders
**Dawyck, Stobo** Extensive collection of conifers, maple and many rare trees. Original Dawyck Beech, very early Larch, Douglas Fir, Western Hemlock, fine Asiatic Silver Firs.

## Edinburgh
**Royal Botanic Gardens** Notable collections of Birch, Maple, Lime, Conifers, Corylus colurna, Tetracentron, Quercus dentata, Fagus orientalis etc.

## East Lothian
**Smeaton House, East Lothian** Wide range of notable conifers, big Italian Maple.

**Whittinghame, near Haddington** A large collection of big conifers.

## Glasgow
**Glasgow Botanic Gardens** An interesting collection of tree ferns (Dicksonia).

## Inverness-shire
**Moniac Glen, near Beauly (Forestry Commission picnic site)** A small area of very tall Douglas Firs (to 51m) and a few other conifers.

## Perthshire
**The Hermitage, Inver, Dunkeld** A few very big trees, one Douglas Fir of 53m.

**Blair Castle, Blair Atholl** Diana's Grove is full of Conifers 45m tall, outstanding Japanese Larch, outside are an early European Larch and original hybrid Larch. St. Brides, just above, has immense Abies procera and Abies magnifica, side by side.

**Keir House, Dunblane** Large number of big conifers and rare maples. Notable Abies, spectabilis, Cupressus torulosa.

**Doune House, Dunblane Valley near Motor Museum** Well spaced huge conifers, small maple and oak collection. Notable Western Hemlock, Wellingtonia (44m), largest Lawson and Nootka Cypresses in Scotland.

**Scone Palace, near Perth** Garden has original Douglas Fir, huge pinetum in widely spaced lines planted 1860 among 1852 trees. Notable Jeffrey's pine, Western Hemlock, Wellingtonia, four massive Sitka Spruces, Noble Firs, and younger rarities.

## Dumfries and Galloway
**Castle Kennedy and Lochinch** Large scale early planting of wide range of conifers, also tender hardwoods. Avenues of unusual species (e.g. Embothrium, Eucalyptus, Araucaria). Notable Bishop Pine, line of Cordyline, Nothofagus spp.

## Northern Ireland
**Castlewellan, Newcastle, Co. Down** An immense collection rich in rare and tender conifers and other trees, many of great size.

**Rowallane, Saintfield, Co. Down** Many fine rare and tender trees, notable Nothofagus collection.

# The Republic of Ireland
**Powerscourt, Co. Wicklow** A huge collection, mainly conifers, many very well grown, rare and big.

**The John F Kennedy Memorial Arboretum, New Ross, Co. Wexford** A rapidly expanding collection on a vast scale. Forest plots.

**Glasnevin Botanic Garden, N. Dublin** A large collection with many fine, very rare trees, outstanding Euodia spp., good rare maples etc.

**Birr Castle, Co Offaly** An enormous and widespread general collection, numerous extreme rarities, notable Wing-nuts, limes, maples, etc.

# The national plant collections

The National Council for the Conservation of Plants and Gardens, a registered charity, was established in 1978 as a countrywide drive "through volunteer membership, to conserve, document, promote and make available Britain's great bio-diversity of garden plants for the benefit of horticulture, education and science." It is the recognised authority for the National Plant Collections Scheme.

On the following pages we list some of the National Collections of some species described in this book. The information is correct at the time of going to press but the collections are constantly changing. You can obtain your own up-to-date copy of the full directory, or find out more about how you might join in the work of the Council, by contacting them at:
The Stable Courtyard, Wisley Garden, Woking, Surrey, GU23 6QP, Tel: 01483 211465, or visit their website: ww.nccpg.com for the latest information.

## Acer

Viscount Ridley, Boston House, Blagdon, Seaton Burn, Newcastle-upon-Tyne, NE13 6DB
Tel: 01670 789236

W L Banks, Hergest Croft Gardens, Ridgebourne, Kington, Herefordshire, HR5 3EG
Tel: 01544 230160

## Aesculus

J Buckland, West Dean Gardens, West Dean, Chichester, Sussex, PO18 0QZ
Tel: 01243 818209

## Alnus

c/o Mr David Christie, Jersey Trees For Life, Le Lavandage, Mont de la Rocque, St Brelade, Jersey, JE3 8BQ
Tel: 01534 746614

Viscount Ridley, Boston House, Blagdon, Seaton Burn, Newcastle-upon-Tyne, NE13 6DB
Tel: 01670 789236

K Ashburner, Stone Lane Gardens, Stone Farm, Chagford, Devonshire, TQ13 8JU
Tel: 01647 231311

## Arbutus

Mr I H B Cathie, Barton House, Moreton-in-Marsh, Gloucestershire, GL56 0PJ
Tel: 01608 674303

## Betula

D Hardman, Head of Horticulture & Estate Management, Royal Botanic Gardens Kew, Wakehurst Place, Ardingly, Haywards Heath, West Sussex, RH17 6TN
Tel: 01444 894054

Mr. & Mrs. Mayall, The Mill House, Brownhill, Ruyton XI Towns, Shrewsbury, Shropshire, SY4 1LR
Tel: 01939 260638 / mob: 07793 365522

W L Banks, Hergest Croft Gardens, Ridgebourne, Kington, Herefordshire, HR5 3EG
Tel: 01544 230160

K Ashburner, Stone Lane Gardens, Stone Farm, Chagford, Devonshire, TQ13 8JU
Tel: 01647 231311

## Carpinus

Estate Manager, Beale Arboretum, West Lodge Park, Hadleywood, Barnet, Hertfordshire, EN4 0PY
Tel: 0208 216 3900

The Curator, The Sir Harold Hillier Gardens & Arboretum, Jermyns Lane, Ampfield, Romsey, Hampshire, SO51 0QA
Tel: 01794 368787

## Castanea

Viscount Devonport, (Collection attention of M Carree), Peasmarsh Place Arboretum, Rye, Sussex, TN31 6XE
Tel: 01797 223398

## Cercidiphyllum

Andrew Powell, Canford School, Canford Magna, Wimborne, Dorset, BH21 3AD
Tel: 01202 841254

## Cornus

The Curator, The Sir Harold Hillier Gardens & Arboretum, Jermyns Lane, Ampfield, Romsey, Hampshire, SO51 0QA
Tel: 01794 368787

Mr. M Jackson, Newby Hall Gardens, Ripon, N. Yorkshire, HG4 5AE
Tel: 01423 322583

C P Bailes, Curator, RHS Garden, Rosemoor, Great Torrington, Devon, EX38 8PH
Tel: 01805 624067

Alan Pullen, 'Secretts' Garden Centre, Old Portsmouth Road, Milford, Nr. Godalming, Surrey, GU8 5HL
Tel: 01483 520550

## Corylus

The Curator, The Sir Harold Hillier Gardens & Arboretum, Jermyns Lane, Ampfield, Romsey, Hampshire, SO51 0QA
Tel: 01794 368787

## Cotoneaster

Mrs J Fryer, Rumsey Gardens, Drift Road, Clanfield,
Waterlooville, Hampshire, PO8 0PD
Tel: 01730 827202

## Eucalyptus

Mr T Hart Dyke, Lullingstone Castle, Eynsford,
Kent, DA4 0JA
Tel: 01322 860762

Dr & Mrs DJ Smith, Meon Orchard, Kingsmead,
Wickham, Hampshire, PO17 5AU
Tel: 01329 833253

## Fagus

The Principal, Northumberland College at
Kirkley Hall, Ponteland, NE20 0AQ
Tel: 01661 860808

## Fraxinus

Prof. P Laybourn, Ashgrove, Waterfoot Row,
Thornton Hall, Glasgow, G74 5AD
Tel: 0141 6443992

## Hamamelis

C G Lane, Witch Hazel Nurseries, The Granary,
Cranbrook Farm, Callaways Lane, Newington,
Sittingbourne, Kent, ME9 7LU
Tel: 01795 843098

Pat Edwards, Swallow Hayes, Rectory Road,
Albrighton, West Midlands, WV7 3EP
Tel: 01902 372624

## Ilex

Mr & Mrs A D Barnes, Fachongle Ganol, Cilgwyn,
Newport, Pembrokeshire, SA42 0QR
Tel: 01239 820688

C P Bailes (Curator), RHS Garden, Rosemoor,
Great Torrington, Devon, EX38 8PH
Tel: 01805 624067

## Juglans

Mr I Bond, Northwick Estate, Upton Wold,
Moreton-in-Marsh, Gloucestershire, GL56 9TR
Tel: 01386 700 667

Andrew Powell, Canford School, Canford Magna,
Wimborne, Dorset, BH21 3AD
Tel: 01202 841254

P G Whaites, The National Trust, Wimpole Hall,
Arrington, Royston, Hertfordshire, SG8 0BW
Tel: 01223 207257

## Laburnum

P Hall, The National Trust, Powis Castle Gardens,
Welshpool, Powys, SY21 8RE

The Curator, Thorpe Perrow Arboretum Ltd.,
Bedale, North Yorkshire, DL8 2PR
Tel: 01677 425323

## Liquidambar

Dr J Gammon, Birchfleet, Nyewood, Petersfield,
Hampshire, GU31 5JQ
Tel: 01730 821636

## Liriodendron

J Buckland, West Dean Gardens, West Dean,
Chichester, Sussex, PO18 0QZ

## Magnolia

M Puddle, The National Trust, Bodnant Garden,
Tal-y-cafn, Colwyn Bay, Clwyd, LL8 5RE
Tel: 01492 650460

M Flanagan, Crown Estate Commissioners,
Windsor Great Park, Windsor, Berkshire, SL4 2HT
Tel: 01753 860222

Lady Quicke, Sherwood Garden, Newton St Cyres,
Exeter, Devon, EX5 5BT
Tel: 01392 851216

Mr C Williams, The Estate Office, Caerhays Castle,
Gorran, St Austell, Cornwall, PL26 6LY
Tel: 01872 501310

C Margrave, Wentworth Castle Gardens, Lowe Lane,
Stainborough, Barnsley, Yorkshire, S75 3ET
Tel: 01226 731269

## Malus

Mr & Mrs B Holmes, The Christobella Charitable
Trust, Barnards Farm, Brentwood Road,
West Horndon, Essex, CM13 3LX
Tel: 01277 811262

University Of Reading & Fast Ltd., Brogdale Farm,
Brogdale Road, Faversham, Kent, ME13 8XZ
Tel: 01795 536250

## Pinus

The Curator, The Sir Harold Hillier Gardens &
Arboretum, Jermyns Lane, Ampfield, Romsey,
Hampshire, SO51 0QA
Tel: 01794 368787

The Curator, Tatton Garden Society, 4 Main Road,
Shavington, Crewe, Cheshire, CW2 5DY
Tel: 01270 664367

## Platanus

D Stone, The National Trust, Mottisfont Abbey,
Nr. Romsey, Hampshire, SO51 0LP
Tel: 01794 340757

## Populus

Richard Cripps, Lackham College, Lacock, Chippenham, Wiltshire, SN15 2NY
Tel: 01249 466710

Dr R Jinks, Forestry Commission Research Agency, Alice Holt Lodge, Wrecclesham, Farnham, Surrey, GU10 4LH
Tel: 01420 22255

## Prunus

Mr M Hall, Batsford Arboretum, Batsford Park, Moreton-in-Marsh, Gloucestershire, GL56 9QB
Tel:  01386 701441

The Ironbridge Gorge Museum Trust, Ironbridge, Telford, Shropshire, TF8 7AW
Tel: 01952 433522 (Damson and Bullace)

University Of Reading & Fast Ltd., Brogdale Farm, Brogdale Road, Faversham, Kent, ME13 8XZ
Tel: 01795 536250

## Pyrus

Three Counties Agricultural Society, Showground, Malvern, Worcestershire, WR13 6NW
Tel: 01684 584900 (Perry Pears)

University Of Reading & Fast Ltd., Brogdale Farm, Brogdale Road, Faversham, Kent, ME13 8XZ
Tel: 01795 536250

Mr J Chapman, Prestberries Cottage, Blackwell's End, Hartpury, Gloucester, Gloucestershire, GL19 3DB
Tel: 01452 700333

Hartpury Historic Land and Buildings Trust, Orchard Centre, Blackwell's End, Hartpury, Gloucestershire, GL19 3DB

## Quercus

The Curator, The Sir Harold Hillier Gardens & Arboretum, Jermyns Lane, Ampfield, Romsey, Hampshire, SO51 0QA
Tel: 01794 368787

M H Amory, Chevithorne Barton, Tiverton, Devonshire, EX16 7QB.

## Sorbus

Dr. RA Benton, Jodrell Bank Science Centre, Macclesfield, Cheshire, SK11 9DL
Tel: 01477 571339

JM Hirst, East Durham & Houghall Community College, Durham City, Durham, DH1 3SG
Tel: 0191 3861351

Mr Glyndwr Marsh, Mount Joy, Newbridge Village, Cadnam, Hampshire, SO40 2NW
Tel: 02380 813049

Viscount Ridley, Boston House, Blagdon, Seaton Burn, Newcastle-upon-Tyne, Northumberland, NE13 6DB
Tel: 01670 789236

## Stuartia

High Beeches Gardens Conservation Trust, The High Beeches, Handcross, Sussex, RH17 6HQ
Tel: 01444 400589

## Syringa

Mr D Lockwood, Nat. Collections Co-ordinator, Leeds City Council, Farnley Hall, Hall Lane, Farnley, Yorkshire, LS12 5HA
Tel: 0113 3957400

Mr & Mrs C Chapman, Norman's Farm, Wyverstone, Stowmarket, Suffolk, IP14 4SE
Tel: 01449 781081

## Taxus

P Brown, University of Bath, Claverton Down, Bath, Somerset, BA2 7AY
Tel: 01225 385552

Colin Morgan, Bedgebury National Pinetum, Bedgebury, Kent, TN17 2SL
Tel: 01580 211781

## Tilia

Viscount Devonport, (Collection, Attention of M Carree) Peasmarsh Place Arboretum, Rye, Sussex, TN31 6XE
Tel: 01797 223398

The Curator, Thorpe Perrow Arboretum, Bedale, North Yorkshire, DL8 2PR
Tel: 01677 425323

Westonbirt Arboretum, The National Arboretum, Westonbirt, Tetbury, Gloucestershire, GL8 8QS
Tel: 01666 881203

## Ulmus

R Greenland, Environmental Services, Brighton & Hove Council, Hove Town Hall, Norton Road, Hove, Sussex, BN3 3BQ
Tel: 01273 292929

## Viburnum

The Rt. Hon. The Lord Kenyon, Gredington, Whitchurch, Shropshire, SY13 3DH
Tel: 01948 830305

Plants Records Officer, RHS Garden, Hyde Hall, Rettendon, Chelmsford, Essex, CM3 8ET
Tel: 01245 400256

# Trees for celebrations and memorials

Trees alive today are the oldest living things on earth: as ancient as the remains of the oldest civilisations yet still growing. In nature they stand as living memorials of ages past, rooted to their spot, the story of the centuries stored in their growth rings. Trees are not simply an important part of our modern lives, they have enriched and ennobled us over vast stretches of time.

This unique longevity has meant that mankind has always turned to trees (and representations of trees) as living metaphors for matters spiritual, and as markers for memorial. The druid's yew grove is an example of the first, the native North American's lodge or totem pole is an example of the second.

Given the massive environmental benefits which even a single small tree triggers, there can be no finer way to mark the important stages in our lives than to plant a tree. Be it birth, marriage or death, a tree – long after the other memories have faded – will be a living reminder of the moments and the people that matter most in our lives. Here are some suggestions:

### To celebrate a birth

#### Cherry
A Christian symbol of sweetness and goodness, and an emblem of the infant Jesus

#### Holly
The tree of good luck and protection

#### Peach
For the Chinese, symbolic of youth, good fortune, and long life

#### Pear
A traditional symbol of health, fortune, and hope. In rural Switzerland a pear tree was planted on the birth of a baby girl

#### Sweet Chestnut
In Christianity, symbolic of goodness, chastity and triumph over temptation

### To mark a marriage

#### Ash
Known as the "venus of the forest" and long associated with love

#### Beech
Known as the trysting tree, where lovers met and into which messages of love were carved

#### Lime
Associated with laughter and fun. Garlands of lime were woven for Aphrodite, the Greek goddess of sensual love and beauty

#### Oak
A very sacred tree, seen as the symbol of fertility for centuries

#### Walnut
Associated with love, marriage, and childbirth by the Greeks

### To commemorate a loved one

#### Birch
Long associated in the Christian tradition with the holy spirit

#### Elder
The tree of sorrow and death in many European nations

#### Larch
Revered in many parts of the world as a symbol of immortality

#### Pine
In China, Pine trees were planted on graves. It represents longevity, courage, and faithfulness

#### Yew
In many cultures as well as in the Christian tradition, symbolic of immortality

## The National Memorial Arboretum

Located at Alrewas, Staffordshire, The National Memorial Arboretum provides a place where trees can be planted to commemorate any milestone – happy or sad. True, there are many trees planted by the great and good to commemorate some outstanding citizens of recent times: heroes and heroines from every walk of life in peacetime and in war. But the Arboretum (which is a registered charity) is there to serve ordinary families, as a 'living Westminster Abbey' where the lives of our parents and grandparents, brothers and sisters and friends can be recalled.

For more information, or to find out how you can support the work of the arboretum, contact:
The National Memorial Arboretum
Croxall Road • Alrewas • Staffordshire • DE13 7AR
Tel: 01283 792333 • Fax: 01283 792034
www.thenma.org.uk

# Further reading

The following books and publications are a valuable source of information and are great reading for those who love trees. Many of these have been an important reference during the writing of this book and the author has particularly valued their information and expertise. Some of the titles are now out of print but they are worth sourcing through second hand bookshops or the Internet.

## FRUIT

**The New Book of Apples**
Joan Morgan and Alison Richards, Ebury Press, London. ISBN 0-09-188398-9

**The English Apple**
Rosanna Sanders, Phaidon. ISBN 0-7148 2498-4

**Fruit (RHS)**
Harry Baker, Mitchell Beazley. ISBN 1-85732-905-8

**The Fruit Garden Displayed (RHS)**
Harry Baker, Cassell Ltd. ISBN 0-304-31112-X

**Forgotten Fruit**
Francesca Greenoak, Andrew Deutsch.
ISBN 233-97396-6

**Pears**
Jim Arbury and Sally Pinhey, Wells and Winter.
ISBN 0-9532136-0-9

**Fruit Past & Present**
RHS. ISBN 1-874431-43-4

**Pruning Hardy Fruits**
Jack Woodward. ISBN 0-304-31103-0

**Cherries**
Norman H Grubb, East Malling Research Station, London. Crosby Lockwood & Son Ltd. 1949.

**The Plums of England**
H.V. Taylor, CBE, DSc, VMH, ARCS
London. Crosby Lockwood & Son Ltd. 1949.

**Success with Apples and Pears to Eat and Drink**
Alan Rowe, Groundnut Publishing.
ISBN 0-9527141-3-2

**La Taille des Arbres Fruities – Mode d'emploi**
Jacques Beccaletto, Denis Retournard, Ulmer.
ISBN 2-84138-232-X

**Forgotten Fruits**
Christopher Stocks, Random House Books.
ISBN 978-1905211807

**Perry Pears**
Luckwill & Pollard, The National Fruit and Cider Institute, University of Bristol 1963

**Apples – A Guide to the Identification of International Varieties**
John Bultitude, Macmillan Press Ltd, London.
ISBN 0-333-34971-7

**Plums**
Jim Arbury & Sally Pinhey,
Craft Print International Ltd. ISBN 981-04-4907-0

**The Fruit Manual**
Robert Hogg, Fifth Edition, London: Journal of Horticulture Office 171 Fleet Street. 1884

**Hazelnuts – Production and Culture**
Martin Crawford, Agroforestry Research Trust.
ISBN 1-874275-27-0

**Walnuts – Production and Culture**
Martin Crawford, Agroforestry Research Trust.
ISBN 1-874275-28-9

**Fruit Varieties Resistant to Pests and Diseases**
Martin Crawford, Agroforestry Research Trust.
ISBN 1-874275-35-1

**Chestnuts – Production and Culture**
Martin Crawford, Agroforestry Research Trust.
ISBN 1-874275-26-2

**Plums – Production, Culture and Cultivar Directory**
Martin Crawford, Agroforestry Research Trust.
ISBN 1-874275-29-7

**Cherries – Production and Culture**
Martin Crawford, Agroforestry Research Trust.
ISBN 1-874275-33-5

## ORNAMENTALS

**Flowering Crab Apples – The Genus Malus**
Fr John L Fiala, Timber Press. ISBN 0-88192-292-7

**The Garden Tree**
Alan Mitchell and Allen Coombes.
ISBN 1-84188-007-8

**Garden Trees**
RHS Plant Guides, Dorling Kindersley.
ISBN 0-7513-17-52

**Garden Plants for Scotland**
Kenneth N.E. Cox & Raoul Curtis-Machin, Frances Lincoln Limited. ISBN 9778-0-7112-2675-3

**The Genus Sorbus
– Mountain Ash and Other Rowans**
Hugh McAllister, Royal Botanical Garden, Kew.
ISBN 1-84246-08-9

**Hawthorn and Medlars**
James B. Phipps, RHS, Timber Press.
ISBN 0-88192-591-8

**The Hillier Manual of Trees and Shrubs**
John Hillier and Allen Coombes, David & Charles.
ISBN 0-7153 9942 X

**Hollies – The Genus Ilex**
Fred C Galle, Timber Press. ISBN 0-88192-380-X

**Japanese Flower Cherries**
Wybe Kuitert, Timber Press. ISBN 0-88192468-7

**Japanese Maples**
J D Vertrees/Peter Gregory. ISBN 0-88192-501-2

**Lilacs – The Genus Syringa**
Fr John Fiala, Timber Press. ISBN 0-88192-001-0

**Magnolias – A Gardeners Guide**
Jim Gardiner, Timber Press. ISBN 0-88192-446-6

**Purpleleaf Plums**
Arthur Lee Johnson, Timber Press.
ISBN 0-88192-255-2

**Willow – The Genus Salix**
Christopher Newsholme. Batsford.
ISBN 0-7134-6881-5

**Wisterias – A Comprehensive Guide**
Peter Valder Florilegium. ISBN 0-646-22049-7

**Witch Hazels**
Chris Lane, RHS, Timber Press. ISBN 0-881292-678-7

## GENERAL

**Collins Photographic Key to the trees of Britain and Northern Europe**
ISBN 0-00-219840-1

**The Downright Epicure**
**– Essays on Edward Bunyard**
Edward Wilson, Prospect Books.
ISBN 1-903018-48-X; 978-1-903018-48-4

**Meetings with Remarkable Trees**
Thomas Pakenham, Phoenix. ISBN 0-75380-237-6

**A Paradise out of a Common Field**
Joan Morgan and Alison Richards.
ISBN 0-7126-2209-8

**RHS Plant Finder**
RHS, Dorling Kindersley Ltd.
ISBN 978-1-4053-4176-9

**Pruning & Training**
Christopher Brickell & David Joyce,
Dorling Kindersley. ISBN 0-7513-0207-4

**The Pruning of Trees, Shrubs and Conifers**
George E Brown, Timber Press. ISBN 88192-319-2

**Tree Medicine**
Peter Conway, MPG Books. ISBN 0-7499-2173-0

**Tree News**
Published 4 times per annum,
contact 01454 642 441 for details.

**Why are Leaves Green?**
Jon Stokes and John White, The Tree Council.
ISBN 978-0-904853-07-0

## PESTS AND DISEASES

**A Colourful Atlas of Pests of Ornamental Trees, Shrubs and Flowers**
David V Alford, Manson Publishing.
ISBN 1-874545-34-0

**Pests of Fruit Crops – A Colourful Handbook**
David V Alford, Manson Publishing.
ISBN 1-84076-051-6; 978-1-84076-051-4

**Pest and Diseases**
Pippa Greenwood and Andrew Halstead.
ISBN 0-75130366-6

## PROPAGATION

**The Grafters Handbook**
R J Garner, Cassell. ISBN 0-304-34274-2

**Practical Woody Plant Propagation**
Bruce Macdonald, Timber Press. ISBN 0-88192-062-2

# Acknowledgements

It has been fortunate to have the assistance of many friends and colleagues in the writing of this book without whom much of the information, layout, artwork and photography would have been so much poorer as a result. I wish to extend my huge appreciation to these very kind and talented people.

## Design and production

To Norman Maitland for his extreme patience, understanding and skill in the way this book is presented, to Irene Maitland for her devotion to accuracy and to Alan Scaife for his engine room endeavours, all of whom make up a formidable team at Maitland Associates.

## Proof reading

To Keith Atkey, for sharing his passion for trees and plants combined with his linguistic flair and virtuosity, so valuable at the proof reading stage.

## Support and inspiration

My grateful thanks to many friends, family and fellow enthusiasts and in particular Les Bisset, Els Brewin, Peter, Patricia and Ken Cox, Mary Ann Crichton Maitland, Martin Crawford, Veronica Cross, Callum Pinney, Hugh and Laura Ermen, Geoff Flogdell, Jim Gardiner, Tony and Liz Gentil, John Massey, John Ravenscroft, Clive Simms, Chris Sanders and Wim Van de Poel. To Andrew Wright and Stephanie Dunn James for their daily encouragement over the months that turned into years, and finally and most importantly to Nikki for her patience.

## Photography

I am indebted in particular to Archie Miles and Claire Higgins for some stunning photographs and to Ronald Houtman for access to his extensive library. Thanks also for some important contributions from Mark Bolton, Richard Borrie, Martin Crawford, Brian Fraser, Jim Gardiner, Sue Griffith, Brian Humphrey, Norman Maitland, Helmut Orth, Charles Parsons, Chris Sanders, Alan Scaife, Dale Swash and Wim Van de Poel. Also to Bluebell Nurseries and Arboretum, Holt Studios, Hillier Nurseries, The Kentish Cobnuts Association and The National Fruit Collections, Brogdale. My apologies to anyone whose photograph has not been properly acknowledged.

## Inspirational locations

The other photographs reproduced for this book have been gathered over 25 years, some of which have been taken in my own garden and at our tree nursery in the beautiful Teme Valley on the borders of Worcestershire/Herefordshire. However, the most valuable contributor has been the many inspirational gardens, arboretums and fruit collections within the UK that I have visited along the way. I wish to mention in particular the following that have given me the greatest pleasure: Batsford Park, Ben More and The Royal Botanic Gardens Edinburgh, Burford House Gardens, Crathes Castle, Dundee Arboretum, Glendoick Garden and Arboretum, Hatton Fruit Garden (East Malling), Ness (The University of Liverpool Botanic Garden), Westonbirt (The National Arboretum), Hergest Croft, Wakehurst Place (The Royal Botanic Gardens Kew), Wisley Gardens (Royal Horticultural Society) for both ornamental and fruit trees, Saville Gardens, and John Massey's private garden.

## Illustrations

The continuing use of the tree shape sketches by Peter Richardson is much appreciated. Also my special thanks to Stephanie Dunn James for her lovely illustrations.

## Additional material

Andrew Forsyth and Jack Cox.

## Support and publication

Firstly my special appreciation to Peter Seabrook who kindly wrote the foreword for the Tree Guide for Gardens in 2001 and has again put his reputation on the line on my behalf. Also to the Tree Council, especially Pauline Buchanan Black and Jon Stokes. Jon, in particular, provided continual encouragement and faith in this book during its genesis. He and the 200 voluntary tree officers of the Tree Council should be commended for their valuable work across the UK.

# Index